Z
2011
.B32
1965

Bateson

A guide to English literature

Oakland Community College
Highland Lakes Library
7350 Cooley Lake Road
Union Lake, Michigan

A GUIDE TO ENGLISH LITERATURE

A Guide to English Literature

BY

F. W. BATESON

ALDINE PUBLISHING COMPANY

Chicago

Preface

Geography is about maps, Biography is about chaps.[1]
And Literature is about—whatever it is that literature *is*
about. The uncertainty may explain why, whereas atlases
and biographical dictionaries abound, the equivalent literary works of reference have hitherto been few and far
between.[2] Alexander Pope ascribed a similar infrequency
to angels' visits.

This pioneering handbook is primarily a bibliographical
labor-saving device. Here are the editions and commentaries that the reader will find it a good idea to go to first
of all if he wants to explore at all seriously any of the classics or classical areas of English literature down to the
present day. Since there are now, generally speaking,
plenty of good modern editions and critical studies, why
make the process of comprehension more difficult than
it need be by using one that is unreliable or out of date?
The *Guide* stops, of course, at or before the point where
original research may be expected to begin, though a special section on literary scholarship makes some attempt
to provide the researcher with some of the indispensable
equipment.

The function of the four interchapters is to assist the

[1] See that minor classic of English humorous verse *Biography for Beginners* (1905) by Edmund Clerihew Bentley.
[2] The bibliographical aids of Tom Peete Cross (rev. Donald
F. Bond 1962), Arthur G. Kennedy (rev. Donald B. Sands
1960), and Richard D. Altick and Andrew Wright (rev. edition
1963) are guides to the more general books *about* English literature, but they omit the literature itself as well as the books
about particular authors and works. Some of the recent literary
histories and period-anthologies contain helpful bibliographies.

reader to a historical point of view toward the literature of the principal periods. They may be regarded as a preliminary catechism that will then enable him to interrogate personally his mental impressions as they arise in the actual process of contact with this or that work or author. There is only one overruling assumption: it is that the sequence of books, authors, styles, and movements which constitute English literature is a chronological continuum. The reader's progress, that is, out of *Othello* into *King Lear* should not differ in kind but only in degree from his progress out of the Middle Ages into the Renaissance.[3]

A quasi-educational purpose is therefore implicit. In effect the *Guide* proposes itself as a new kind of literary history. The conventional history of literature has often tended to become a substitute for the reading of the literature it describes: the better the history the greater the temptation to substitute it. Since George Saintsbury, let us say, was obviously wiser than one is oneself, is it not likely that his impressions of Fielding's *Tom Jones* will be superior to one's own impressions of that often tedious novel? Why not, then, accept them gratefully as such? And in that case will there be any need to struggle through those two long volumes oneself? The argument conceals a fallacy, but at least a reading of Saintsbury does not compel a reading of *Tom Jones*. On the other hand, the present combination of reading lists and interchapters *cannot* be a substitute for anything else. Meaningless as literature in themselves, they may nevertheless provide the necessary preliminary to meaningful reading.

Some oddities of arrangement derive from these assumptions. Thus, authors are not arranged as might be

---

[3] After years of work on the *Oxford Shakespeare* the great Elizabethan scholar R. B. McKerrow became convinced "that any satisfactory study of the works of Shakespeare, or indeed probably of any other author, must take full account of the order in which they were written, and that it is advisable actually to study them, so far as possible, in that order" (*Prolegomena for the Oxford Shakespeare*, 1939, p. vi).

expected in a single alphabetical series—with Auden (an English author, if an American citizen) coming between John Aubrey (b. 1626) and Jane Austen (b. 1775). Instead there are four chronological compartments—with the divisions *circa* 1500, 1650, and 1800—in which authors succeed each other in the order of their births. An alphabetical order is easier no doubt for the casual enquirer to use, but is anything learned from its application? To learn that Marlowe and Shakespeare—or Keats and Carlyle— were born in the same year is, on the other hand, to acquire a fact of considerable critical importance.[4] Indeed, much of the silliness of some modern criticism derives directly from its indifference to what might be called this chronological principle. (A work of literature is what it is, thematically and stylistically, because *inter alia* its composition occurred at a certain point in historical time.) But the skeptic and the incurably unchronological can, of course, always use the index.

The compiler has actually used at one time or another the great majority of the books and editions here listed. At one time he had hoped not to include a single item with which he was not himself familiar, but the tidal waves of recent scholarly publications have made it physically impossible for him to keep that admirable resolution. If errors of fact or opinion have crept in, as they are sure to have done, they will be penitently corrected in the second edition. The most difficult decision of all has been to draw the line between excessive inclusion and gross omission, and the line may not always have been a consistent one. Since there are several bibliographies of our three major authors, for example, the sections on Chaucer, Shakespeare, and Milton have been made more selective than those on the lesser writers. Editions cited are restricted to those with explanatory notes or other editorial matter; early editions and mere reprints

---

[4] It has seemed an unnecessary refinement to arrange authors born in the same year by the month of their birth, though Marlowe was in fact born earlier in 1564 than Shakespeare.

are therefore not recorded. The *Guide* is intended to cover everything of critical importance down to the end of 1963 (with many 1964 items), but short essays and articles have had to be excluded except in a few special cases. Unless indicated otherwise the place of publication may be assumed to be either the United Kingdom or the United States and the commentaries, etc., to be written in English.

Chapters I to IX are meant for the student and general reader rather than the research specialist (who should supplement these lists with the special section allotted to him, Chapter XI below). There is also a general section on literary criticism (Chapter X). By "English literature" is meant the best or "standard" English authors, together with the standard editions of their writings and the standard commentaries and biographies. In the absence of a standard work or edition the next-best thing is provided, which is usually the most recent contribution and is therefore likely to be still in print or at least easily accessible. Editions described as "definitive" can be assumed to be fully annotated; otherwise, if the presence of notes is not indicated there are probably few or none at all. A "critical" edition is one with a definitive text that lacks adequate explanatory notes.

Chapter XI ("Literary Scholarship") is largely by Professor Harrison T. Meserole of the Pennsylvania State University, who is also preparing a companion *Guide to American Literature*.

F. W. Bateson

Corpus Christi College, Oxford

Contents

Abbreviations and Conventions

BCB	British Council Booklet ("Writers and Their Work" Series)
CBEL	*The Cambridge Bibliography of English Literature*
CHEL	*The Cambridge History of English Literature*
DNB	*Dictionary of National Biography*
EETS	Early English Text Society
ELH	*A Journal of English Literary History*
MP	*Modern Philology*
OED	*The Oxford English Dictionary*
OHEL	*The Oxford History of English Literature*
PMLA	*Publications of the Modern Language Association of America*
PQ	*Philological Quarterly*
RES	*Review of English Studies*
SP	*Studies in Philology*
STC	*Short-Title Catalogue*
TLS	*The* (London) *Times Literary Supplement*

A list of the standard abbreviations of all the literary journals now current will be found in *PMLA*'s annual bibliography (most of them appear in Chapter XI below). *The MLA Style Sheet* has a useful list of the abbreviations permissible in scholarly footnotes (op. cit., ibid., etc.). In spite of their convenience, I have tried to eschew such abracadabra in this guide.

The place of publication of books and journals is Great Britain or the United States unless otherwise indicated; the date given is that of first publication in *either* the United States *or* Britain (publication is not always simultaneous).

A GUIDE TO ENGLISH LITERATURE

I. General Works on English Literature

1. BIBLIOGRAPHIES AND READING LISTS[1]

The most elaborate of the general bibliographies is
CBEL (*The Cambridge Bibliography of English Literature*), edited by F. W. Bateson (paradoxically, of Oxford), 4 vols., 1940. This lists every English author and
book with any claim to literary distinction from Anglo-
Saxon times to *c.* 1900. Semi-literary matter, such as political pamphlets, newspapers, travel books, schoolbooks,
sermons, and scientific treatises, is also included in considerable detail. There are long lists of modern books and
articles about English literature in all its aspects down to
c. 1935, and a substantial Supplement by George Watson
(1957) brings this secondary material down to *c.* 1955.
The arrangement is chronological and by genres within
five main periods. Vol. IV is the Index. George Watson's
one-volume abbreviation of the whole work (1958) covers
some four hundred authors in all and includes the principal twentieth-century figures as well. A detailed twentieth-century volume is imminent and Watson is editing a
revision of the original work.

Useful period-bibliographies are to be found in each
volume both of the *Oxford History of English Literature*
and, on a smaller scale, of *The Pelican Guide to English
Literature* (see below for both).

The best of the single-author, -period, and -genre bibliographies are listed in their appropriate sections. For

1 This section provides a rapid conducted tour among the indispensable research tools; those who want more should turn immediately to Chapter XI below ("Literary Scholarship").

most authors and purposes *CBEL* will be found to suffice. Supplementing it are the various annual lists of the previous year's work in the English field. Three of these have a special importance: (i) the English Association's *The Year's Work in English Studies* (from 1919; short, often rather uncritical, summaries of the more important books and articles); (ii) the Modern Humanities Research Association's *Annual Bibliography of English Language and Literature* (from 1920; more comprehensive than *The Year's Work* but limited to the bare titles); (iii) *PMLA's* annual bibliography (a very thorough list of titles; confined until 1956 to the work of American scholars). But, useful though these general lists are, they are merely catalogues. The annual period-lists in a number of American journals are virtually complete and often add authoritative critical comments on the more important publications. The division of labor has been as follows: *1500–1660, SP* (from 1917); *1660–1800, PQ* (from 1926; outstandingly valuable comments; the 1925–60 lists have been reissued with general indexes by Louis A. Landa, etc., 4 vols., 1950–62); *1800–1837, ELH* (1937–49, thereafter *PQ;* includes other European literatures); *1837–1900, MP* (1933–52, thereafter *Victorian Studies;* lists for 1932–44 reissued by William D. Templeman, 1945, and those for 1945–54 by Austin Wright, 1956, both with general indexes). In addition, *Studies in English Literature* (founded 1960) includes valuable critical surveys of "Recent Studies" in 1500–1660 (drama separately), 1660–1800, and 1800–1900 periods.

The reader who wants more modest assistance—even more modest than is provided in this manual—will find most of what he requires either in A. C. Baugh's *A Literary History of England* (1948), which has reliable bibliographical footnotes throughout, or in the American omnibus anthologies such as G. B. Harrison's *Major British Writers* (rev. 1959) with its "Reading Suggestions" for each author included.

2. LITERARY HISTORIES

GENERAL

The most ambitious of the general histories are *CHEL*
(*The Cambridge History of English Literature*, ed. A. W.
Ward and A. R. Waller, 14 vols., 1907–16; general index,
1927) and its Oxford counterpart *OHEL* (*The Oxford
History of English Literature*, ed. F. P. Wilson and B.
Dobrée, 12 vols. in 14 parts, of which 8 have been issued
1945–63). The principal difference between *CHEL* and
OHEL is that in the former each chapter is by a different
scholar, usually a specialist in the topic discussed, whereas
each volume or part of *OHEL* is by a single author
(usually but not always an Oxford man) from beginning
to end. *CHEL*, though seriously out of date now for the
major figures and topics, is still extremely useful for the
semi-literary areas. *OHEL* has its dull volumes as well as
one brilliant *tour de force* in C. S. Lewis's *The Sixteenth
Century* (*excluding Drama*), but it never fails to be an
efficient guidebook—except in the twentieth-century volume, which is virtually restricted to eight major figures
—and is especially useful for the middling authors who
don't get full-length books written about them.

The two best modern one-volume histories are probably
A. C. Baugh's *A Literary History of England* (1948) and
Hardin Craig's shorter *A History of English Literature*
(1950). Baugh's collaborators were Kemp Malone, Tucker
Brooke, George Sherburn, and Samuel C. Chew; and
Craig's were George K. Anderson, Louis I. Bredvold,
and Joseph Warren Beach—most of them nice elderly
American professors with the virtues and limitations of
their tribe. Both of these can now be obtained in separate
paperback parts (the Craig series rev. 1962).

Of the older histories, George Saintsbury's one-volume
A Short History of English Literature (1898, last rev.
1957) is the only one with any life left in it. Saintsbury's

opinions and verdicts have worn extraordinarily well and his criticism remains endlessly readable, if never profound.

A quite different note from *CHEL*'s and *OHEL*'s—and from the efficient Americans' too—is struck in Boris Ford's *The Pelican Guide to English Literature* (7 vols., 1954–61), which is a paperback collaborative venture dominated by the critical ideals of F. R. Leavis of Cambridge and his *Scrutiny* associates. The emphasis, except for an irrelevant initial chapter in each volume on "The Social Context," is critical rather than historical. A stimulating if occasionally infuriating collection; Vol. VII (twentieth century) is particularly provocative.

A more modest affair is *Annals of English Literature, 1435–1925* by J. C. Ghosh and E. G. Withycombe (1935, rev. R. W. Chapman and D. M. Davin 1961, with extension to 1950), a sort of skeleton history which simply lists each year's principal publications but is remarkably inclusive and reliable.

The "English Men of Letters" series—launched by John Morley in the 1870s and supplemented from time to time up to *c.* 1940 to a total of some 60 volumes—forms a kind of literary history because of the uniform treatment and length, though each volume (from Chaucer to Meredith) was in fact restricted to a single author; the contributors ranged from Trollope, Leslie Stephen, and Henry James to J. B. Priestley. A modern equivalent is the British Council's "Writers and Their Work" series (ed. successively T. O. Beachcroft and B. Dobrée, 1950–   ), which now includes over 140 English authors of all periods, each with a booklet to himself of forty to sixty pages with a comprehensive but unannotated bibliography. The contributors are partly academics and partly literary journalists, and the series is especially useful for twentieth-century authors (fifty have been done already). The "Writers and Critics" series of paperbacks (ed. A. Norman Jeffares, twenty-five items, many Americans, etc., by 1963) is more ambitious; each runs to 120 pages or more and some of the volumes are first-rate.

SCOTTISH LITERATURE

Three recent surveys—John Speirs's *Scots Literary Tradition* (1940, rev. 1962), James Kinsley's *Scottish Poetry* (1955; ten essays by different authors), and Kurt Wittig's *Scottish Tradition in Literature* (1958)—all have their uses, though they are all rather superficial. Simply as a literary guidebook Wittig's is perhaps the best because of its greater range and continuity. David Craig's *Scottish Literature and the Scottish People* (1961), a much abler work, is restricted to the period from 1680 to 1830.

POETRY

George Saintsbury: *A History of English Prosody from the Twelfth Century* (3 vols., 1906–10). Readable and thorough if now rather old-fashioned. A good prosodic handbook is Enid Hamer, *The Metres of English Poetry* (1930).

T. S. Eliot: *The Use of Poetry and the Use of Criticism* (1933). An acute if unmethodical survey of the English critic-poets from Sidney to Eliot himself.

F. W. Bateson: *English Poetry and the English Language* (1934, rev. 1961); *English Poetry: a Critical Introduction* (1950).

F. R. Leavis: *Revaluation: Tradition and Development in English Poetry* (1936). From the Metaphysicals to the Romantics. Well worth disagreeing with.

Leicester Bradner: *Musae Anglicanae: A History of Anglo-Latin Poetry, 1500–1925* (1940).

Moody E. Prior: *The Language of Tragedy* (1947). Critical examination of English poetic drama.

E. M. W. Tillyard: *The English Epic and Its Background* (1954). From Homer to Gibbon; Tillyard counts Thucydides, Malory, Bunyan, etc., as prose epics.

Bernard Groom: *The Diction of Poetry from Spenser to Bridges* (1956). An unpretentious account of the distinctive vocabularies of the major poets.

Josephine Miles: *Eras and Modes in English Poetry*

(1957). An informative and sensitive statistical investigation.

DRAMA

Allardyce Nicoll's A History of English Drama, 1660–1900 (6 vols., 1952–59)—a revision of a series of separate period-histories (1923–46)—has the advantage of including everything, even if the critical comments are often naïve or inept. Volume VI is "A Short-Title Alphabetical Catalogue of Plays Produced or Printed in England from 1660–1900." Similar catalogues for the periods to 1660 can be found in E. K. Chambers's Mediaeval Stage (2 vols., 1903) and Elizabethan Stage (4 vols., 1923) and their sequel Gerald E. Bentley's Jacobean and Caroline Stage (6 vols., 1941–56). The nearest approach to a critical history of the English drama is William Archer's racy The Old Drama and the New (1923). A useful work of reference is Phyllis Hartnoll's Oxford Companion to the Theatre (1951, enlarged 1957).

PROSE FICTION

Ernest A. Baker's History of the English Novel (10 vols., 1924–39), though pedestrian and uninspiring, is remarkably thorough. Three shorter histories of the English novel in the older manner are those of Walter Raleigh (1891; up to Scott only), George Saintsbury (1913; Saintsbury's best fiction criticism is in scattered introductions to various eighteenth-century and nineteenth-century novels), and Robert M. Lovett and Helen S. Hughes (1932; efficient if superficial). The more modern analytical approach is to be found at its best in Arnold Kettle's Introduction to the English Novel (2 vols., 1952–53) and Walter Allen's English Novel (1955), but both omit the minor novelists. Edward Wagenknecht's Cavalcade of the English Novel (1943, rev. 1954), though uncritical, has comprehensive bibliographies.

William K. Wimsatt and Cleanth Brooks's Literary Criticism: a Short History (1957) has now superseded George

Saintsbury's enjoyable but theoretically naïve *History of Criticism and Literary Taste in Europe* (3 vols., 1900–4; English chapters extracted 1911 as *A History of English Criticism*). Though labeled "Short" (in fact it runs to 777 pages) the Wimsatt–Brooks survey is remarkably inclusive—especially for English and American criticism. References are given in it to the crucial articles and essays, as well as to the relevant books.

3. ANTHOLOGIES

GENERAL

G. B. Harrison's *Major British Writers* (2 vols., 1954, enlarged 1959) can be recommended. Harrison allows nearly a hundred pages to each of his authors (there are twenty-two in all, from Chaucer to T. S. Eliot), and his team of editors, a different one for each author, includes such first-rate scholar-critics as C. S. Lewis (for Spenser), Bertrand H. Bronson (for Johnson and Boswell), Northrop Frye (for Byron), I. A. Richards (for Shelley), and Lionel Trilling (for Arnold). Prose fiction has been excluded, but there are plenty of notes and some good introductions. *Masters of British Literature* (2 vols., 1958) follows a similar formula, though the list of editors is less impressive; care has clearly been taken to avoid any unnecessary duplication of Harrison's authors and extracts.

POETRY

F. T. Palgrave: *The Golden Treasury of the Best Songs and Lyrical Poems in the English Language* (1861; fully annotated by J. H. Fowler, 5 vols., 1901–28). Often reprinted, sometimes with supplementary poems, and a landmark in the history of English taste. Palgrave was responsible for the arrangement and the notes, but he left the final choice of poems to be included to Alfred Tennyson.

A. T. Quiller-Couch: *The Oxford Book of English*

Verse, 1900 (rev. and enlarged 1939). Still the best one-volume selection. A defect is that, though the poets are in strict chronological order, each poet's poems are not arranged in the order of their composition; there are no notes.

Cleanth Brooks and Robert Penn Warren: *Understanding Poetry* (1938, rev. 1950 and 1960). The first and best of the new-style American anthologies, without notes but with elaborate critical analyses of some of the poems. A creditable effort is made to get to grips with the principal technical problems; the revised editions recant the original anti-historicism.

W. H. Auden and Norman Holmes Pearson: *Poets of the English Language* (5 vols., 1950). Arranged chronologically and ending *c.* 1900. The period introductions by Auden are brilliant and the choice of poems (not confined to short pieces as Palgrave, Quiller-Couch, and Brooks–Warren are) reflects more accurately than any other collection the preferences of informed critical opinion today. Glosses are supplied by E. Talbot Donaldson for the medieval poems, but there are no explanatory notes. A number of American poets are also included.

Iona and Peter Opie: *An Oxford Dictionary of Nursery Rhymes* (1951, rev. 1952). A scholarly collection with good notes.

PROSE

Hugh Sykes Davies: *The Poets and Their Critics* (2 vols., 1943–62). Extracts from criticisms, early and modern, of the principal English poets; Vol. I, Chaucer to Gray and Collins; Vol. II, Blake to Browning.

Kenneth Allott: *The Pelican Book of English Prose* (5 vols., 1956). Each volume has a separate editor who provides a long critical-historical introduction.

James Sutherland: *The Oxford Book of English Talk* (1953).

Miriam Allott: *Novelists on the Novel* (1959). From Richardson to Aldous Huxley.

The best of the period-anthologies, e.g. Kenneth Sisam's *Fourteenth-Century Verse and Prose,* Eleanor P. Hammond's *English Verse between Chaucer and Surrey,* G. Gregory Smith's *Elizabethan Critical Essays,* J. E. Spingarn's *Seventeenth-Century Critical Essays,* Helen Gardner's *The Metaphysical Poets,* and the six Oxford verse collections (from E. K. Chambers's *Sixteenth-Century Verse* to W. B. Yeats's *Modern Verse*), will be found under the appropriate headings below.

4. MISCELLANEOUS WORKS OF REFERENCE

James Murray, Henry Bradley, W. A. Craigie, and C. T. Onions: *A New English Dictionary on Historical Principles* (20 vols., 1888–1928; reissued with Supplement as *The Oxford English Dictionary,* 13 vols., 1933). The *OED* is indispensable for students of all ages if only as a preventive to slovenly or unhistorical reading. *The Shorter Oxford Dictionary* (ed. William Little, 2 vols., 1933), though decidedly a second-best, will solve many problems and is more reliable on the current standard pronunciations.

H. W. Fowler: *A Dictionary of Modern English Usage* (1926). Problems of grammar and style arranged alphabetically; the best book ever on how to write good English.

E. Cobham Brewer: *Dictionary of Phrase and Fable* (1870, rev. 1949). Indispensable for idioms, myths, and allusions.

Karl Beckson and Arthur Ganz: *A Reader's Guide to Literary Terms* (1961). Often needs supplementing from P. Vivian's more modest *A Dictionary of Literary Terms* (1908) and M. H. Abrams's revision of D. S. Norton and P. Rushton's *Glossary of Literary Terms* (1957). Sylvan Barnet, Morton Berman, and William Burto, *A Dictionary of Literary Terms* (1960), is similar to Abrams though less free from error.

John Bartlett: *Familiar Quotations* (1855, latest rev. 1955). An American compilation with an American bias.

The Oxford Dictionary of Quotations (1941, rev. 1953). Much better than Bartlett for verse quotations but weak for prose.

Granger's Index to Poetry (ed. R. J. Dixon, 1953; supplement 1957). Indexes over 600 modern anthologies (to 1955), including the period Oxford collections. First edition 1904.

Paul Harvey: *The Oxford Companion to English Literature* (1932, rev. 1946). Useful for plots, names of dramatis personae, etc.

Joseph T. Shipley: *Dictionary of World Literature* (1945, rev. 1953). Articles vary enormously in quality, but some of the longer ones, e.g. "Neo-classical Criticism" by R. S. Crane, are excellent.

Leslie Stephen and Sidney Lee: *Dictionary of National Biography* (63 vols., 1885–1900, reprinted in 21 vols.). Supplements every decade. Although superseded for the major figures, *DNB* is still invaluable for minor or occasional writers. For ordinary reference purposes the one-volume *Concise Dictionary* (1939), which merely abbreviates the entries, omitting none and coming down to 1930, is generally adequate.

William Matthews: *British Diaries between 1442 and 1942* (1950). *British Autobiographies Published or Written before 1951* (1955). Chronological lists with brief summaries of each item.

Subject-Index of the London Library (4 vols., 1909–55). More detailed than the *CBEL* index, though not confined to English literature.

The works of reference listed above are the ones most likely to be of general use to the literary student. Some of them are only marginally or intermittently concerned with English literature. Others on more specialized or semi-literary topics will be found throughout the book. The *Guide to Reference Books* (latest ed. 1951; 3 Supplements for 1950–58), begun by Isadore G. Mudge and continued by Constance M. Winchell, is well worth dipping into for its informative comments on each item; though mainly extra-literary, it will be found useful for the lesser dictionaries and for such things as concordances and indexes. A. J. Walford's *Guide to Reference Material* (1959, Supplement 1963) is similar and easier to find one's way about in.

II. The Approach to Medieval Literature

1. WHEN DOES ENGLISH LITERATURE BEGIN?

Matthew Arnold's warning in "The Study of Poetry" against what he called the "historical fallacy" still stands. The fallacy is to confuse the evidential value of works of literature—that is, considered as documents merely defining chronological stages in the development of a literature, a genre, a "movement," or indeed of an individual author—with their "real" or permanent value. The existence of a book—or of several books—does not prove anything: they may be *bad* books, or just trivia. It is true Arnold's illustrations of the fallacy, apart from a passing deprecation of any comparing of Caedmon with Milton, were all drawn from Old or Middle French. But that was because in 1880, the date of "The Study of Poetry," Old and Early Middle English were still in the exclusive keeping of the philologists and the antiquarians. Literary criticism proper still began with Chaucer. But for some two generations now eminent scholars with persuasive tongues and unquestioned literary sense like W. P. Ker, R. W. Chambers, and J. R. R. Tolkien have been staking out quite as large claims for our own early literature as Arnold's French contemporaries were making in his time for the *Chanson de Roland* and Chrétien de Troyes. And the scholars have been joined more recently by some talented and vociferous literary critics, notably C. S. Lewis and John Speirs.

A good deal of what is claimed for our earliest literature may be conceded. Under cross-examination, however, much of the modern enthusiasm has turned out to be either social-sentimental (the writings are good because they reflect a less corrupt world than ours), or else historically fallacious in a new way, the scholarly emphasis now being not so much on "origins" (good because first) as on "traditions" (good because maintaining the lines of communication). No doubt the prestige of T. S. Eliot's "Tradition and the Individual Talent" (1919) has had something to do with this latest refinement in the legerdemain of learning. Its classic example is R. W. Chambers's *On the Continuity of English Prose from Alfred to More* (1932).[1] To Chambers—and the most hardhearted reader soon finds himself infected with Chambers's own romantic excitement—the worthy anonymous author of *Ancren Riwle* "might have done almost anything." Richard Rolle's honest utilitarian prose is, he assures us, "excellent"; Walter Hilton's is "glorious." Roper's charming but decidedly naïve and even clumsy life of Sir Thomas More exhibits, along with other virtues, a "passionate narrative power." And so on, the literary excellences multiplying in a direct ratio to the hypothetical continuity of the prose styles. Arnold's sniffs can be imagined.

The crucial question that Chambers and his fellow enthusiasts have begged is the degree of "real" (literarily significant) continuity between pre-Conquest and post-Conquest literature. No doubt a certain continuity is discernible between some Old English homilies and saints' lives and their Early Middle English equivalents. But have the latter any "permanent" value? Are they worth reading today by anybody except a specialist? Is the continuity more than a "historical" one? A complementary question that has also been left unanswered is the "real" relationship between the acknowledged masterpieces of the two periods. Is there in fact *any* connection between *Beowulf* and the *Canterbury Tales?* Will a knowledge of Old English poetry "really" help a modern reader, except at the most superficial level, to appreciate more fully the carols,

---

[1] An acute and well-informed revaluation of Chambers's thesis is to be found in Norman Davis's "Styles in English Prose of the Late Middle and Early Modern Period" (*Les Congrés et Colloques de l'Université de Liège*, XXI [1961], 165–81).

ballads, and miracle plays, or even *Piers Plowman* and
Sir Gawain and the Green Knight?[2] It has not been
proved; it does not seem likely to be proved.

The degree of linguistic continuity has also been ex-
aggerated. The implication of the conventional tripartite
division into "Old English" (the term that has now dis-
placed "Anglo-Saxon"), "Middle English," and "Modern
English" is that the connection between Old English (the
language spoken in England between the sixth and the
twelfth centuries A.D.) and Middle English (its successor
from *c*. 1150 to *c*. 1500) is similar to that between Middle
English and Modern English (from *c*. 1500 to the present
day). In fact, however, Middle and Modern English merge
into each other gradually and almost imperceptibly,
whereas the change from Old to Middle English was
rapid and drastic, a linguistic revolution. The proper historical parallel is with the similar, though slower, transi-
tions on the Continent from Latin to French, Italian, and
Spanish. At one end of the process there is what is now a
dead language. (Old English, as standardized in the West
Saxon of Alfred and his successors, possessed a system of
genders, case-endings, and verb declensions almost as
elaborate and inflexible as those of classical Latin.) A Dark
Age then intervenes—in England the old ties, linguistic and
cultural, almost collapsed under the impact of the Scan-
dinavian and, especially, the Norman invasions—and a new
language emerges everywhere, which is virtually unin-
flected, with a greatly simplified gender system, varying
considerably from district to district, and essentially
Modern English, French, Italian, and Spanish. To obscure
or minimize the linguistic hiatus in the interest of an
etymological continuity is to miss the all-important human

[2] The re-emergence of the alliterative meter in the middle
of the fourteenth century is an interesting "historical" fact, but
it has little "real" significance because of the crudity with which
the Middle English poets used it. Chaucer's Parson described it,
correctly, as "rum, ram, ruf."

point: Cicero would not have understood the *Chanson de Roland* or Dante; the author of *Beowulf* would not have understood the *Canterbury Tales*. But with a few marginal glosses to help them, the modern Frenchman and Italian on the one hand, and the modern Englishman or American on the other, *can* manage the *Chanson de Roland*, Dante, and Chaucer. They are a part, respectively, of modern French, Italian, and English literatures; Cicero and *Beowulf* are not.

Kenneth Sisam, one of the most distinguished of modern Anglo-Saxon scholars, has proposed the end of the twelfth century as "the starting-point for a study of modern [English] literature."[3] It is a sensible compromise. Chaucer, with whom even T. H. Ward's *The English Poets*[4] began, is too late: *Beowulf* is the poem of another culture altogether. The point is not only that there is a line of continuous transmission running from such things as *The Owl and the Nightingale* and the *Ancren Riwle* to the fourteenth century and beyond, which does not run between them and the Old English masterpieces, but that Early Middle English literature at its best *is* literature. The great English poems of the Age of Chaucer—which is also that of *Piers Plowman* and *Sir Gawain and the Green Knight*—do not spring out of a sub-literature, like Defoe's novels; they are the culmination of a sophisticated literary movement which began two hundred years earlier.

[3] *Fourteenth-Century Verse and Prose* (1921), p. x. *The Oxford English Dictionary* chose 1150 as the *terminus a quo* of the English language. R. W. Chambers is even more precise: "If a line must be drawn between Old English and Middle English, it would, I think, have to come between the man who wrote the Peterborough Annal for 1131, and the man who wrote (perhaps about 1155) the Peterborough Annal for 1132" (*On the Continuity of English Prose*, 1932, p. lxxxvi).

[4] The most elaborate of the Victorian anthologies. Arnold was the uncle of Ward's wife (the once famous Mrs. Humphry Ward) and helped him to plan the collection, as well as contributing the general introduction ("The Study of Poetry") and the accounts of Gray and Keats.

(It is true many of the intermediate works in the series have not survived.[5])

Old English literature is, of course, well worth study for its own sake. The English medievalist will need to acquaint himself with it in some detail, as he will need to acquaint himself with Old Norse, Old and Middle French, Middle High German, and the whole range of Latin literature, classical, post-classical, and medieval. But for the modern student of English literature *as a whole,* these disciplines must remain marginal luxuries. He has also, after all, a duty to the Latin, Greek, and Hebrew classics, and the Italian, Spanish, and French Renaissances, as well as to the later European literatures, and he must find his way about the political, social, and intellectual contexts of English literature proper too, including American literature. Under these circumstances a nodding acquaintance with the language and literature of the Anglo-Saxons is all that it is reasonable to demand. If he has a facility for languages and can stumble through "The Wanderer," "The Seafarer," "The Dream of the Rood," and perhaps "The Battle of Maldon," in the original, so much the better. He will certainly want to read *Beowulf*—and perhaps the other heroic fragments as well—but most of it will necessarily have to be in translation. (The prose version by Clark Hall, which has recently been revised by C. L. Wrenn with an illuminating introduction by J. R. R. Tolkien, is no doubt the one to use.)

But if the conscientious student of English literature can certainly dispense with the full rigors of Anglo-Saxon vocabulary and grammar, a "real" critical estimate cannot be reached even in later Middle English without the cooperation of scholarship. Fortunately, Chaucer's language, like Gower's, is fairly easy, but the brilliant "Gawain-poet" —the anonymous author probably of *Pearl,* among other things, as well as of *Sir Gawain and the Green Knight*—

[5] See R. M. Wilson, *The Lost Literature of Medieval England* (1952).

is often impenetrable without the help of good notes and a glossary. Nor is it enough for the modern reader just to know the dictionary meanings of each word and sentence. The language used in a particular passage will often not release its special shades of meaning until it is related to the literary context in which the passage occurs. And here, with one or two honorable exceptions such as G. R. Owst's *Literature and Pulpit in Medieval England* (1933) and Ernst Robert Curtius' *Europäisches Literatur und lateinisches Mittelalter* (English translation 1952), the scholars have been less helpful so far.

What exactly, it may be asked, is the "context" of a work of literature? A rough answer might be that context is the layer or layers of meaning that literature super-adds to language. But Aristotle's distinctions in Chapters I to III of the *Poetics* still provide the best point of critical departure. In addition to language, the *mode of communication*, as Aristotle has it, with the limitations and emphases a particular language imposes at each stage of its evolution, there is *manner of presentation* (drama, narrative, oratory, the letter, etc.), that is, a series of author-audience relationships, each with its own technical problems and conventions. Finally, according to Aristotle,[6] there are the "objects of imitation," that is, *subject matter*, which means in practice the topics and themes in which the author and his original public took a special interest.

Aristotle's triad provides at any rate a tidy prescriptive formula. Here are the three questions which the modern reader must learn to ask himself if he is to make contact —Arnold's "real estimate"—with a medieval author.

[6] Aristotle puts the "objects of imitation" second, but their logical position in his analysis is *third:* the *Iliad* is (i) a Greek (ii) narrative poem (iii) about the Trojan War.

2. The Mode of Communication and Its Literary Consequences

In the four centuries that followed the Norman Conquest, England was trilingual. Broadly speaking, up to 1350 or even later, the ruling class spoke and wrote in French, while the country's official and intellectual life was conducted in Latin. English, the speech of the middle and lower classes, was hardly ever *written* at all, except for purposes of religious edification. But in the second half of the fourteenth century, English began to displace French and Latin more or less everywhere. (The non-literary evidence of this linguistic revolution is summarized in G. G. Coulton's *Chaucer and His England* [1908]). Inevitably, however, because of the suddenness with which English rose in the social scale, it retained—even in the hands of courtiers such as Chaucer and Gower, or intellectuals such as Wyclif and Hilton—much of its popular nature. An important literary consequence is that Middle English poetry—unlike Old English poetry—has almost no conventional "poetic diction" until the fifteenth century. The most disconcerting characteristic, however, of fourteenth- and fifteenth-century Middle English for the modern reader is its plethora of varying forms and pronunciations. Those simple outlines of Chaucer's English obligingly provided in modern editions of his poems are always tiresomely peppered with qualifications—"sometimes," "often," "usually, "occasionally." There *was* no standard or King's English in the fourteenth century, largely because until Henry IV no King of England had spoken English as his native tongue since Harold. Instead there were dozens of overlapping regional dialects, each as "correct" as the next. The immediate literary effect of the dialectal differences in pronouns, inflectional endings, pronunciation, and vocabulary was to make stylistic finish, "the best words in the best order," an ideal almost impossible to attain. Even in London no two speakers could be counted on to agree which the best words and word-order were. One must not, therefore, expect a Middle English equivalent either of *la poésie pure*, with its "vowel music" and elaborate verbal patterns, or of the delicate linguistic precision that almost any eighteenth-century satirist seems to exhibit. It is true Chaucer's early poems are full of the rhetorical figures that Geoffrey de Vinsauf, Matthieu de Vendôme, and the others had codified, but he was never able to maintain this artificial elegance for more than a few lines at a time. The commentators are fond of pointing out the *interpretatio* (variations)—complete with *sententia* (moral generalization), *contentio* (antithesis), *circumlocutio*, oxymoron, chiasmus, and suspension—of the opening lines of the *Parliament of Fowls:*

> The lyf so short, the craft so long to lerne,
> Th' assay so hard, so sharp the conquerynge,
> The dredful joye, alwey that slit so yerne . . .

But they all omit the rest of the stanza, in which Chaucer gets off the rhetorical high horse with an almost ludicrous haste:

> Al this mene I by Love, that my felynge
> Astonyeth with his wonderful werkynge
> So sore, iwis, that whan I on hym thynke,
> Nat wot I wel wher that I flete or synke.

Instead of a climax in the same resounding end-stopped iambics, the rhythm has suddenly become that of common speech:

> Al this mene I . . .

(That is, four stressed syllables in a row.) The "iwis" of the last line but one is also the merest padding, and the stanza ends with a grotesque image apparently of Chaucer bathing!

The *Parliament* is one of Chaucer's earlier poems, and

the lapse from decorum was perhaps unintentional. Later, however, a playing off of the low with the high style became one of his regular devices. He even evolved a sort of "low" rhetoric of his own with the popular proverb displacing the *sententia* and such phrases as "shortly for to telle" and "nevere was ther seyn with mannes ye/ So noble array" displacing respectively *occupatio* (the continued refusal to describe this or that—a device by which this or that is in fact described) and hyperbole. Chaucer is noticeably more comfortable in these native and colloquial figures of speech than in the "colours of rethoryk." The English language was not ripe as yet for a Milton or a Mallarmé. The fact that Lydgate, Chaucer's most indefatigable disciple, keeps on eulogizing his master's "flowers of rethorick eloquence" only confirms the doubts everybody has always had about Lydgate's literary sense.[7] Even in the fifteenth century, though English had by then largely lost its semi-servile status, the problem of linguistic "correctness" had not been consciously realized. The Scottish Chaucerians did better than the English, perhaps because when they imitated Chaucer they were really writing in an almost dead language, of which the "rules," as it were, were all to be found in his poems.

The absence of any concept or criterion of "correctness" in Middle English speech helps to account for the peculiarities of Middle English prosody. A compromise had to be worked out between the accentual Old English verse and the French syllabic system. In theory the Middle English octosyllabic couplet consists of four stresses, as the Old English alliterative line had done, though with the number of syllables between each stress now reduced to one. In practice, however, irregularity prevailed. Few consecutive Middle English lines have the "correct" number either

---

[7] Lydgate's real point—which is echoed in most of the fifteenth-century compliments to Chaucer—is that with Chaucer English poetry becomes a conscious art comparable to that of the Greeks, Romans, Italians, and French. It is in this sense that he is the "Father" of our poetry.

of stresses or of syllables. Chaucer's prosody—which was shared by Gower and the other Court poets—has not much more than the appearance of a greater syllabic regularity, and even that is truer of our overedited modern texts than of the original manuscripts. J. M. Manly's great Chicago edition, based on all the manuscripts and early printed texts, has in fact left us with a text that is far less smooth metrically than that of the earlier editors. Moreover, such regularity as Chaucer obtained—in deference to his French and Italian models—was more fiction than fact. The inflectional endings, especially the unstressed final -e (which Chaucer certainly expected to be pronounced, however faintly, at the end of the line), provide the principal fiction. With a few exceptions they count or do not count as a syllable entirely as metrical convenience dictates. In other words, the reader must know the meter before he can begin to read the poem—a condition no poet is entitled to impose. (It is the fallacy of classical meters in English: a meter must always emerge naturally from the text's own speech-rhythms, which are themselves conditioned by the sense.) Chaucer's frequent omission of the first unstressed syllable of the line and his insertion of an extra syllable at the caesural pause have been excused as "licenses." As naturally read, however, such lines do not in practice differentiate themselves from the "correctly" decasyllabic ones. We do not notice them. The actual metrical norm in the *Canterbury Tales* varies from nine to twelve syllables in just the same way as the blank verse of a Jacobean dramatist. Juggling with the final -e will usually produce a line that adds up to ten (or with a final -e at the end of the line eleven) syllables, but the essential rhythm is in fact preserved whether the -e is sounded more or less faintly or dropped altogether. Chaucer is not to be scanned like Pope or Tennyson by counting syllables. The desperate hypothesis that men such as Hoccleve, who had known Chaucer personally, could not read his verse as well as a twentieth-century prosodist, derives from this failure to distinguish between the fiction of a quasi-French syllabic regularity and the accentual reality. With Chaucer—as with Langland, the Gawain-poet, and even Wyatt—it is the total *stress weight* of the syllables that determines the equivalence between one line and the next. The precise number of the unstressed syllables, because they have next to no weight, has next to no metrical significance; what is important is to get the degrees of stress right.

The prosodic principle on which Chaucerian verse is constructed was defined by George Gascoigne in *Certain Notes of Instruction concerning the Making of Verse or Rime in English* (1575):

> . . . our father *Chaucer* hath used the same libertie
> in feete and measures that the Latinists do use: and
> who so ever do peruse and well consider his workes,
> he shall finde that although his lines are not alwayes
> of one selfe same number of Syllables, yet, beyng
> redde bye one that hath understanding, the longest
> verse, and that which hath most Syllables in it, will
> fall (to the eare) correspondent unto that which
> hath fewest sillables in it: and like wise that whiche
> hath in it fewest syllables shalbe founde yet to con-
> sist of woordes that have suche naturall sounde, as
> may seeme equall in length to a verse which hath
> many moe sillables of lighter accentes. And surely I
> can lament that wee are fallen into suche a playne
> and simple manner of wryting, that there is none
> other foote used but one; whereby our Poemes may
> justly be called Rithmes, and cannot by any right chal-
> lenge the name of a Verse.[8]

Gascoigne's complaint against the tyranny of syllabic regularity has been met since his time by the elaboration, notably by Milton, of metrical fictions similar to Chaucer's. Although our prosody is primarily accentual it has had

[8] *Elizabethan Critical Essays*, edited by G. Gregory Smith (1904), I, 50.

to be made to look syllabic too. By Gascoigne's time the pressure to conform syllabically had become greater because the ideal of linguistic "correctness," of which it is an offshoot, was very much in the air. Chaucer could take his metrics more lightheartedly. Dialectal pronunciations provided a nice range of rhymes. Thus the modern *merry* usually appears in his poems as *murye* (the southwestern form), but if this did not suit the rhyme he could also use *mirye* (the northeastern form) or *merye* (the southeastern form). And the final unstressed *-e*—normally pronounced in his time by the older generation and by southerners, but not by younger speakers or northerners —was equally obliging. Under the veneer of a French orthodoxy, rhetorical and prosodic, the essential Chaucer (like the essential Gawain-poet, who had a similar Court veneer) managed to remain as uncommitted as the English language itself was in his time.

3. The Manner of Presentation: Oral Delivery

The two styles that are juxtaposed in the first stanza of *The Parliament of Fowls* are best thought of as two different tones of voice. In the three rhetorical lines with which the poem opens, Chaucer is out to impress us; the phrases are noticeably bookish and pedagogic. But he cannot—or at any rate does not—keep it up. A mode of communication without "correctness" to stiffen it and give it authority could not aspire to the grand style (of which verbal decorum is a prerequisite), except for brief moments. And so with a shrug of his shoulders and an apologetic smile Chaucer changes the tone of his voice, which becomes abrupt, intimate, and humorous. The narrator's abandonment of generalization for personal comment is perhaps the most striking difference between the two halves of the stanza. At first it is an anonymous voice, the conventional literary man's, who is speaking to us from a raised dais as it were; then the impersonal narrator comes down into the audience and Chaucer himself, or a persona calling itself Chaucer, becomes vividly present.

Chaucer's two voices—which enter via the "gentils" and "churls" into the whole presentation of the *Canterbury Tales*—exploit for purposes of drama the most serious technical limitation of Middle English literature: its dependence on oral recitation. The more ambitious works were always read aloud; the popular tale or romance was recited by a minstrel; the lyrics and ballads were sung either solo or in unison (at least for the refrains). Theatrical presentation of a kind had also begun in the miracle plays. But reading in the modern sense—silently, to oneself—though already normal, apparently, for Latin and French—had scarcely begun in English. Unlike Provence, where each poet had a professional reciter, the Middle English poet had, therefore, to *act* his own poetry as though it was a dramatic monologue.[9]

The frontispiece to the Cambridge (Corpus Christi) manuscript of *Troilus and Criseyde* shows Chaucer reading the poem to Richard II, the royal family, and other members of the English Court. Some of the younger courtiers, who are reclining on the ground, do not seem to be paying much attention to what Chaucer is saying. A public reading of any length tends to be monotonous at any time. Chaucer's brilliant solution of the problem was to include his audience in the narrative by direct appeals to them— or sometimes to groups within the audience, such as the lovers or the ladies—to confirm his own interpretation of his "auctour" or source. And complementing this pseudo-chorus of an oral audience (who were not expected, of course, to respond verbally to the second-person-plural appeals), Chaucer gradually evolved his own pseudo-narrator, a little thick in the head, without any personal experience of sexual love, who was and was not Chaucer himself.

The pseudo-narrator is perhaps the most interesting of

[9] The oral facts are tabulated by Ruth Crosby in two articles in *Speculum*, XI (1936), XIII (1938).

the literary conventions that originated in the practice of oral delivery. We meet him not only in Chaucer but also in *Piers Plowman*, whose grotesque Long Will is not quite William Langland, just as the diffident lover of the *Confessio Amantis* is only nominally John Gower (the identity is not revealed until Book VIII). Some of the convention's refinements deserve attention. Chaucer's Lollius, for example, the nonexistent Latin historian of the Trojan War, is a nice example of the *pseudo-source*. Boccaccio's *Il Filostrato*, the actual source of *Troilus and Criseyde*, is never mentioned in the poem, and the principal episodes that Chaucer attributes to Lollius are in fact his own invention. The pseudo-source is here a sort of cushion, therefore, between the pseudo-narrator and the pseudo-audience. The only audience the historical Chaucer was seriously interested in, as the epilogue to *Troilus* makes plain, was his friends "moral Gower and philosophical Strode," whom he expects to *read* the poem to themselves. A somewhat similar device is Malory's "French book." Over and over again Malory refers the reader to this usually nonexistent French source. The passage at the very end on Arthur's four knights who join a Crusade is typical. Eugène Vinaver adds a note here in the standard modern edition of the *Morte d'Arthur:*

> Once again Malory's reference to the French book is meant to conceal his departure from it. In no French version do Arthur's knights appear as crusaders.

It is almost as if Chaucer and Malory were exchanging winks with the more sophisticated members of their audiences. The apparatus of realism—for example, the introduction of a real Southwark innkeeper to act as master of ceremonies on the pilgrimage to Canterbury, or Malory's elaborate identification of Astolat with Guildford—has been provided for the simpler souls in the audience. The literary heart of their matter is much less naïve.

4. Subject Matter: The Middle English Mind

With *Piers Plowman* (completed *c.* 1377), *Troilus and Criseyde* (written *c.* 1385), the *Canterbury Tales* (1387–94), and *Sir Gawain and the Green Knight* (*c.* 1390?), English literature suddenly came of age. The suddenness is as remarkable as the superiority in literary quality over the earlier prose and verse. These four superb poems, each of epic length and achievement, are among the classics of world literature—and they were all written within twenty years of each other. Nor do they stand alone. Although exact dates are difficult to determine, this was also the period, more or less, of the best miracle plays, the first ballads, and some of the best carols, as well as of such minor masterpieces as Chaucer's early poems, the *Pearl,* and Gower's *Confessio Amantis.* It cannot be a coincidence that this literature all belongs to the generation immediately succeeding the bubonic pandemic of 1348–49 that is now known as the Black Death. In Toynbeean terms the generation of Langland, Chaucer, and the Gawain-poet was a "response" to the "challenge" of the Black Death. A society that loses one third of its population in some fifteen months must adjust itself violently if it is to survive. And somehow, though few of the details seem to be known, England did adjust itself; in the process the feudal world and its ecclesiastical complements, threatened for some time, at last began to disintegrate and a new social order to take its place. The Elizabethans looking back at it called it Merry England. Merry or not, English became its official language instead of French and Latin, and a new hierarchy of values was soon ordering church, state, and the individual's private life.

The collapse of villeinage is the affair of the economic historian, but the decline of the "gentils" and the upsurge of the villeins had their literary effects too. It is, in a sense, what the *Canterbury Tales* is all about. The topic to which the Pilgrims keep on returning is love and marriage. At the heart of the new scheme of values is a new sympathy with sexual love. The medieval church had been built on a morality of asceticism to which *pulchritudo* was detestable because it was the continuous source of temptation to a clergy forbidden both to marry and to "burn." But in a country that suddenly finds itself depopulated, procreation becomes one of the essentials of the society's survival,[10] and *pulchritudo* returned to its proper place in the values of *l'homme moyen sensuel*. Moreover, because it had achieved its new status from below, human (sexual) love often carried with it remnants of the half-buried pre-Christian fertility cults. The summer of the Robin Hood ballads,

> when the shawes be sheyne,
> And leves be large and long,

is a more realistic mating season than the May of the French dream-visions, perhaps because the Christian veneer of the courtly love-game is absent. Hood himself, the cunning disguiser and invincible fighting man, seems to descend from Odin, as incidentally does the "Blind Harry" who speaks the superb "Manner of the Crying of a Play" that is attributed to Dunbar, the most brilliant of the Middle Scots poets. The modern reader of the fifteenth-century ballad, especially the supernatural ones, cannot but be conscious of the implicit pagan roots; in F. J. Child's definitive *English and Scottish Popular Ballads* (1882–98) the specifically Christian references are few and far between.[11] In Malory, too, Fate is the ultimate enemy, a concept that is at least ethically preferable to the French clockwork of Fortune's Wheel.

The paganism of the later fourteenth century is notice-

[10] Chaucer's Host's regret that the Monk was forbidden to beget children will be remembered. See *Canterbury Tales* B 3133 ff.

[11] See Lowry C. Wimberly, *Folklore in the English and Scottish Ballads* (1928, rev. 1959).

ably more genial and optimistic than either that of the
ballads and Malory or that of the Anglo-Saxon poets. In
Chaucer and the Gawain-poet, and even in Langland, the
will is free and the universe infinitely various. Here is God's
plenty! The originally Platonic doctrine of plenitude—whose
history from the *Timaeus* to Pope's *Essay on Man* has been
traced in A. O. Lovejoy's brilliant *The Great Chain of Being* (1936)—had undergone an Aristotelian stratification
into hierarchies in the Middle Ages. But the original exu-
berance was always liable to erupt and upset "degree"—as
it did in the Dea Natura of Bernardus Sylvestris and Alanus
of Lille. Chaucer's ambivalent irony did not exclude either
interpretation. In this evasion of an intellectual commit-
ment Chaucer's philosophy of life conforms to the mode of
popular allegory that characterizes post-Black Death England. It might be called proverbial allegory. A proverb is
a generalization that is still not detached from the typical
concrete instance that embodies it:

> Our economists of today theorize about the "inevita-
> bility of gradualness." Our ancestors of the less cere-
> bral fifteenth century meant much the same thing,
> but they might say "Little by little the cat eateth up
> the bacon flickle," or "Feather by feather the goose is
> plucked."[12]

A kind of thinking goes on in the proverb but it is pre-
conceptual. The proverb-coiner has the urge to generalize,
though his mind is unable to reach the final stage of an abstraction under which the particular examples of a principle can fall. In this sense *Piers Plowman* is an enlarged or
extended proverb, and a similar process is clearly at work
in *Sir Gawain* and the "Merchant's Tale," though the progress toward abstraction has not gone so far in them as in
Langland. This English proverbial allegory is the opposite,
therefore, of the allegory of the *Roman de la Rose*—or *The*

[12] *Oxford Dictionary of Proverbs* (1935), p. xii.

Faerie Queene for that matter—where concept precedes personification. With Langland, on the other hand, we begin with Piers the honest yokel and it is only gradually and almost imperceptibly that he grows into Do-wel, Do-bet, and Do-best. In other words, generalization works itself out in the process of narration. The audience does not know that Piers is a symbol both of mankind and of Christ until the narrative eventually compels it to make the identification. (Paganism wakes up and finds itself Christianity.) Moreover, in making the identification we have the feeling that our discovery is only repeating a similar conversion in Langland himself. The relationship is not that of preacher and congregation so much as a conspiracy of author and audience, who are exploring the nature of reality simultaneously and together. The remarkable Christian mystics of the period, Richard Rolle and his followers and the author of the beautiful anonymous *Cloud of Unknowing*, were also, therefore, a part of the Peasants' (spiritual) Revolt. John Ball's strange letter to his Essex followers— with its combination of Christian Utopianism and gibberish, proverbial wisdom and cryptic references to *Piers Plowman*—sums up in dramatic popular allegory the aspirations of Chaucer's England:

> John Sheep, sometime Saint Mary priest of York and now of Colchester, greeteth well John Nameless and John the Miller and John Carter, and biddeth them that they be ware of guile in borough and standeth together in God's name, and biddeth Piers Plowman go to his work and chastise well Hob the Robber, and taketh with you John Trueman and all his fellows and no more and look shape you [appoint for yourselves] to one head and no more.

> John the Miller hath ground small, small, small;
> The King's Son of Heaven shall pay for all.
> Beware or ye be woe,
> Knoweth your friend from your foe.

Haveth enough and sayeth "Ho,"
And do well and better, and flee-eth sin,
And seeketh peace, and hold you therein.

And so biddeth John Trueman and all his fellows.[13]

[13] I have modernized the spelling. The original text can be
found in Sisam's *Fourteenth-Century Verse and Prose* (1921),
pp. 160–61.

III.   A Middle English Reading List

1. Bibliographies, Literary Histories, and Anthologies

BIBLIOGRAPHIES

The Middle English section of *CBEL* (Vol. I, 1940–see
above, p. 1), was mainly the work of John Edwin Wells,
whose *Manual of the Writings in Middle English, 1050–
1400* (1916; nine Supplements, 1919–52) is an indispensable if uninspiring work of reference, which lists and summarizes almost every book and article about Middle English literature down to 1945 as well as describing the
various Middle English works themselves. The Modern
Language Association of America is preparing a one-
volume revision to consolidate Wells, bring it up to date,
and extend it to 1500; in the meantime annual lists in
PMLA (unfortunately restricted to the work of American
scholars until 1956) provide a current record of Middle
English scholarly output. Wells included some fifteenth-
century items such as the romances and the drama; other
aspects are covered by H. S. Bennett in the Bibliography to
his *OHEL* volume (*Chaucer and the Fifteenth Century*,
1947, pp. 240–318), which has an alphabetical catalogue
of authors and anonyma and is also good on background
topics.

LITERARY HISTORIES

W. P. Ker's short *English Literature, Medieval* (1912)
has been reissued as *Medieval English Literature* (1942)
with a Supplementary Note by R. W. Chambers, who
calls it "a classic of English Criticism"; if not quite that, it

is at any rate an eminently readable and sensible survey. A longer and more ambitious work is Margaret Schlauch's *English Medieval Literature and Its Social Foundations* (Warsaw, 1956), which conceals under its Marxist framework a fresh and acute reappraisal of the whole range of English literature from *Beowulf* to the Renaissance. This is probably the best critical introduction to the period now available. Dorothy Everett, who had been assigned the earlier Middle English period for *OHEL*, died with only a few chapters completed; they have now been printed in her posthumous *Essays on Middle English Literature* (1955), which also includes two informative essays on Chaucer's verbal artistry. Her *OHEL* period is now being undertaken by J. A. W. Bennett, the author of *The Parlement of Foules* (1957) and the present editor of the period's quarterly, *Medium Aevum*. It is unlikely, however, to supersede R. M. Wilson's *Early Middle English Literature* (1939, rev. 1951), which is both thorough and sensible. The *OHEL* volumes by E. K. Chambers (1945) and H. S. Bennett (1947) cover the fifteenth century between them, though the division of labor follows no obvious logical principle; H. S. Bennett's volume also includes a long, rather dull chapter on Chaucer. Two far livelier if more restricted surveys are R. W. Chambers's *On the Continuity of English Prose* (1932), which argues, with effective quotations, that the prose style first found in Alfred characterizes all the best English prose to More and even later, and C. S. Lewis's *The Allegory of Love* (1936), which traces—with all sorts of fireworks and perversities en route—the history of the love-allegory from the *Roman de la Rose* to Spenser. Incidentally, Lewis's notion that courtly love was necessarily adulterous even in England is neatly disposed of by Gervase Mathew in *The Essays Presented to Charles Williams* (1947), a collection edited, ironically enough, by Lewis himself. Lewis's last contribution to medieval studies was *The Discarded Image* (1964; a wide-ranging survey of the classical bases). John Speirs's *Medieval English Poetry* (1957), an attempt to assess the literary qualities of what he calls "the non-Chaucerian tradition" (i.e., lyrics, romances, alliterative poems, and miracle plays), is enthusiastic but amateurish; George Kane's *Middle English Literature: a Critical Study of the Romances, the Religious Lyrics, Pier's Plowman* (1951), on the other hand, is severely professional. (But both are well worth reading.) As much can hardly be said of C. S. Baldwin's *Medieval Rhetoric to 1400* (1928, reissued 1959) or J. W. H. Atkins's *English Literary Criticism: the Medieval Phase* (1943), though they, too, are useful to dip into. But Geoffroi de Vinsauf (who was apparently an Englishman, even if he lived in France and wrote in Latin) and his fellow rhetoricians are best consulted in Edmond Faral's edition of *Les Arts Poétiques du XIIe et du XIIIe Siècle* (Paris, 1924). The specialist journals catering especially for this period are *Speculum* (1926–) and *Medium Aevum* (1932–). Some interesting specimens of the more sophisticated critical methods now fashionable in medieval studies will be found in *Critical Approaches to Medieval Literature* (ed. Dorothy Bethurum, 1960).

ANTHOLOGIES

The most recent general anthology is the Bruce Dickins and R. M. Wilson *Early Middle English Literature* (1951), which was intended to cover the twelfth and thirteenth centuries on the lines of Kenneth Sisam's *Fourteenth-Century Verse and Prose* (1921, rev. 1937). The extracts are shorter, however, than in Sisam and there is no equivalent to Sisam's masterly introduction, which is in effect a miniature literary history of the whole period. Rolf Kaiser's bulky *Alt- und Mittel-englische Anthologie* (rev. as *Medieval English,* Berlin, 1961) includes specimens, with textual notes, of almost everything of interest from the beginnings to *c.* 1500 except *Beowulf* and Chaucer; explanatory notes and a glossary are promised in a second volume. R. S. Loomis and R. Willard's *Medieval English Verse and Prose in Modernized Versions* (1948) also omits Chaucer, but its specimens are useful elsewhere as introduction or short cut; other modernizations, rather too "poetic" perhaps for most tastes today, will be found in Jessie L. Weston's *Romance, Vision, and Satire* (1912, restricted to alliterative pieces) and her *Chief Middle English Poets* (1914). Eleanor P. Hammond's *English Verse between Chaucer and Surrey* (1927), the best general selection of fifteenth- and early sixteenth-century poetry, has separate introductions and notes to the twenty poets included as well as a long General Introduction which is especially useful on fifteenth-century prosody. The only prose selection is William Matthews's first-class *Later Medieval English Prose* (1963); the texts, from Mandeville and Wyclif to Caxton, are slightly modernized (introduction and headnotes especially interesting on prose style).

2. Special Studies

Charles L. Kingsford: *English Historical Literature in the Fifteenth Century* (1913). Includes letter collections.

Joseph Wright: *An Elementary Middle English Grammar* (1928).

James P. Oakden: *Alliterative Poetry in Middle English* (2 vols., 1930–35).

Gerald R. Owst: *Literature and Pulpit in Medieval England* (1933). Influence of popular preachers—especially useful for Langland.

George G. Coulton: *Medieval Panorama: the English Scene from Conquest to Reformation* (1938).

Carleton Brown and R. H. Robbins: *The Index of Middle English Verse* (1943). First-line index of every extant Middle English poem with details of editions, etc.

Edith Rickert: *Chaucer's World* (ed. Clair C. Olson and M. M. Crow, 1948). Extracts from a wide range of medieval documents translated into modern English to illustrate Chaucer's social background.

Fernand Mossé: *A Handbook of Middle English* (tr. James A. Walker, 1952). The best linguistic introduction.

H. Kurath and S. H. Kuhn: *Middle English Dictionary*

(1952–   ; in progress). Designed to supersede *OED* for the period.

Medieval England, edited by Austin L. Poole (rev. 2 vols., 1958). Nineteen essays by different experts on various aspects of English life and culture.

3. LYRICS, ROMANCES, DRAMA, BALLADS

LYRICS

A good short general selection of Middle English lyrics is E. K. Chambers and Frank Sidgwick's *Early English Lyrics, Amorous, Divine, and Trivial* (1907), which has brief notes. For the reluctant beginner a better point of departure might be Speirs's chapter on "Carols and Other Songs and Lyrics" in his *Medieval English Poetry* (1957); Speirs prints twenty-six poems in full and is engagingly enthusiastic about their merits. Similar but more scholarly and more comprehensve is R. T. Davies's *Medieval English Lyrics* (1963) which includes 187 pieces (to Wyatt), sensible introductory notes, and modern versions on opposite pages where necessary. The whole extant corpus of Middle English lyrical verse is available, with a full apparatus of introductions and notes, in three volumes edited by Carleton Brown (*Thirteenth Century,* 1932; *Fourteenth Century* [religious verse], rev. G. V. Smithers 1952; *Fifteenth Century* [religious verse], 1939), supplemented by Richard L. Greene's *Early English Carols* (1935; Selection 1962), and R. H. Robbins's *Secular Lyrics of the Fourteenth and Fifteenth Centuries* (1952), and *Historical Poems of the XIVth and XVth Centuries* (1959). The famous *Harley Lyrics,* so called because they are preserved in the British Museum MS. Harley 2253–"Alysoun," "Lenten is come with love to towne," etc.–have been edited by G. L. Brook (1948, rev. 1956). Lawrence Minot's rather dreary political lyrics are also available (ed. Joseph Hall, 1887, rev. 1914), and Frances M. M. Comper's *Life of Richard Rolle* (1928) includes his mystical lyrics. There is a sane critical discussion of the religious lyrics of the period by George Kane in his *Middle English Literature* (1951); Arthur K. Moore's *Secular Lyric in Middle English* (1951) is thorough but rather heavy going.

ROMANCES

With the two exceptions of *Sir Gawain and the Green Knight* (see p. 42 below) and Malory's *Morte d'Arthur* (see p. 44 below) the English medieval romances are not of much literary interest, the runner-up being perhaps the alliterative *Morte d'Arthur* (ed. James D. Bruce, EETS, 1903). The most elaborate edition of the romances is Walter H. French and C. B. Hale's *Middle English Metrical Romances* (1930). An excellent summary of the Arthurian romances, their problems, and their background is available in *Arthurian Literature in the Middle Ages* (1959) by R. S. Loomis and others; Loomis's *Development of Arthurian Romance* (1963) is a much shorter introduction to the same material. Geoffrey of Monmouth's *Historia Regum Britanniae* is available, with other early Arthurian texts, in Edmond Faral's *La Légende Arthurienne* (3 vols., Paris, 1929); its historical pretensions have recently been exposed by J. S. P. Tatlock in the masterly *Legendary History of Britain* (1950). The Everyman series includes translations or modernizations of Geoffrey of Monmouth, Layamon's *Brut*, both the alliterative and the stanzaic *Morte Arthure*, and all Chrétien de Troyes's Arthurian romances except the *Perceval*. For the Alexander romances the standard work is F. P. Magoun's edition of *The Gests of Alexander* (1929). Other romances now obtainable in annotated modern editions include Thomas Chestre's *Sir Launfal* (ed. A. J. Bliss, 1960) and *Kyng Alisaunder* (ed. G. V. Smithers, 2 vols., EETS, 1952–57). A critical discussion of the metrical romances will be found in George Kane's *Middle English Literature* (1951). Laura Hibbard's *Medieval Romance in England* (1924, rev. 1959) is the standard work on the non-cyclic romances.

DRAMA

A. W. Pollard's *English Miracle Plays, Moralities, and Interludes* (1890, final rev. 1927) only prints five miracle plays, but its long and lucid introduction is still useful. On the other hand, A. C. Cawley's collection in the Everyman series (1956) includes fourteen miracle plays, all with short explanatory footnotes, as well as *Everyman* itself. His edition of the six pieces by the "Wakefield Master" (1958) is more scholarly and is fully annotated. Martial Rose's *The Wakefield Mystery Plays* (1963) can also be recommended. Joseph Q. Adams's *Chief Pre-Shakespearean Dramas* (1924) retains its value because of its inclusiveness; the notes are very short but almost everything of dramatic interest down to *c.* 1570 has been packed into its 712 pages. Another general collection is *Representative Medieval and Tudor Plays*, edited by R. S. Loomis and H. W. Wells (1942). Unfortunately the four cycles (York, Towneley, Chester, and "Ludus Coventriae") are only available in EETS and similar nineteenth-century editions without adequate annotation, and many of the often interesting single plays and fragmentary cycles are in the same condition. The standard accounts are E. K. Chambers, *The Medieval Stage* (2 vols., 1903), and Hardin Craig, *English Religious Drama of the Middle Ages* (1955), both descriptive rather than critical. Karl Young's *The Drama of the Medieval Church* (2 vols., 1933), the classic account of the liturgical drama, sets the English beginnings in their wider European context.

THE BALLADS

The most convenient edition is the Cambridge one-volume abbreviation (1904) of Francis J. Child's exhaustive *English and Scottish Popular Ballads* (5 vols., 1882–98; reissued 3 vols., 1957). The shorter edition prints 301 of the 307 ballads in the larger collection, though it reduces the number of versions of each ballad to the two or three most interesting ones. George L. Kittredge, Child's pupil and successor at Harvard, provides a long introduction that is still valuable, and there are detailed headnotes to each ballad. Bertrand H. Bronson is bringing out an indispensable supplement in *The Traditional Tunes of the Child Ballads* (Vol. I, 1959). No modern editor has attempted to supersede Child and only a handful more ballads of the "Child" type have turned up this century; *The Viking Book of Folk Ballads* (ed. Albert B. Friedman, 1956) is a selection of interest because it abandons the "Child" formula and gives the musical airs. The printed street ballads, ignored by Child, can be sampled in *The Common Muse: an Anthology of Popular British Ballad Poetry, XVth–XXth Century,* edited by V. de Sola Pinto and A. E. Rodway (1957). The best single book on the ballads is probably G. H. Gerould's *The Ballad of Tradition* (1932), but M. J. C. Hodgart's shorter *Ballads* (1950) in Hutchinsons' University Library series is an excellent introduction to the whole subject.

4. Single Works and Authors

(In approximately chronological order; the *CBEL* references are to *The Cambridge Bibliography of English Literature* [1940] and its Supplement [1957], which has the same pagination.)

Ancren Riwle (late twelfth century). Edited (from Cotton MS.) by Mabel Day (EETS, 1952); edited (from Caius College MS.) by R. M. Wilson (EETS, 1952); edited (from Royal MS.) by Albert C. Baugh (EETS, 1956); edited (from Bodleian MS.) by Frances M. Mack (EETS, 1963). Parts 6 and 7 have also been edited with full explanatory notes and glossary by Geoffrey Shepherd (1960). The most recent translation into modern English is by M. B. Salu (1956). (*CBEL,* I, 179 f.)

The Owl and the Nightingale (*c.* 1200). Edited by J. W. H. Atkins (1922, with translation); edited by J. H. G. Grattan and G. F. H. Sykes (EETS, 1935; parallel texts of the two manuscripts); edited by Eric G. Stanley (1960; excellent introduction and notes). (*CBEL*, I, 181 f.)

Layamon (early thirteenth century). *Brut.* Critical edition in preparation by G. L. Brook and R. F. Leslie (EETS, Vol. I, 1963). Selections by Joseph Hall (1924) and J. A. W. Bennett (1964). (*CBEL*, I, 163 f.)

The Lay of Havelok (late thirteenth century). Edited by W. W. Skeat (1868; final rev. by Kenneth Sisam, 1915). Translated by A. J. Wyatt, 1913. (*CBEL*, I, 148 f.)

Sir Orfeo (early fourteenth century). Good edition by A. J. Bliss (1954). (*CBEL*, I, 151 f.)

Richard Rolle (*c.* 1300–1349). *English Writings*, edited by Hope Emily Allen (1931); *Minor Works*, edited and translated by Geraldine E. Hodgson (1923); *Selected Works*, edited by G. C. Heseltine (1930). For Rolle's life and writings, see Hope Emily Allen (1927) and Frances M. M. Comper (1928; includes edition of Rolle's lyrics). Conrad Pepler's *English Religious Heritage* (1950) is a competent introduction to the later English medieval mystics, including Julian of Norwich (*c.* 1343–*c.* 1415), Walter Hilton (d. 1396), and the author of *The Cloud of Unknowing* (*c.* 1370), as well as Rolle. (*CBEL*, I, 191 f.)

"Sir John Mandeville." *Travels*, edited by Paul Hamelius (EETS, 2 vols., 1919–23). See Josephine W. Bennett's masterly *Rediscovery of Sir John Mandeville* (1954). There is a modern English version of Mandeville by Malcolm Letts (2 vols., 1953). (*CBEL*, I, 191.)

John Wyclif (*c.* 1325–1384). *Select English Writings*, edited by H. E. Winn (1929; useful introduction and notes). Mathew Spinka's *Advocates of Reform* (1953) includes translations from Wyclif and others (to Erasmus) with a good introduction. The standard life is that by Herbert B. Workman (2 vols., 1926). For the Wycliffite Bible, see Margaret Deanesly's *Lollard Bible* (1920). (*CBEL*, I, 203 f., 307 f.)

John Gower (1330?–1408). Complete works, edited (with notes) by G. C. Macaulay (4 vols., 1899–1902); Macaulay's edition of *Confessio Amantis* is also obtainable separately (EETS, 2 vols., 1900–1). Latin works translated by Eric W. Stockton (1962). C. S. Lewis has an entertaining chapter on Gower in his *Allegory of Love* (1936). (*CBEL*, I, 205 f.)

William Langland (*c.* 1332–*c.* 1400). *Piers Plowman:* edited by W. W. Skeat (EETS, 6 vols., 1863–84; rev. 2 vols. 1884 with *A, B,* and *C* texts in parallel columns); edited by Thomas A. Knott and David C. Fowler (1952; *A* text only, no explanatory notes); edited by George Kane and E. Talbot Donaldson (definitive edition; *A* version 1960, notes and *B* and *C* versions in preparation). The most recent prose version is J. F. Goodridge's Penguin paperback of the *B* text (1959), which has a good introduction and adequate notes. There is an unannotated version of the *B* text by H. W. Wells (1935) with a critical introduction by Nevill Coghill, who has also brought out his own selection (1949). The best book to date on *Piers Plowman* is E. Talbot Donaldson's *Piers Plowman: The C-Text and Its Poet* (1949), which is not in fact confined to the *C* text. Robert W. Frank (1957) expounds the *Vitae* (*B* text) convincingly; Elizabeth Salter's survey (1960) is a sensible introduction; and Nevill Coghill's British Academy lecture (1945), if not exactly sensible, is at least very ingenious. John Lawlor's study (1962), which concentrates on the literary aspects, can be recommended to nonspecialists. (*CBEL*, I, 197 f.)

Geoffrey Chaucer (*c.* 1343–1400). Standard edition by F. N. Robinson (1933, rev. 1957), which prints everything positively ascribable to Chaucer and has a summarized biography as well as thorough separate introductions and notes; the glossary is inferior to that in W. W. Skeat's elaborate Victorian edition (7 vols., 1894–97), and for the text of the *Canterbury Tales* Robinson has been superseded by the monumental J. M. Manly and Edith Rickert

edition based on all the extant manuscripts (8 vols., 1940).
For the undergraduate or beginner E. T. Donaldson's generous selection (1958) is preferable because of the excellent footnotes and separate critical discussion of each work
or tale. A. C. Baugh's *Chaucer's Major Poetry* (1964) is
fuller but less critical, though the notes are first-class.
Some of the editions of separate works are valuable
—notably R. K. Root's *Troilus and Criseyde* (1926, rev.
1945) and D. S. Brewer's *Parlement of Foules* (1960);
for a quick reading, A. C. Cawley's *Canterbury Tales*
(1958) and J. Warrington's *Troilus* (1963), both in the
Everyman series, provide marginal glosses and short explanatory footnotes. The technical aids include: Eleanor
P. Hammond's *Chaucer Bibliography* (1908), with its sequel by Dudley D. Griffith (1955); Caroline F. E. Spurgeon's *Five Hundred Years of Chaucer Criticism and Allusion, 1357–1900* (3 vols., 1925); Robert D. French's
Chaucer Handbook (1927, rev. 1947; a factual record);
the concordance by John S. P. Tatlock and Arthur G. Kennedy (1927); and for the *Canterbury Tales* the elaborate
Sources and Analogues, edited by W. F. Bryan and Germaine Dempster (1941).

Chaucer criticism has multiplied recently, but apart
from Dryden (preface to *Fables,* 1700) and Aldous Huxley (a brilliant essay on the pagan element in Chaucer in
On the Margin, 1921), no first-rate literary critic has ever
ventured into this field except C. S. Lewis (not quite first-
rate?), who has written provocatively on *Troilus* both in
The Allegory of Love (1936) and in "What Chaucer Really
Did to *Il Filostrato*" (*Essays and Studies of the English
Association,* XVII, 1932). The scholars have done much
useful work at the footnote level, but a defective literary
sense vitiates or limits most of their more ambitious discussions. Partial recent exceptions are perhaps Charles Musca-
tine's *Chaucer and the French Tradition* (1957), J. A. W.
Bennett's *The Parlement of Foules: an Interpretation*
(1957), and Wolfgang Clemen's *Chaucer's Early Poetry*
(1963). John Speirs's bold attempt to apply modern critical
methods in *Chaucer the Maker* (1951) did not unfortu-

nately fulfill its excellent intentions. A recent stylistic study, Robert O. Payne's *The Key of Remembrance* (1964), is intermittently suggestive, as is also (if less so) the unrelenting pursuit of biblical analogues in D. W. Robertson's learned *Preface to Chaucer* (1964). Of the older books, the lectures by J. L. Lowes (1934) seem to wear best, though W. C. Curry's *Chaucer and the Medieval Sciences* (1926, rev. 1960) is still indispensable in its special field. And G. L. Kittredge's short and infuriating study (1915) still has its admirers. The scholar-critics have generally been at their best in articles or essays rather than books. Specimens of their scattered works are to be found in the paperback collections edited by E. Wagenknecht (1960) and R. Schoeck and J. Taylor (2 vols., 1960–61). (*CBEL*, I, 208 f.)

"The Gawain-poet" (flourished *c.* 1390). *Sir Gawain and the Green Knight*, edited by J. R. R. Tolkien and E. V. Gordon (1925, rev. 1936), is the standard edition, but much useful supplementary information is provided in the Israel Gollancz and Mabel Day edition (EETS, 1940). The translation by James L. Rosenberg (1959) has a useful introduction by James R. Kreuzer; the best critical discussion to date is Marie Borroff's stylistic and metrical study (1962). *Pearl* has been excellently edited by E. V. Gordon (1953). Both poems are also available together in Everyman's Library (ed. A. C. Cawley, 1962). There are editions of *Patience* by H. Bateson (1912, rev. 1918) and of *Purity* (Cleanness) by Robert J. Menner (1920). (*CBEL*, I, 135 f., 201 f.)

Chaucer Apocrypha. Vol. VII of W. W. Skeat's edition of Chaucer (1897) contains many of the poems once ascribed to Chaucer, including *The Testament of Love* by Thomas Usk (d. 1388) and such fifteenth-century pieces as the *Tale of Beryn* and *The Cuckoo and the Nightingale*. D. A. Pearsall's edition of *The Flower and the Leaf* and *The Assembly of Ladies* (1964) has a good introduction, notes, and glossary. (*CBEL*, I, 254.)

John Barbour (1316?–1395). *The Bruce:* standard edition by W. W. Skeat (EETS, 4 parts, 1870–89; rev. for Scottish Text Society, 2 vols., 1893–94). (*CBEL*, I, 166 f.)

Thomas Hoccleve (*c.* 1368–*c.* 1450). Works, edited by F. J. Furnivall and Israel Gollancz (EETS, 3 vols., 1892–1925). (*CBEL*, I, 252 f.)

John Lydgate (*c.* 1370–*c.* 1450). Minor poems, edited by H. N. MacCracken and M. Sherwood (EETS, 2 vols., 1910–33). Most of the longer poems have also been edited by EETS. The best critical discussion of Lydgate is in Eleanor P. Hammond's *English Verse between Chaucer and Surrey* (1927), which also includes generous extracts from his work. W. F. Schirmer's life has been revised and translated by A. Keep (1961). A critical selection is in preparation by Norton Smith. (*CBEL*, I, 250 f.)

James I of Scotland (1394–1437). *The Kingis Quair:* standard edition by W. Mackay Mackenzie (1939). (*CBEL*, I, 256 f.)

Reginald Pecock (*c.* 1390–*c.* 1461). Definitive study by V. H. H. Green (1945). (*CBEL*, I, 260 f.)

Paston Letters. Excellent selection, with notes and glossary, by Norman Davis (1958). See also H. S. Bennett, *The Pastons and Their England* (1922, rev. 1931). (*CBEL*, I, 266.)

Robert Henryson (1429?–1508?). Standard edition of poems by G. Gregory Smith (Scottish Text Society, 3 vols., 1906–14; introduction in Vol. I especially valuable); the single-volume edition by H. Harvey Wood (1933, rev. 1958) is perfectly adequate for most purposes; there is also a scholarly selection by Charles Elliott (1963; good notes). The only recent study is by Marshall W. Stearns (1949), though E. M. W. Tillyard has a helpful account of "The Testament of Cressid" in *Five Poems* (1948). (*CBEL*, I, 257 f.)

Sir Thomas Malory (flourished *c.* 1470). Standard edition (from recently discovered Winchester MS.) by Eugène Vinaver (3 vols., 1947, rev. 1948 and 1963) has a persuasive, if often erroneous, critical introduction and elaborate notes. Vinaver's edition of Malory's last book has been issued separately with corrections (1955); the single-volume edition of Vinaver's complete text (1960) is without introduction and notes. The best general study is still Vinaver's earlier *Malory* (1929), but J. A. W. Bennett has edited some interesting *Essays on Malory* (1963) by a number of scholars, including C. S. Lewis. (*CBEL*, I, 263.)

William Caxton (*c.* 1422–1491). Good popular introduction by Nellie S. Aurner (1926), which prints most of Caxton's Prologues and Epilogues in an appendix; complete edition of these (with full biography) by W. J. B. Crotch (EETS, 1928). See also H. S. Bennett, *English Books and Readers, 1475–1557* (1952). (*CBEL*, I, 261 f.)

William Dunbar (*c.* 1460–*c.* 1520). Standard edition by John Small and others (Scottish Text Society, 3 vols., 1884–93). The single-volume edition by W. Mackay Mackenzie (1932, rev. Bruce Dickins 1961) prints all the poems with short notes and a glossary; James Kinsley's selection (1958) is oddly capricious in its omissions. There is a solid life by J. W. Baxter (1952). (*CBEL*, I, 258 f.)

Gavin Douglas (*c.* 1474–1522). Poetical works, edited by John Small (4 vols., 1874; includes a biography). Definitive edition of translation of *Aeneid* by D. F. C. Coldwell (Scottish Text Society, 4 vols., 1957–   ), whose *Selections* (1964) provide an excellent introduction to all Douglas's work (full notes and glossary). See Lauchlan M. Watt's *Douglas's Aeneid* (1920) and the sparkling section in C. S. Lewis's *OHEL* volume. (*CBEL*, I, 259 f.)

Stephen Hawes (*c.* 1475–1523?). *The Passetyme of Pleasure,* edited by William E. Mead (EETS, 1928). C. S.

Lewis has a section on Hawes in *The Allegory of Love* (1936). (*CBEL*, I, 253 f.)

John Skelton (1460?–1529). Poems: edited by Alexander Dyce (2 vols., 1843; still the most fully annotated edition); edited by Philip Henderson (1931, rev. 1948; uncritical but complete). Also an EETS edition of *Magnificence* by R. L. Ramsay (1906). Skelton's "aureate" translation of Diodorus Siculus has been well edited by F. M. Salter and H. L. R. Edwards (2 vols., EETS, 1956–57). The best modern studies are by William Nelson (1939) and H. L. R. Edwards (1949), both being primarily biographical. (*CBEL*, I, 408 f.)

IV.   The Approach to Renaissance Literature

Like Romanticism—the inevitable parallel because of both periods' bias towards individualism for its own sake —the Renaissance has recently lost much of its Victorian glamour. To Walter Pater, whose *The Renaissance* (1873) is still well worth reading in spite of the affected style, it was "the name of a many-sided but yet united movement, in which the love of the things of the intellect and the imagination for their own sake, the desire for a more liberal and comely way of conceiving life, make themselves felt, urging those who experienced this desire to search out first one and then another means of intellectual or imaginative enjoyment, and directing them not only to the discovery of old and forgotten sources of this enjoyment, but to the divination of fresh sources thereof—new experiences, new subjects of poetry, new forms of art." Pater's emphasis, it will be seen, was not on the "old and forgotten sources"—not, therefore, on the *rebirth* as such of classical art and culture, so much as on the new forms of aesthetic activity the classical revival (also known as Humanism) may or may not have stimulated. The crucial words are *new, liberal, comely.*

A sophisticated version of Pater's Renaissance, adjusted to an anti-Victorian view of English literary history, made its appearance in T. S. Eliot's "The Metaphysical Poets" (1921). With Milton and Dryden, according to Eliot, who was adopting two of Remy de Gourmont's favorite terms, "a dissociation of sensibility set in" displacing the unified sensibility of writers like Shakespeare, Chapman, and Donne, who had been able to think and feel at the same time. "The poets of the seventeenth century, the successors of the dramatists of the sixteenth, possessed a mechanism of sensibility which could devour any kind of experience." Why they felt an urge to "devour" is explained in "Four Elizabethan Dramatists" (1924), one of Eliot's most persuasive essays. Here the final impression the English Renaissance leaves is said to be one of "artistic greediness." Its writers wanted "every sort of effect together" and were unwilling "to accept any limitation and abide by it." Their philosophy, ultimately, was one "of anarchism, of dissolution, of decay."

At the merely aesthetic level Eliot's Renaissance is not so different from Pater's. But his instinctive, pre-critical admiration is accompanied by a distrust of what lay behind or beneath the brilliant surface. And since 1924 everybody's suspicions have increased as the historical context of the Elizabethan achievement has become clearer. Unlike the Victorian aesthetes, we are uncomfortably aware of the social matrix of the English Renaissance—a continuous inflation (with the opportunities it provided the new capitalism of enormous profits or total ruin), unprecedented technical progress (which included gunpowder as well as the printing press), immensely efficient dictatorships, ruthless colonial exploitation (with syphilis, according to D. H. Lawrence, the most influential import of all), a hysterical religious fanaticism, and an omnivorous credulity (alchemy, astrology, and witchcraft flourished as never before). *New* no doubt, scarcely *liberal*, not by any means always *comely*.

Keynes's "rash generalization" (his own words) in *A Treatise on Money*, that Shakespeare, like "the larger proportion of the world's great writers and artists," was the product of "the atmosphere of buoyancy, exhilaration and the freedom from economic cares felt by the governing class, which is engendered by profit inflations" has been given short shrift by L. C. Knights in *Drama and Society in the Age of Jonson* (1937). The Elizabethan governing class was *not* free from economic cares. On the contrary, the economic instability was their nightmare, and the desperate devices to which James I and Charles I were driven to survive economically were a direct cause, as Keynes must have known, of the Civil War. But if Knights disposed of Keynes, he did not dispose of the overwhelming social impact of the sixteenth-century price-revolution. In a less naïve sense than Keynes's, Shakespeare's plays *were* the product of the inflation, because at bottom they are the objective correlatives of a morality that had been developed in the process of his society's adjustment to inflation. The price-revolution reached England *c.* 1525, when the prices of most commodities, including food, began to rise (rents and wages, on the other hand, remaining more or less at the old levels). Economists have still not made up their minds about the causes of the inflation, though the inflow of Spanish-American silver almost certainly had something to do with it, and at the time, except to one or two advanced thinkers, such as Bodin, no rational explanation at all was available. Prices continued to rise, without anybody in the least understanding why, until *c.* 1650, when this inflation came to an end as mysteriously as it had begun.

The disturbing effect of the sixteenth-century inflation can be compared with that of the Black Death. Once again, with demoralizing suddenness and without any apparent human intervention, England found itself a different place, with many of its basic traditional assumptions —for example, that a day's labor could be counted on to support a man and his family for a day—inexplicably losing their meaning. It was another Toynbeean "challenge," but different from that of the fourteenth century because (i) though there were many recurrences of bubonic plague, it never returned on the same scale as in 1348–49, as inflation was to do, and (ii) its effects were obvious for all to see, whereas the Elizabethan inflation was continuous for over a hundred years and *invisible*, except indirectly.

The two differences, though not the whole story by any means, may help to explain some of the respective but very different excellences of Chaucer and Shakespeare.

Translated into the simplest human terms the sixteenth- and early seventeenth-century inflation meant that a son's money income had to be nearly twice that of his father if the new generation was to maintain a comparable standard of living. Generally speaking, there were two ways in which the family income could be doubled. One was for the son to work twice as hard as his father. This might be called the middle-class or Puritan solution; its effect upon orthodox Christian theology is the subject of R. H. Tawney's sociological classic *Religion and the Rise of Capitalism* (1926). The alternative solution, one more characteristic of the specifically Renaissance ethos, was for the son to go out into the world and carve a fortune there. For the son of a gentleman the prospect that offered the biggest rewards, social and financial, was a place at Court. The initiative and determination which could bring dazzling monetary rewards to the middle-class "undertaker" or entrepreneur, were rewarded at a Renaissance Court by the even more dazzling possibility of the favor of the quasi-divine Renaissance Prince. It is true a Prince's smiles were not an immediately marketable commodity ("glory" and "gold" are incommensurable orders of value), but as the Court took the place of modern Cabinet and modern Civil Service combined, the opportunities for pickings were considerable—even for those who were only favorites of a favorite. To succeed, however, it was necessary to be, or at least to seem, properly qualified; hence the dozens of "courtesy books," of which much the most interesting is Castiglione's *Il Cortegiano* (translated into English by Sir Thomas Hoby in 1561). And among the qualities required of a courtier, along with horsemanship, fencing, dancing, and the like, was the ability to write a love song or turn a copy of complimentary verses. George Puttenham's *The Art of English Poesy* (1589) is the most

elaborate English textbook of this aspect of courtliness.[1]
(The Queen accepted its dedication and Puttenham tactfully uses some of her dreary poems as examples of poetic
craftsmanship.) Although not a book to read through at
a sitting, it makes an excellent introduction, with its anecdotes of Court life and its encyclopedia of metrical forms
and figures of speech, to the intellectual and technical
bases of Court poetry. Puttenham's object was "to make
of a rude rimer, a learned and a Courtly Poet"; "learned,"
however, not in any academic sense but in the require-
ments of "decorum," the basis of which was "experience,"
a quality ten times as valuable, according to Puttenham,
as book-learning.

Decorum, with its implication of a conscious cultiva-
tion by the individual of a behavior appropriate to the
nuances of each social occasion, was a key Renaissance
term. Closely connected with it is "bravery" or a general
magnificence of appearance. Decorum, which permitted
simple clothes, speech, and manners in the country, de-
manded their opposite at Court. Here, therefore, was a
criterion of linguistic "correctness," both in the courtier's
speech and for Court poetry, that had not been available
for Chaucer or the fifteenth century. In the formal speech
of Court occasions, and so in the Court poetry which was
the reflection of such occasions, the courtier was expected
to be "brave" ("gallantly arrayed in all his colors" is how
Puttenham puts it of the poet) without seeming indeco-
rously artificial or unnatural (at Court a proper magnificence *was* natural). Sidney makes the point when discussing oratory:

> I have found in divers smal learned Courtiers, a
> more sound stile, then in some professors of learning,
> of which I can gesse no other cause, but that the
> Courtier following that which by practice he findeth
> fittest to nature, therein (though he know it not)

[1] The quotations are from the excellent edition by Gladys D.
Willcock and Alice Walker (1936).

doth according to art, though not by art: where the
other using art to shew art and not hide art (as in
these cases he shuld do) flieth from nature, and indeed abuseth art.[2]

Sidney's "practice" is here the product of Puttenham's
"experience." But to be "smal learned" was not, of course,
an indispensable qualification. The best Court poets—
Wyatt, Sidney, Greville, Donne, Lord Herbert, Thomas
Carew—were highly educated men. Without an expert
knowledge of rhetoric, "bravery" could not be had. But
the art had not to obscure the speaking voice. The require-
ment was not a matter of "sincerity," but of a realism to
counterpoise the magnificence. The *Arcadian Rhetoric*
(1588) of Abraham Fraunce, a textbook that explicitly
defines tropes and figures as "Braverie of speach," insists
with Puttenham on "discretion" and the continual danger
of "affectate curiosity." Fraunce, like Sir John Hoskyns
(Donne's friend and the author of *Directions for Speech
and Style*, a later, more sophisticated textbook), draws
most of his examples from the *Arcadia*, to most of us
today a tediously overwritten work, though that Sidney
was himself aware of the dangers of rhetoric is proved by
his sarcasms about "swelling Phrases," "coursing of a letter" (alliteration), and "*Nizolian* paper bookes" (a phrase-
book or gradus) in *The Defence of Poesy*. Sidney's own
criterion is, essentially, dramatic effectiveness. Discussing
"that *Lyricall* kind of Songs and Sonets" he complained,
"truly many of such writings, as come under the banner
of unresistable love, if I were a mistresse, would never
perswade mee they were in love: so coldly they applie,
firie speeches, as men that had rather redde lovers writings.
. . ." Which does not mean, as nineteenth-century critics
thought, that these poets had to be really in love and ad-
dressing a real mistress, but that the *illusion* of such a situation had to be communicated. And at the English Court,
where everybody knew everybody, a necessary conse-

[2] *The Defence of Poesy* (1595).

quence of the realistic "I" was the illusion or convention of an identifiable mistress. Penelope Devereux was indispensable to Sidney as sonneteer, though not necessarily in any other capacity. His marriage to Frances Walsingham in 1583, before the Astrophel cycle of sonnets had even been completed, seems to have been a happy one.

Sidney's "professors of learning" and "Nizolian" copyists were learned in the ordinary academic sense—the educational products not of "experience" and "practice" but of authority and logic. Although he does not identify them for us, they were probably middle-class Puritans turned university wits. The type was a variant upon those sons who worked twice as hard as their fathers; the Oxford and Cambridge men worked their heads off at school and college instead of in shop or counting-house, sometimes losing some of their Puritanism in the process. They are the first professional authors in English, with their most splendid representatives in Spenser, the son of the London journeyman tailor, and Milton, the son of the London scrivener-usurer. If they are to be called Renaissance, it is with an important difference from the Court group. The "correctness" that such Puritan intellectuals aspired to was the neo-classic critics' version of decorum as it was being formulated by the contemporary Continental commentators on Aristotle's *Poetics*. As systematized by the elder Scaliger in *Poetices Libri Septem* (1561), the neo-classic "rules" have an impressive logical rigor, and the Elizabethan "scholarship-boy" with literary instincts but no native literary tradition to work in (his pastors and masters had cut away the medieval roots), may be forgiven his fascination. But the neo-classic system only provided models and patterns. Unlike the Court poet, whose lyrical "bravery" was a literary correlative of his aspiration to royal favor, the Puritan or professional poet had no human material with which to fill the neo-classic molds. (The intellectual correlative of the new capitalism was the new science.) At its norm this poetry is dismally "literary," an imitation of an imitation; at its best, however, it is saved, almost in spite of itself, at least in *The Faerie Queene* and *Paradise Lost,* on the one hand by the unconscious terrors and appetites that have seeped through, and on the other by the sheer mental energy of its structures.

A third area in the English Renaissance's cultural map must not be overlooked. Both the aspiring courtier and the industrious Puritan were never more than a generation or two from the half-pagan, half-Christian democracies of village and borough, with the vigorous juries, guilds, and vestries they had perfected in the fifteenth century. Some of the finest folk songs and traditional ballads seem to date from this period (the Percy Folio, our earliest text for many, was only compiled about 1650), and they come from the other side of the Renaissance pale, which did not extend more than a hundred miles at most to the west and north of London. Oral poetry was of course on the defensive. Puttenham's contemptuous reference to the "blind harpers" and their "reports of *Bevis of Southampton, Guy of Warwick, Adam Bell,* and *Clymme of the Clough* and such other old Romances or historicale rimes, made purposely for recreation of the common people at Christmas dinners and brideales" is a more typical sixteenth-century reaction than Sidney's well-known tribute. Nevertheless, though rejected at Court, the culture of the people was part of the unconscious inheritance of even the age's most "modern" writers. Proverbs and proverbial lore, the Testaments of the folk until they were superseded by the Authorized Version, circulated in all classes of society, as M. P. Tilley's valuable *Dictionary of the Proverbs in England in the Sixteenth and Seventeenth Centuries* (1950) has conclusively demonstrated.

It is the collision and partial fusion of the three modes of speech—of court, city, and country—that gives Renaissance English its special virtues of vividness and complexity. With the class barriers partly broken down by inflation, there followed a greater linguistic mobility than in the fifteenth century; the amalgamation of speech that characterized the upper classes of southern and eastern England preceded any similar assimilation of attitudes or philosophies. Hence the pervasive "ambiguity" of the speech of the period—most suggestively explored by William Empson in *Seven Types of Ambiguity* and *The Structure of Complex Words*—which was a linguistic reflection of the underlying social ambivalances. Much of the "bravery" of the Renaissance style derives from the reader's sense of an intellectual daring that *enjoys* the proximity to logical contradiction. Dr. Johnson, an unsympathetic critic, complained that with Donne, Cowley, and the other metaphysical poets, "the most heterogeneous ideas are yoked by violence together." Some violence cannot be denied, but in the best Court poetry—of which metaphysical poetry was only the central phase—the reader has no sense of the failure of incompatible ideas to exist side by side. The surprising juxtapositions in "The Flea," for example, one of Donne's most popular poems, were a faithful reflection of a society in which the traditional hierarchies of church and state were in fact in dissolution. The Elizabethans, believing in themselves, were not afraid to believe in the ultimate beneficence of a reversal of the values to which they had found themselves committed. And they liked a similar paradoxical excitement in their poetry.

2. DRAMATIC SPEECH

Wyatt, who has as good a claim as anyone to be the first Renaissance Englishman, wrote his earliest "ballets" in the 1520s; Chaucer's last Canterbury Tales date from *c.* 1394. In the century and a quarter between—except for Skelton and the Scotch poets an inglorious period for Court literature—the best poetry had been the popular oral poetry of songs, carols, and ballads. But the invention of the printing press and the remarkable increase in literacy at this time were the beginning of the end of oral poetry, except at such sub-literary levels as the nursery rhyme or the obscene jingle. Wyatt's poems, although often nominally lute-songs, are essentially poems to be *read*—privately, to oneself, the eye lingering or rereading whenever it becomes necessary or desirable. The minute corrections in Wyatt's own handwriting in the Egerton MS. (now in the British Museum) demonstrate by their attention to minutiae of phrasing, imagery, and rhythm that this is a poetry of art, of "the best words in the best order." Wyatt's contemporaries and followers recognized his pioneering achievement as a poetic craftsman, the Elizabethan tributes to him and Surrey resembling those of the Augustans to Waller and Denham and of the Romantics to Chatterton. But there is an important difference between Wyatt's attitude to words and word-order and Waller's or Chatterton's. Wyatt's poetry, though composed on paper and intended to be read privately, is made out of the spoken language and is intended to create the illusion of speech. The typical Wyatt poem—whether song, sonnet, epigram, or "satire"—is a soliloquy or monologue, in which the "I" makes the same immediate impact as the dramatis persona in a play. Some of the revisions in the Egerton MS., when a regular iambic line loses a syllable (e.g. by a monosyllable taking the place of a disyllable), seem to show Wyatt deliberately aiming at dramatic pause in his rhythms. His masterpiece "They fle from me that sometyme did me seke" is constructed entirely on this principle. In line 2, for example,

With naked fote stalking in my chambre,

the reader's ear anticipates *footstep* (or some equivalent disyllable) and the absence of the unstressed syllable creates a pause before *stalking,* the pause emphasizing most effectively the stealthiness with which the approach is being made. Wyatt's innovation of ending the sonnet with a couplet—for which his Italian and French models had provided no precedent—is a device of the same type. The effect is something like the decasyllabic couplet at the end of a blank-verse scene in an Elizabethan or Jacobean play.

The poem's conclusion is marked off with a decisive dramatic finality. It is true the balance between octave and sestet, so important to Petrarch and his followers, is destroyed in the process, but Wyatt and his English successors, who almost all end their sonnets with a rhyming couplet, were not interested in the principle of metrical balance. Their concern was effective dramatic speech.

In Chaucer and his contemporaries the emphasis was primarily on *dramatic action*. Except in a few uncharacteristic passages of French rhetoric, our attention is hardly ever detained in them by the actual word or phrase. Instead we are hurried along from what is said to the situation that the words communicate or create. And so the word itself becomes almost transparent. With Renaissance literature, on the other hand, whether it is prose or poetry, the words have all the immediacy and resonance of speech —a speech that itself controls and determines the nature of the dramatic action. The literary unit, therefore, is a speech unit, a phrase or a single sentence, as is clearly demonstrated by the large number of memorable items bequeathed by English Renaissance literature to any dictionary of quotations. The conventional literary unit, such as sonnet, narrative poem, or play, instead of determining what is said in the sentence or phrase, tends to be determined—in the best English Renaissance literature when it is at its best—*by* the smaller units. The smaller unit can even stand by itself, enacting on its own small scale its own miniature drama. The phrase is often, indeed, of superior literary value when it does stand by itself, detached from its context. Shakespeare's "That time of year thou may'st in me behold" is certainly one of the best of the *Sonnets,* but it is a poor thing compared to its own fourth line when we allow the nine magic words to stand by themselves:

Bare ruined choirs, where late the sweet birds sang. . . .

Renaissance literature presupposes a reader or auditor who will translate the writer's page or the actor's words

into visual images that the mind's eye can contemplate
on an imagined stage. (The public theaters, without scen-
ery or lighting and with only the most rudimentary prop-
erties, relied upon the audience's active imaginative cooperation with the dramatists' words.) Such mental
spectacle is the specific "bravery" that the modern reader
of the Elizabethans and Jacobeans must above all learn
to cultivate. Since the spectacle is essentially dramatic,
there is no leisure as a rule for description. What is described even in *The Faerie Queene* and *Hero and Leander*
is a scene in action, with a limited number of identifiable
men and women in continuously changing interrelation-
ships. So far as there is any recurring structural principle
it is the negative one of mutability, change for its own
sake, which is the metaphysical version of the 1550–
1650 inflation; it followed that the relationships between
the dramatis personae *must* change, the human situations *must* develop. The point of poetic interest is therefore not so much the immediate situation *per se* (present
tense) as the tensions between it and what came before
(past tense) and what is still to come (future tense). In
Donne's "Extasie," for example,

> All day the same our postures were,
> And we said nothing all the day . . .

the lovers, simply by the improbable claim they make of
one day's total immobility, invite us to contrast it with
what must have preceded it as well as with what is to
come next. Again, to take another familiar single-sentence
masterpiece, in Webster's line

> Cover her face; mine eyes dazzle; she died young . . .

the single sentence is a miniature three-act play. The face
is to be covered in order that it may not be visible now,
but before it is covered its dazzling beauty has already
been revealed, and it is only after the revelation of her
beauty that we discover the young Duchess is dead.

To look for a positive structural principle in English

Renaissance literature is to miss its essential point. Mutability, though certain, is after all unpredictable. Each human situation, therefore, is unique, *sui generis;* its outcome cannot be foretold by examining earlier human situations of approximately the same type, and it cannot be used as a yardstick of the proper behavior of others who may find themselves later in the same position. The dramatic presentation of such a situation will be unlikely to fit naturally into a pre-existent mold, such as the classical genres, and it can have no "moral" because a similar situation is unlikely to recur. In the circumstances of Renaissance mutability the only assistance the writer can give the reader is to provide his writings with titles that will suggest or summarize the point of departure or the general direction that each poem will take. Donne seems to have been the first poet to make the title an essential part of the meaning of a short poem, though in a bungling way Tottel's editor had realized as early as 1557 that Wyatt's and Surrey's *Songs and Sonnets* also need descriptive titles. The dramatists followed Donne's lead, Jonson realizing before Shakespeare the potentialities of this device as a kind of commentary or program note: *Everyman in His Humour,* 1598; *Measure for Measure,* 1604. The genre-labels persist (Hemminge and Condell did their best for Shakespeare with the tripartite comedies, histories, and tragedies, in that order), but they had become so vague and structurally irrelevant as to be almost meaningless. The conventional classical divisions—epic, tragedy, ode, comedy, satire, pastoral, etc.—had been based on subject matter and on mode of presentation; that is, on extra-verbal considerations. The English Renaissance, with its instinctive reliance on dramatic speech as the determinant of literary structure, did not exactly discard the genres. It was rather that the precepts of Aristotle and Horace, and their Italian and French neo-classic heirs, were not relevant to their critical interests, which were always technical rather than theoretic. Apart indeed from Sidney and Puttenham, the literary critics of this period are unrewarding, except on technical issues—as in the interchange of letters between Spenser and Gabriel Harvey and the Campion–Daniel controversy, both on the use of classical meters in English. Even Jonson, who clearly had the makings of a first-class literary critic, did not in fact achieve more than occasional vigorous *obiter dicta*.

Milton, like Spenser (his "original," as he told Dryden), is something of a special case. (The Renaissance had run its course by the time he reached full literary maturity in the 1650s.) Milton is a Humanist, like More or Jonson or Hooker. A closer parallel, on a lower level, might be with the Scotch *littérateur* Drummond of Hawthornden, whose feelings about the metaphysical poets Milton certainly shared. Drummond is pontificating to his friend Arthur Johnstone:

> *Poesie* is not a thing that is in the finding and search, or which may be otherwise found out, being already condescended upon by all nations, and as it were established *iure gentium* amongst Greeks, Romans, Italians, French, Spaniards. Neither do I think that a good piece of *Poesie* which Homer, Virgil, Ovid, Petrarch, Bartas, Ronsard, Boscan, Garcilasso (if they were alive and had that language) could not understand, and reach the sense of the writer.[3]

It is the bracketed qualification that gives Drummond's case away. Homer and the others were *not* alive, and if they had been they would not have been able to write in English. Drummond, whose literary remains were edited by Milton's nephew Edward Phillips, is an almost perfect specimen of the ivory-tower poet. In his daily life Drummond spoke and heard broad Scots all the time, but his verse and prose, both of which are imitation-Sidney, are in pure English. Like Drummond, though for different reasons, Milton never felt the attractive magnet of the Court. Or if he did at one time, as *Arcades* and *Comus*

---

[3] Quoted by W. P. Ker, *The Art of Poetry* (1923), pp. 10–11.

perhaps suggest, it was an attraction that soon passed. *Lycidas,* like his earliest poems, is the perfection of grammar-school poetry—what the Humanists, following Quintilian, called *imitatio.* Ivory-tower poetry can achieve greatness under one condition: its composition by a poet of intelligent, sensitive, maladjusted, and neurotic temperament. Spenser and Milton seem to fulfil this condition; Marvell is the third great neurotic of the period. This is not to deny other elements of interest in their writings but it is to the neurotic contradictions in those writings, in part no doubt to be derived from their Puritanism, that the modern reader looks for the fundamental oppositions and discordancies that their tortured imaginations were somehow able to balance and reconcile.

3. THE EGO AND FORTUNE

Two concepts dominated the mind of Renaissance England. One was the Ego, the other was Hap or Fortune. The two concepts were indeed each other's complement. The Ego, retreating into itself or encouraging itself to a stoical endurance, had developed a new self-consciousness under the impact of the blows or favors of what it felt to be the nature of things—an unpredictable, uncontrollable, non-human a-moral and yet quasi-personal force. One aspect of this force was no doubt the product of the economic inflation. The motto of Sir Thomas Gresham, the Keynes of the period, was *Fortune à moi.* But a more obvious agent or embodiment of Fortune was the Renaissance Prince. The whims of most of the Tudors and Stuarts were even more unpredictable than any economic process. As Perlin, a French traveler here in 1558, remarked, "One day one sees a man as a great lord, the next he is in the hands of an executioner." Ralegh's career was the type; "Fortune tossed him up of nothing and to and fro to greatness and from thence down to little more than that wherein she found him" (Sir Robert Naunton, *Fragmenta Regalia*). George Cavendish, who had been Wolsey's gentleman-usher, wrote his moving life of his old master in these terms. Wyatt, another victim—though unlike his poetic disciple Surrey he saved his head—took it for granted:

> as they say, one happy howre
> May more prevayle than Ryght or Myght;
> Yf fortune then lyst for to lowre,
> What vaylyth Right?

Even Prospero's magic only equipped him with a pre-science of the moment when "bountiful Fortune" was to prove herself his "dear lady." Those who were less success-ful consoled themselves as Ralegh did: "For conversation of particular greatness and dignity there is nothing more noble and glorious than to have felt the force of every for-tune. . . . He only is to be reputed a man whose mind cannot be puffed up by prosperity nor dejected by any adverse fortune."[4]

Such stoic fatalism is scarcely distinguishable from the tragic sense. The typical Renaissance tragedy—whether compressed into a lyric or expanded into five acts—enacts a conflict between the Ego and Fortune. In the lyric the author is able to speak in the first person singular, though Marlowe's own voice, and those of Chapman and Web-ster, are as audible in their plays as the "I" of Wyatt's, Sidney's, and Donne's poems. It is an unembarrassing "I" because it was both personal and representative, and the reader has no sense of prying into bedrooms because the particular mistress, even if we can put a name to her (Ann Boleyn, Penelope Devereux, Ann More), also in-cludes and represents Fortune, *"la donna mobile"* par ex-cellence. In Wyatt's case in particular it is an almost ab-stract relationship. The lady's physical entity is lost sight of entirely in her mutability and her cruelty. Shakespeare's comic heroines, though equally unpredictable and all-pow-

[4] I owe the Perlin and Ralegh quotations to Lewis Einstein's chapter on "The Vicissitudes of Fortune" in his *Tudor Ideals* (1921), an important and unjustly neglected book.

erful, are the instruments of a more benign Fortune. In the tragedies, on the other hand, it is the Ego and its variants or subdivisions who occupy most of the scenes, and Fortune itself tends to be out of sight, though never out of mind—or at most to have delegated some of its functions to lesser agents like ghosts, witches, or Machiavellian villains. The central dichotomy includes and explains the characteristic Renaissance combination of acute psychological realism and the widest factual improbability. The Ego was observed and recorded with fascinated or disgusted honesty, not only by Shakespeare but by all the great Renaissance writers (with the Humanist exceptions). For them the Ego, the individual rational moral human personality, represented reality, which they called Nature. But beyond the Ego's immediate range or knowledge almost anything seemed to be possible. There Fortune, who was Nature's antithesis, ruled absolutely, a metaphysical Tudor Prince to be propitiated or even influenced but never understood. It was left to Bacon, the trumpeter of the scientific revolution, to call Fortune's bluff:

> . . . chiefly, the mould of a man's fortune is in his own hand. *Faber quisque fortunae suae,* saith the Poet. And the most frequent of external causes is, that the folly of one man is the fortune of another.[5]

[5] *Essays*, No. XL, "Of Fortune." The poet is Plautus (misquoted by Bacon).

V.   A Renaissance Reading List, 1500–1650

1. Bibliographies, Literary Histories, Criticism, and Anthologies

BIBLIOGRAPHIES

For most purposes *CBEL* (Vol. I, 1940, pp. 317–912) with its Supplement (1957) is the most useful bibliography of the period, because it lists the modern editions and commentaries as well as the original editions. For more recent books and articles "Literature of the Renaissance" (published annually in *SP* since 1917) should always be consulted—or the much less complete section in *The Year's Work in English Studies* of the English Association. A contemporary record of great historical value, and some human interest, is the *Transcript of the Register of the Company of Stationers, 1554–1640* (ed. E. Arber, 5 vols., 1875–94, reissued 1950). Its sequel, the *Register for 1640–1708* (ed. G. E. B. Eyre, 3 vols., 1913–14, reissued 1950) is of less importance, because after 1640 so many of the books of literary interest evaded registration. A. W. Pollard and G. R. Redgrave's *A Short-Title Catalogue of Books Printed in England, Scotland, and Ireland, and of English Books Printed Abroad* (1926, revised edition in preparation by W. A. Jackson) lists virtually every edition of every book printed within its terminal dates, as well as giving the principal libraries where copies are to be found; an even better sequel for 1641–1700 has been compiled by Donald Wing (3 vols., 1945–51). These, however, are tools for the researcher rather than the literary student, who will probably find the bibliographies attached to the two *OHEL* volumes—C. S. Lewis's on the sixteenth

century, excluding drama (1954), and Douglas Bush's on
the first half of the seventeenth century (1945)—more
rewarding. A catalogue within the period that has set new
standards in descriptive bibliography, and as such should
interest even the merely literary student, is W. W. Greg's
*A Bibliography of English Printed Drama to the Resto-
ration* (4 vols., 1939–60). The analytical bibliography in
which Greg was a pioneer (with his friend R. B. McKerrow) receives further treatment in Chapter XI below.

LITERARY HISTORIES

The most ambitious recent surveys are C. S. Lewis
and Douglas Bush's *OHEL* volumes referred to above.
Lewis (Vol. III) confines himself to the nondramatic literature of the sixteenth century and Douglas Bush (Vol.
V) also excludes drama. The former is a remarkable tour
de force, continuously lively and provocative without any
serious gap in the information provided. The effect of a
George Saintsbury *redivivus* is enhanced by the oddly old-
fashioned preferences (Wyatt gets low marks, Spenser and
Sidney are the heroes). The best chapters are perhaps the
extra-literary ones on the changing intellectual climates of
opinion, but even at his most perverse Lewis is always
enormously readable. Bush's book is also readable, if a
little old-fashioned, at least on Milton. Its weakness is
that, unlike Lewis, Bush is only a minor literary critic and
his opinions as such are rarely of much interest, but as a
guide, especially to the minor figures, the book is of great
value because it is both tidy and thorough. In comparison, C. F. Tucker Brooke's survey of the period in A. C.
Baugh's *Literary History of England* (1948) and Hardin
Craig's even shorter one in his own *History of English
Literature* (1950)—both now obtainable separately—are
merely competent textbooks.

There are several scholarly surveys of separate aspects
of English Renaissance literature, such as F. S. Boas's
University Drama in the Tudor Age (1914), Wolfgang
Clemen's *Die Tragödie vor Shakespeare* (1955, English

tr. 1961), W. W. Greg's *Pastoral Poetry and Pastoral Drama* (1906), Miss M. C. Bradbrook's *The Growth and Structure of Elizabethan Comedy* (1955), Una Ellis-Fermor's *Jacobean Drama* (1936, rev. 1961), Richard F. Jones's *The Triumph of the English Language; a Survey of Opinions concerning the Vernacular* (1953), George Williamson's *The Senecan Amble: a Study in Prose Form from Bacon to Collier* (1951), and H. J. C. Grierson's classical *Cross Currents in English Literature of the Seventeenth Century* (1929), though Jones and Williamson are useful for the numerous out-of-the-way quotations they assemble rather than for their own comments. The most rewarding academic work—apart from the remarkable scattered articles by M. W. Croll on prose style (still uncollected)—has been on the poetry of the period. The serious student will at least dip into Douglas Bush's *Mythology and the Renaissance Tradition in English Poetry* (1933), Janet G. Scott's *Les sonnets élisabéthains* (Paris, 1929; for the French and Italian sources), Veré L. Rubel's *Poetic Diction in the English Renaissance* (1941; Skelton to Spenser), Rosemond Tuve's original and suggestive *Elizabethan and Metaphysical Imagery* (1947), Hallet Smith's *Elizabethan Poetry* (1952), J. W. Lever's *The Elizabethan Love Sonnet* (1956), and R. Ellrodt's detailed analysis of the Metaphysicals (3 vols., Paris, 1960; in French). Such works should, of course, be supplemented by the contemporary rhetorics, especially Abraham Fraunce's *The Arcadian Rhetorike* (1588; ed. Ethel Seaton, 1950), John Hoskins's *Directions for Speech and Style* (ed. H. H. Hudson, 1936), and Alexander Gil's *Logonomia Anglica* (1621; ed. O. Jiriczek, 1903), as well as by Puttenham, Sidney, and Jonson. One or two of the best *Festschrift* collections belong to this period, notably the H. J. C. Grierson (1938) and F. P. Wilson (1959) tributes. The Grierson volume includes contributions by Mario Praz, Pierre Legouis, T. S. Eliot, and H. W. Garrod among others and is in fact a microcosm of seventeenth-century literary scholarship. Some useful paperback anthologies of modern articles in the period include: *Shakespeare's Contemporaries,* edited by Max Bluestone and Norman Rabkin (1961; thirty-three items); *Elizabethan Drama,* edited by R. J. Kaufmann (1961; nineteen longish articles), and *Seventeenth-Century English Literature* (1962), *Seventeenth-Century English Poetry* (1962)—both the last edited by W. R. Keast.

RECENT CRITICISM

With the possible exception of Coleridge (who, however, cannot be trusted outside Shakespeare), T. S. Eliot is probably the most perceptive critic the English Renaissance has ever had; his *Elizabethan Essays* (1934, rev. 1963 with unfortunate omissions) assembles all the essays on the dramatists, from Marlowe to Ford, including the brilliant "Preface to an Unwritten Book" called "Four Dramatists" (omitted as "callow" 1963 ed.!); *On Poetry and Poets* (1957) adds "Sir John Davies"; "The Metaphysical Poets" and "Andrew Marvell" are in the *Selected Essays* (1932), which also includes all the dramatic essays. The chapter on the period in *The Use of Poetry and the Use of Criticism* (1933) is of less interest. William Empson's *Seven Types of Ambiguity* (1930, rev. 1947) finds its most telling examples in this period, though some serious errors on George Herbert have been exposed by Rosemond Tuve (*A Reading of Herbert,* 1952); his *Versions of Pastoral* (1935) has acute essays on Elizabethan double plots, Marvell's "Garden," and *Paradise Lost.* L. C. Knights's *Explorations* (1946) has four essays on Shakespeare (an especially good one on the sonnets), one on Bacon, and one on Herbert; *More Explorations* (1964) contains some later essays on this period. James Smith's articles in *Scrutiny* have not been collected, but those on *As You Like It* and "Metaphysical Poetry" at any rate are brilliant performances. Another Cambridge work, one written in the shade of Empson as well as Eliot, is Miss M. C. Bradbrook's *Themes and Conventions of Elizabethan Tragedy* (1935). There is little else of much critical distinction in this field outside Shakespeare and Milton; Miss M. M. Mahood's *Poetry and Humanism* (1950), P. Cruttwell's *The Shakespearean Moment* (1954), which is not confined to Shakespeare, and A. Alvarez's *The School of Donne* (1961) are clever works on the period by the younger critical generation in England. In America the emphasis has until recently been on scholarship and on theory rather than on criticism, though Cleanth Brooks's *The Well-Wrought Urn* (1947), which discusses Shakespeare, Donne, Herrick, and Milton *inter alios*, should not be overlooked.

ANTHOLOGIES

A good general anthology for the sixteenth century, with plenty of relevant notes, is a critical desideratum; the seventeenth century is well enough served in Ruth C. Wallerstein and Ricardo Quintana's *Seventeenth-Century Verse and Prose* (2 vols., 1951), which provides solid scholarly introductions and good explanatory footnotes (Vol. I, with twenty-two authors sharing its 450 pages, ends with Marvell and Vaughan; Shakespeare, Milton, and the drama are left out). On the whole the best collections have been those organized on a genre basis, such as J. W. Hebel and H. H. Hudson's *Poetry of the English Renaissance, 1509–1660* (1929), which has introductions and notes—unlike the two Oxford books (sixteenth century edited by E. K. Chambers, seventeenth century edited by H. J. C. Grierson and G. Bullough), which are fat but indigestible. Similar to the Hebel–Hudson volume are Norman E. McClure's *Sixteenth-Century Poetry* (1954) and R. C. Bald's *Seventeenth-Century Poetry* (1959)—both annotated and nearly 600 pages long. The complementary Hebel–Hudson selection from the period's prose (1952) is also competent, and the poetry and prose are obtainable together (1953). Grierson's *Metaphysical Lyrics and Poems* (1921) has now been superseded by Helen Gardner's Penguin *Metaphysical Poets* (1957), a good selection if under-annotated. Specimens of the prose are provided in M. A. Shaaber's substantial and competent edition (1957). There are two important fully annotated collections of the period's literary criticism: *Elizabethan Critical Essays* (ed. G. Gregory Smith, 2 vols., 1904; useful notes, introduction now out of date) and *Critical Essays of the Seventeenth Century* (ed. J. E. Spingarn, 3 vols., 1908–9; introduction still the best available to the topic). O. B. Hardison's collection of English Renaissance criticism (1963) is less inclusive than Gregory Smith, though he has several pieces omitted by Smith. The collections of plays, of which there have been dozens since Robert Dodsley's *Select Collection* (12 vols., 1744), are becoming less necessary as more dramatists receive critical editions. J. M. Manly's *Specimens of Pre-Shakespearean Drama* (2 vols., 1897–98) is useful because of its wide range, and *Representative English Comedies* (ed. Charles M. Gayley and others, 3 vols., 1903–14) is still occasionally worth consulting because of its critical emphasis. The current non-Shakespeare collections are those by C. F. Tucker Brooke and N. Burton Paradise (1933; thirty plays), C. R. Baskervill, V. B. Heltzel, and A. H. Nethercot (1934; forty-two plays), and Hazelton Spencer (1934; twenty-eight plays), all of which have short notes. Richard C. Harrier's *Anthology of Jacobean Drama* (2 vols., 1963) has much fuller notes but only eight plays. The original Mermaid series (1887–1909) had no pretension to scholarly accuracy but is still the pleasantest medium in which to read such Jacobean and Caroline dramatists as Beaumont and Fletcher, Massinger, Middleton, Ford, and Shirley. The New Mermaids (general editor Philip Brockbank, 1964–   ) provide fuller annotation but unfortunately far fewer plays per volume. A good modern series that combines scholarship, critical sense, and legibility is the Revels Plays (general editor Clifford Leech, 1958–   ); each play (Kyd's *Spanish Tragedy*, Webster's *White Devil*, Middleton's *Changeling*, etc.) obtains a separate volume. Nor should Charles Lamb's *Specimens of English Dramatic Poets* (1808) be overlooked (best edition by I. Gollancz, 2 vols., 1893). R.

Ashley and E. M. Moseley's *Elizabethan Fiction* (1953) prints Gascoigne, Lyly, Nashe, Deloney, and an excerpt from Sidney's *Arcadia*. Prose fiction is also available in Charles C. Mish's more adventurous *Anthology of Short Fiction of the Seventeenth Century* (1963), which has ten unfamiliar tales, all pre-Restoration, with substantial headnotes.

Some more restricted collections and selections of considerable interest are (in order of publication): (i) *Early English Classical Tragedies* (ed. J. W. Cunliffe, 1912: *Gorboduc* and its Senecan successors); (ii) *English Madrigal Verse* (ed. E. H. Fellowes, 1920); (iii) *A Cabinet of Characters* (ed. Gwendolen Murphy, 1925; includes some later characters too); (iv) *The Pepys Ballads* (ed. Hyder E. Rollins, 8 vols., 1929–32: street ballads of Pepys's own time and earlier). (The earliest poetical miscellanies—from Tottel's [1557] to *A Poetical Rhapsody* [1602]—have also been edited by Rollins in exemplary detail.) (v) Paul M. Zall's edition of 15th and 16th century jestbooks (1963).

2. Special Studies

L. D. Einstein: *The Italian Renaissance in England* (1902).

E. K. Chambers: *The Elizabethan Stage* (4 vols., 1923). Volumes III and IV give short accounts of every known Tudor play.

Edwin Nungezer: *A Dictionary of Actors before 1642* (1929).

F. O. Matthiessen: *Translation: an Elizabethan Art* (1931). A critical appreciation.

H. O. White: *Plagiarism and Imitation during the English Renaissance* (1935).

L. B. Wright: *Middle-Class Culture in Elizabethan England* (1935).

Willard Farnham: *The Medieval Heritage of Elizabethan Tragedy* (1936).

Howard Baker: *Induction to Tragedy* (1939). So-called "Senecan" tragedies are primarily medieval.

Mario Praz: *Studies in Seventeenth-Century Imagery* (2 vols., 1939–47). Not confined to England.

D. C. Allen: *The Star-Crossed Renaissance: the Quarrel about Astrology and Its Influence in England* (1941).

G. E. Bentley: *The Jacobean and Caroline Stage* (5 vols., 1941–56). Includes elaborate *catalogue raisonné* of every known play of the period.

T. W. Baldwin: *William Shakespeare's Small Latine and Less Greeke* (1944). What was taught in Elizabethan schools.

F. P. Wilson: *Elizabethan and Jacobean* (1946). Interesting literary odds and ends.

Benjamin Boyce: *The Theophrastan Character in England* (1947).

M. P. Tilley: *A Dictionary of Proverbs in England in the Sixteenth and Seventeenth Centuries* (1950).

Louis Babb: *The Elizabethan Malady* (1951). Melancholy.

Madeleine Doran: *Endeavours of Art: a Study of Form in Elizabethan Drama* (1954). Of great critical interest.

Louis L. Martz: *The Poetry of Meditation* (1954). Influence of Loyola on Donne, etc. *The Meditative Poem* (1963) is a well-edited collection of meditative verse by Martz.

Alfred Harbage: *Theatre for Shakespeare* (1955). Useful summary of all that is known about Elizabethan theaters, production, acting, etc.

A. Lytton Sills: *The Italian Influence in English Poetry from Chaucer to Southwell* (1955).

Wylie Sypher: *Four Stages of Renaissance Style* (1955). Analogies between the arts, 1400 to 1700.

Jean-Jacques Denonain: *Thèmes et Formes de la Poésie "Metaphysique"* (Paris, 1956).

Irving Ribner: *The English History Play in the Age of Shakespeare* (1957).

T. W. Craik: *The Tudor Interlude: Stage, Costume, and Acting* (1958).

A. B. Kernan: *The Cankered Muse* (1959). Satire.

H. A. Mason: *Humanism and Poetry in the Early Tudor Period* (1959). More, Wyatt, etc.

Joan M. Lechner: *Renaissance Concepts of the Commonplaces* (1962). An important supplement to the studies in Renaissance Rhetoric.

Margaret Schlauch: *Antecedents of the English Novel, 1400–1600* (1963).

Hugh M. Richmond: *The School of Love* (1964). Stuart love lyrics.

3.   THE PRINCIPAL WRITERS

(Arranged in chronological order of birth. The *CBEL* references are to *The Cambridge Bibliography of English Literature* [4 vols., 1940] and its Supplement [1957], which has the same pagination as the parent work.)

Sir Thomas More (1478–1535). Definitive Yale edition in progress, edited by R. S. Sylvester and Louis Martz (Vol. II, 1963). English works, edited by W. E. Campbell and A. W. Reed (2 vols., 1927–31; incomplete). Selection, edited by P. S. and H. M. Allen (1924). *Utopia* (Latin text and Ralph Robinson's translation): edited by J. H. Lupton (1895); edited by G. Sampson and A. Guthkelch (1910). *Correspondence*, edited by Elizabeth F. Rogers (1947). Early lives, edited by E. V. Hitchcock (EETS 1932, 1935, 1950). R. W. Chambers has written much the best recent life (1935) as well as the slighter *The Place of More in English Literature and History* (1937). *L'Univers de Thomas More* (Paris, 1963) by Germain Marc'hadour is an elaborate and scholarly account of More's life and times. For *Utopia* see J. H. Hexter's study (1952). H. A. Mason's *Humanism and Poetry in the Early Tudor Period* (1959) has some suggestive chapters on More and his circle. (*CBEL*, I, 666 f.)

William Tindale (d. 1536). Good selection, edited by S. L. Greenslade (1938). See also under "English Bible," p. 84 below. (*CBEL*, I, 668.)

Sir David Lindsay (1485–1555). Poetical works, edited by Douglas Hamer (Scottish Text Society, 4 vols., 1931–36). *Satire of the Three Estates*, edited by James Kinsley (1954); *Squire Meldrum*, edited by James Kinsley (1959). (*CBEL*, I, 897 f.)

John Heywood (1497?–1580?). Interludes, edited by John S. Farmer (1905). Epigrams, edited by B. A. Mulligan (1956). See Ian Maxwell, *French Farce and John Heywood* (Melbourne, 1946). (*CBEL*, I, 518 f.)

Sir Thomas Wyatt (1503?–1542). *Collected Poems*, edited by Kenneth Muir (1949; helpful introduction but almost no explanatory notes). Uncritical texts in *Silver Poets* (ed. G. Bullett, 1947). Muir has also edited some interesting hitherto unknown poems (1961). There is a well-documented appreciation by Hallet Smith (*Huntington Library Quarterly*, IX, 1946), and a sensible discussion of the sonnets by J. W. Lever in *The Elizabethan Love Sonnet* (1956). Kenneth Muir's *Life and Letters* (1963) is now the standard biography. Concordance by Eva C. Hangen (1941). H. A. Mason's *Humanism in Poetry in the Early Tudor Period* (1959) contains a long and perceptive account of Wyatt. For the style see R. Southall, *The Courtly Maker* (1964). (*CBEL*, I, 411 f.)

Roger Ascham (1515–1568). English works, edited by W. Aldis Wright (1904; complete texts but without notes, etc.). Detailed biographical and critical study by Lawrence V. Ryan (1963). (*CBEL*, I, 671.)

Henry Howard, Earl of Surrey (1517?–1547). Poems, edited by F. M. Padelford (1920, rev. 1928; thorough but pedestrian). Uncritical texts in *Silver Poets* (ed. G. Bullett, 1947). Well-edited selection by Emrys Jones (1964). Study by Edwin Casady (1938). (*CBEL*, I, 412 f.)

George Puttenham (*c.* 1530–1590). *The Arte of English Poesie,* good edition by Gladys D. Willcock and Alice Walker (1936). (*CBEL,* I, 865.)

Thomas Sackville, Earl of Dorset (1536–1608). "Induction" and "Complaint of Henry Duke of Buckingham" in *A Mirror for Magistrates* (critical edition of whole collection by Lily B. Campbell, 2 vols., 1938–46). *Complaint of Buckingham,* edited by Marguerite Hearsey (1936); *The Tragedie of Gorboduc,* edited by J. W. Cunliffe (in *Early English Classical Tragedy,* 1912). For a clever modern disparagement, see Donald Davie, *Essays in Criticism,* IV, 1954. (*CBEL,* I, 413 f.)

George Gascoigne (1539?–1577). Complete works, edited by J. W. Cunliffe (2 vols., 1907–10; no notes). *A Hundreth Sundrie Flowers* (ed. with notes C. T. Prouty, 1942). Detailed life by C. T. Prouty (1942). (*CBEL,* I, 414 f.)

Prayer Book (*The Book of Common Prayer,* 1549, etc.). The standard account is still that by Francis Proctor (rev. Walter H. Frere, 1902). For a bibliographical survey see Stanley Morison, *English Prayer Books* (1943, enlarged 1949). (*CBEL,* I, 676 f.)

Sir Walter Ralegh (1552?–1618). Poems, edited by Agnes M. C. Latham (1929, rev. 1951); uncritical text in *Silver Poets* (ed. G. Bullett, 1947). M. C. Bradbrook's *The School of Night* (1936) is an acute study of Ralegh's literary relationships. See also P. Edwards (1953), W. Oakeshott (1960), and A. L. Rowse (1962). (*CBEL,* I, 827 f.)

Edmund Spenser (1552?–1599). The Variorum works (ed. E. Greenlaw, C. G. Osgood, F. M. Padelford, and others, 9 vols., 1932–49, with excellent index 1957) supersedes all earlier editions, though W. L. Renwick's competent edition of the minor poems (4 vols., 1928–34) is perhaps easier to consult. Of the one-volume editions, E. de Selincourt's (1912) gives a good text, but there are no notes and the introduction is verbose and uncritical. Fred-

eric I. Carpenter's *Reference Guide to Spenser* (1923)—
Supplements to 1935 and 1960 by Dorothy F. Atkinson
(1937) and Waldo F. McNeir and Foster Provost (1962)
—is indispensable for the scholar; most of us manage with
H. S. V. Jones's *Spenser Handbook* (1930). The fullest
life is that by A. C. Judson (1945) in the Variorum edition
(see above). Of the older critics, W. L. Renwick (1925)
is perhaps the most sensible and C. S. Lewis (especially
the last chapter of *The Allegory of Love*, 1936) the most
brilliant. The most ambitious of the recent studies is H.
Berger's analysis of *Faerie Queene*, Book 2 (1957), though
this is often unreliable and obscure; A. C. Hamilton's interpretation of the allegory in the context of Elizabethan
criticism (1961) is a much sounder introduction to Spenser. There is some excellent criticism in *Form and Convention in the Poetry of Spenser*, edited by W. Nelson (1961),
who has also brought out a good book of his own (1963).
Graham Hough's *Preface to the Faerie Queene* (1962)
provides a sound, strictly literary interpretation, as does
Thomas P. Roche of Books 3 and 4. They are less original
than Alastair Fowler's brilliant exploration of the poem's
structure in *Spenser and the Numbers of Time* (1964).
Concordance by C. G. Osgood (1915). (*CBEL*, I, 417 f.)

Fulke Greville, Baron Brooke (1554–1628). Poems and
dramas, edited by Geoffrey Bullough (2 vols., 1939),
though not complete, contains almost everything of interest except the life of Sidney (edited by Nowell Smith,
1907). (*CBEL*, I, 421.)

John Lyly (1554?–1606). Complete works, edited by
R. Warwick Bond (3 vols., 1902), is sound if old-fashioned.
A better edition of *Euphues* is that by Morris W. Croll
and Harry Clemons (1916). Excellent general study by
G. K. Hunter (1962). (*CBEL*, I, 524 f.)

Sir Philip Sidney (1554–1586). Albert Feuillerat's edition (4 vols., 1912–26) is complete, with both versions of
Arcadia, but has no introductions or explanatory notes. For

the verse it is now superseded by William A. Ringler's well-annotated and definitive edition (1962). Uncritical text of the verse in *Silver Poets* (ed. G. Bullett, 1947). *Elizabethan Critical Essays,* edited by G. Gregory Smith (Vol. I, 1904), includes a critical edition of *The Defence of Poesie.* The most scholarly of the lives is still that by Malcolm W. Wallace (1915), though Mona Wilson (1931) is more readable and John Buxton (1954, rev. 1964) is interesting on Sidney's Continental tour and friendships. K. O. Myrick has written a helpful account of *Sidney as a Literary Craftsman* (1935), and Robert Montgomery's more ambitious *Symmetry and Sense* (1961) can also be recommended. See also Sidney's version of the Psalms (*The Psalms of Sir Philip Sidney and the Countess of Pembroke,* 1963), which includes his sister's superb renderings. (*CBEL,* I, 419 f.)

George Peele (1557?–1596). A definitive edition is now in progress under the general editorship of C. T. Prouty (life of Peele by D. H. Horne in Vol. I, 1952). Until its completion, reference must be made to A. H. Bullen's less ambitious edition (2 vols., 1888). (*CBEL,* I, 526 f.)

Robert Greene (1558–1592). J. Churton Collins's edition of the plays and poems (2 vols., 1905) still holds the field in spite of many errors and omissions. G. B. Harrison has edited eight of the pamphlets (1923–27), and there have been separate editions of one or two of the plays and romances, such as Daniel Seltzer's competent *Friar Bacon and Friar Bungay* (1963). See René Pruvost's elaborate study of the romances (Paris, 1938; in French). (*CBEL,* I, 529 f.)

Thomas Kyd (1558–1594). Standard edition by F. S. Boas (1901; rev. 1955). Good separate edition of *The Spanish Tragedy* by Philip Edwards (1959). There is a concordance by Charles Crawford (3 parts, Louvain, 1906–10). (*CBEL,* I, 525 f.)

Thomas Lodge (1558?–1625). See the studies by N. Burton Paradise (1931) and E. A. Tenney (1935). The complete works, edited by Edmund Gosse (4 vols., 1883), is uncritical. *Rosalynde* has been edited by W. W. Greg (1907; rev. 1931). (*CBEL*, I, 527 f.)

George Chapman (1559?–1634). Standard editions: plays by T. M. Parrott (2 vols., 1910–14); poems by Phyllis B. Bartlett (1941); Homeric translations by Allardyce Nicoll (2 vols., 1956). (But the editions of *Bussy D'Ambois* by Jean Jacquot [Paris, 1960] and N. Brooke [1963] supersede Parrott's.) There is no satisfactory life, but Swinburne's critical study (1875) is of some interest, and G. de F. Lord has an acute study of Chapman's *Odyssey* (1956). C. S. Lewis's defense of the continuation of Marlowe's *Hero and Leander* (Proceedings of British Academy, XXXVIII, 1952) should not be missed by connoisseurs. (*CBEL*, I, 609 f.)

Francis Bacon (1561–1626). The complete Bacon, edited by James Spedding, R. L. Ellis, and D. D. Heath (14 vols., 1857–74, now being reissued 1961–), has stood the test of time remarkably well. There is no first-class edition of the *Essays* (E. A. Abbot's [2 vols., 1879] is perhaps the least inadequate), but R. F. Jones has collected all the literary works in a useful volume (1937) and J. Max Patrick's similar selection (1963) has helpful notes. L. C. Knights has an interesting essay on "Bacon and the Seventeenth Century Dissociation of Sensibility" in his *Explorations* (1946). See also D. G. James, *The Dream of Learning* (1951). Bacon's philosophy is ably expounded by F. H. Anderson (1948). Elaborate bibliography by R. W. Gibson (1950). (*CBEL*, I, 868 f.)

Robert Southwell (1561?–1595). For the poems and devotional writings, see Pierre Janelle (Clermont–Ferrand, 1935). There is a biography by Christopher Devlin (1956). (*CBEL*, I, 421 f.)

Samuel Daniel (1563?–1619). A. C. Sprague has edited most of the poems and "A Defence of Ryme" (1930); Laurence Michel's *Philotas* (1949) and *The Civile Wars* (1958) are the only critical editions. There is a general study by Joan Rees (1964). (*CBEL*, I, 422 f.)

Michael Drayton (1563–1631). The edition by J. William Hebel, Kathleen Tillotson, and Bernard H. Newdigate (5 vols., 1931–41) is complete and definitive. There is also a sound life by Newdigate (1941), but almost no criticism except Oliver Elton's unambitious study (1905). (*CBEL*, I, 423 f.)

Christopher Marlowe (1564–1593). Standard edition by R. H. Case and others (6 vols., 1930–33; *Edward II* rev. F. N. Lees 1955), including a soberly factual life by C. F. Tucker Brooke, supersedes Tucker Brooke's unannotated one-volume edition (1910). An elaborate edition of *Faustus* by W. W. Greg (1950) is confined to textual reconstruction. The most thorough of the biographies is that by John E. Bakeless (2 vols., 1942). T. S. Eliot's short essay in *The Sacred Wood* (1920) is probably the best critique of Marlowe, but there are good things both in Paul Kocher's scholarly study (1946), in Harry Levin's somewhat pretentious *The Overreacher* (1952), and in J. B. Steane's stylish "critical study" (1964; good on the poetry). There is a concordance by Charles Crawford (5 parts, Louvain, 1911–32). (*CBEL*, I, 531 f.)

William Shakespeare (1564–1616).
Editions. Photo-facsimile of 1623 folio by Helge Kökeritz and C. T. Prouty (1955). Similar facsimiles of the principal quartos in progress begun under general editorship of W. W. Greg (1939–). The most generally useful modern edition of Shakespeare is probably the New Arden (general editors U. Ellis-Fermor and H. F. Brooks, 39 vols., 1951–), now almost complete, though for a few plays, the sonnets (ed. Hyder E. Rollins, 2 vols., 1944), and the poems the New Variorum (general editors H. H.

Furness senior and junior) is a good deal more thorough.
The New Cambridge (principal editor J. Dover Wilson,
39 vols., 1921–   ) is livelier and often more acute than
either, if somewhat marred by Wilson's textual fantasies,
and the serious student will consult all three editions. The
rival Oxford edition planned by R. B. McKerrow is now in
progress (*Coriolanus*, ed. Alice Walker, 1964). Their only
rivals of consequence are G. L. Kittredge's very able edition of sixteen of the principal plays (1946), the less ambitious Pelican paperbacks (general editor Alfred Harbage;
excellent short notes), and John Munro's *London Shakespeare* (6 vols., 1957; short on explanatory notes except
for textual *cruces*). The best modern one-volume editions
textually are Kittredge's (1936), Peter Alexander's (1951),
and C. J. Sisson's (1954), but these are all without notes;
that of William A. Neilson and C. J. Hill (1942) has short
notes; those of G. B. Harrison (1948; twenty-three plays)
and Hardin Craig (1951) are fuller. *The Shakespeare
Apocrypha*, edited by C. F. Tucker Brooke (1908), prints
without notes fourteen plays which have been ascribed to
Shakespeare, including the partly authentic *Sir Thomas
More* and *The Two Noble Kinsmen*.

Works of Reference. Earlier collections of the sources
are now being superseded by Geoffrey Bullough's meticulous *Narrative and Dramatic Sources of Shakespeare* (5
vols., 1957–   ). See also, for an evaluation of the material, Kenneth Muir's *Shakespeare's Sources* (2 vols.,
1957–   ). The standard life is still that of E. K. Chambers (2 vols., 1930), a judicious and comprehensive work
to which later research has added little. The most up-to-
date account is Peter Alexander's tightly packed Home University volume (1964). C. T. Onions's *Shakespeare Glossary* (1911, rev. 1953), based on the *OED*, clarifies most
of the linguistic obscurities, and the best of the concordances is that by John Bartlett (1894). F. E. Halliday's
Shakespeare Companion (1952) is an unpretentious
Shakespeare encyclopedia which is useful for running
down the odd fact. Helge Kökeritz' *Shakespeare's Pronun-*

ciation (1953) is elaborate and authoritative, though some of his conclusions have been questioned; Hilda M. Hulme's *Explorations in Shakespeare's Language* (1962) is perhaps of greater critical interest. Two specialist journals, *The Shakespeare Quarterly* (from 1949) and *Shakespeare Survey* (annually from 1948), report the previous year's theatrical productions, scholarship, and criticism. For earlier work there is a bibliography by W. Ebisch and L. L. Schücking (1931; Supplement 1937), which has been continued to 1958 by Gordon R. Smith (1963).

Criticism. The earlier criticism is to be found in whole or in part either in D. Nichol Smith's selection in the World's Classics series (1916) or in F. E. Halliday's *Shakespeare and His Critics* (1949). Another World's Classics volume (ed. A. Bradby, 1936) is devoted to criticism published between 1919 and 1935, and a third (1963) to 1935–60 criticism. A paperback collection of more recent essays on Shakespeare has been assembled by Leonard F. Dean (1957); J. C. Levenson has a similar one on *Hamlet* (*c.* 1959), and Laurence Lerner an especially useful one on the tragedies, separately and in general (1963). Ten of the annual British Academy lectures have also been exhumed by Peter Alexander (1964; lecturers include A. C. Bradley, Granville-Barker, McKerrow and C. S. Lewis).

Since Johnson (*Johnson on Shakespeare,* good selection by Walter Raleigh, 1908), Hazlitt (*Characters of Shakespeare's Plays,* 1817), and Coleridge (*Shakespearean Criticism,* ed. T. M. Raysor, 2 vols., 1930), the outstanding Shakespearean critics seem to have been: (i) A. C. Bradley (*Shakespearean Tragedy,* 1904; valuable Shakespeare essays also in *Oxford Lectures on Poetry,* 1909, and *A Miscellany,* 1929); (ii) Harley Granville-Barker (*Prefaces to Shakespeare,* 5 series, 1927–48); (iii) Elmer E. Stoll (*Shakespeare Studies,* 1927, rev. 1942; *Art and Artifice in Shakespeare,* 1933); (iv) G. Wilson Knight (*The Wheel of Fire,* 1930, rev. 1949; *The Imperial Theme,* 1931; *The Crown of Life,* 1947). Shakespeare's imagery is analyzed both by Caroline Spurgeon (1935) and, more perceptively, by Wolfgang Clemen (Tr. English 1951). On the early plays the best book to date is Miss M. C. Bradbrook's *Shakespeare and Elizabethan Poetry* (1951); the histories have been ably resurveyed by E. M. W. Tillyard (1944), Lily B. Campbell (1947), and Irving Ribner (1957); a good book on the comedies has still to be written. A suggestive introduction to the poetic interpretation of Shakespeare is D. A. Traversi's *Approach to Shakespeare* (1938) —as is Miss M. M. Mahood's *Shakespeare's Wordplay* (1957) to Shakespeare's more serious puns. Outstanding discussions of one or more plays are J. Dover Wilson's *What Happens in Hamlet* (1935) and *The Fortunes of Falstaff* (1943), and R. B. Heilman's *This Great Stage: Image and Structure in King Lear* (1948). On Shakespeare's text the more important recent contributions have been R. B. McKerrow's *Prolegomena for the Oxford Shakespeare* (1939), W. W. Greg's *Editorial Problem in Shakespeare* (1942, rev. 1951 and 1955) and *The Shakespeare First Folio* (1955), Alice Walker's *Textual Problems of the First Folio* (1953), and Charlton Hinman's microscopic *Printing and Proof-reading of the First Folio* (2 vols., 1963). J. C. Adams discusses the staging of the plays in persuasive detail in *The Globe Playhouse* (1942). (*CBEL*, I, 539 f.)

Thomas Campion (1567–1620). Works, edited by Percival Vivian (1909). See also Miles M. Kastendieck (1938). (*CBEL*, I, 425 f.)

Thomas Nashe (1567–1601?). Works, edited by Ronald B. McKerrow (5 vols., 1904–10, reissued with corrections by F. P. Wilson and W. W. Greg, 1958), is the definitive edition with detailed life, commentary, notes, and index. The only recent study is by G. R. Hibbard (1962). (*CBEL*, I, 533 f.)

Sir Henry Wotton (1568–1639). Life and letters, edited by Logan Pearsall Smith (2 vols., 1902). (*CBEL*, I, 426.)

Sir John Davies (1569–1626). Poems, edited by Clare Howard (1941); uncritical text in *Silver Poets* (ed. G. Bullett, 1947). E. M. W. Tillyard discusses "Orchestra" in *Five Poems* (1948); T. S. Eliot's short essay is in *On Poetry and Poets* (1957). (*CBEL*, I, 426 f.)

John Donne (1571/2–1631). Poems, edited by H. J. C. Grierson (2 vols., 1912; best edition, but commentary in Vol. II is now partly out of date and several of the poems included are now known not to be Donne's). *The Divine Poems*, edited by Helen L. Gardner (1952) supersedes Grierson for these poems, as does Frank Manley's detailed edition of *The Anniversaries* (1963). *Songs and Sonnets* has been edited by Theodore Redpath (1956; more notes than Grierson but often uncritical); a definitive edition by Helen Gardner is announced. The definitive edition of the sermons is by George R. Potter and Evelyn M. Simpson (10 vols., 1953–61), and ten sermons also have been edited separately by Mrs. Simpson (1963). Selections from poetry and prose both by John Hayward (1929, rev. 1962) and Charles M. Coffin (1952). Concordance by H. C. Combs and Z. R. Sullens (1940). J. B. Leishman's *The Monarch of Wit* (1951, rev. 1962), the fullest study to date, is somewhat erratic critically. Perhaps the most helpful appreciations are Doniphan Louthan's lively *The Poetry of Donne* (1951) and Frank Kermode's British Council pamphlet (1957); K. W. Gransden's modest study (1954) is also sensible and readable. Clay Hunt's analyses, at great length, of seven key poems (*Donne the Craftsman*, 1954) and M. A. Rugoff's *Donne's Imagery* (1939) are more specialized. *A Garland for Donne* (ed. Theodore Spencer, 1932) includes T. S. Eliot's "Donne in Our Time," a repudiation of Eliot's earlier enthusiasms. For two clever depreciations see J. E. V. Crofts (in *Essays and Studies of the English Association*, XXII [1937]), and C. S. Lewis (in the Grierson *Festschrift*, 1938). Joan Webber's *Contrary Music* (1963) is a sound introduction to the prose. Helen Gardner has assembled the principal critical essays on Donne in a useful paperback (1963); Frank Kermode's *Discussions of John Donne* (1963) is more of an anthology of Donne criticism (from Ben Jonson). An edition of the letters promised by I. A. Shapiro and the forthcoming life by R. C. Bald are expected to supersede Edmund Gosse's uncritical *Life and Letters of Donne* (2 vols., 1899). Bibliography by Geoffrey Keynes (1914, rev. 1958). (*CBEL*, I, 441 f.)

Thomas Dekker (1572?–1632). Plays, edited by Fredson Bowers (4 vols., 1953–60; detailed textual apparatus only, commentary by Cyrus Hoy to follow). Plague-pamphlets, edited by F. P. Wilson (1925). There is an elaborate study by M. T. Jones-Davies (2 vols., Paris, 1958; in French). (*CBEL*, I, 619 f.)

Ben Jonson (1572–1637). Standard edition (with excellent notes, almost nothing left out) by C. H. Herford, Percy and Evelyn M. Simpson (11 vols., 1925–52). Complete plays, edited by F. E. Schelling (Everyman's Library, 2 vols., 1910; no notes). Selection with good introduction by Harry Levin (1939). Complete poems: edited by Bernard H. Newdigate (1936; glossary but no notes); edited by William B. Hunter, Jr. (1963; short explanatory footnotes). Selected poems, edited by George B. Johnston (1954; short notes). Good edition of *Bartholomew Fair* by E. A. Horsman (1960). Life, in Herford–Simpson edition (Vols. I, II, 1925). Interesting discussion of the plays and their economic background in L. C. Knights's *Drama and Society in the Age of Jonson* (1937), and of Jonson's dramatic prose by Jonas A. Barish (1960). See also G. E. Bentley, *Shakespeare and Jonson: Their Reputations in the Seventeenth Century Compared* (2 vols., 1945), and Edward B. Partridge's critical survey of the comedies, *The Broken Compass* (1958). T. S. Eliot's brilliant essay will be found in *The Sacred Wood* (1920) as well as in his *Selected Essays* (1932). The best modern Jonson criticism has been assembled by J. A. Barish (1963). (*CBEL*, I, 613 f.)

Joseph Hall (1574–1656). Definitive edition of poems by A. Davenport (1949). (*CBEL*, I, 697, 841.)

Thomas Heywood (1574?–1641). No modern edition of plays except A. W. Verity's Mermaid selection (1888; five plays), but R. W. Van Fossen has a good edition of *A Woman Killed with Kindness* (1961). Arthur M. Clark's pioneer study (1931) has been superseded by Michel Grivelet's elaborate survey (Paris, 1957; in French). T. S. Eliot's essay is in *Selected Essays* (1932). (*CBEL*, I, 622 f.)

Cyril Tourneur (1575?–1626). Complete Works, edited by Allardyce Nicoll (1929; some notes but not enough). *Atheist's Tragedy*, well edited by I. Ribner (1964). See T. S. Eliot (*Selected Essays*, 1932) and John Peter (*Complaint and Satire*, 1956). *The Revenger's Tragedy* is probably by Middleton (see below). (*CBEL*, I, 628 f.)

John Marston (1576–1634). Standard edition of poems by A. Davenport (1961). Latest edition of plays by H. Harvey Wood (3 vols., 1934–39). For *The Malcontent*, see the admirable separate edition by G. K. Hunter (1963). Detailed study (in French) by A. José Axelrad (Paris, 1955). See also T. S. Eliot (*Selected Essays*, 1951) and John Peter (*Satire and Complaint*, 1956). (*CBEL*, I, 627 f.)

Robert Burton (1577–1640). *Anatomy of Melancholy:* edited by A. R. Shilleto (3 vols., 1893; best edition); edited by Floyd Dell and Paul Jordan–Smith (2 vols., 1927; short notes, Latin tr. into English); edited by H. Jackson (3 vols., 1932). Bibliography by Paul Jordan-Smith (1931). (*CBEL*, I, 829 f.)

Thomas Middleton (1580–1627). Works, edited by A. H. Bullen (8 vols., 1885–86); Mermaid selection edited by A. C. Swinburne and Havelock Ellis (2 vols., 1887–90; ten plays). *The Changeling*, edited by N. W. Bawcutt (1958), is the only modern critical edition. Excellent study of the tragedies by Samuel Schoenbaum (1955); for the comedies see Wilbur D. Dunkel (1925). T. S. Eliot's essay in *For Lancelot Andrewes* (1928) is reprinted in his *Selected Essays* (1932). (*CBEL*, I, 611 f.)

John Webster (1580?–1625). Standard edition by F. L. Lucas (4 vols., 1927). Good edition of *The White Devil* by John Russell Brown (1960). Critical studies by Elmer E. Stoll (1905), Rupert Brooke (1916), Clifford Leech (1951; excellent short introduction), and Travis Bogard (1955; more critically ambitious). R. W. Dent's meticulous *Webster's Borrowing* (1960) is indispensable but disconcerting. (*CBEL*, I, 629 f.)

Phineas (1582–1650) and Giles Fletcher (1585–1623). Poetical works, edited by F. S. Boas (2 vols., 1908–9; no notes). Phineas's *Venus and Anohises*, also edited by Ethel Seaton (1926; definitive). For Phineas see Abram B. Langdale (1937). (*CBEL*, I, 444 f.)

Edward Herbert, Baron Herbert of Cherbury (1583–1648). Poems: edited by G. C. Moore Smith (1923); plain texts in *Minor Poets* (ed. R. G. Howarth, 1931). Autobiography, edited by Sidney Lee (1886, rev. 1906). *Religio Laici*, edited and translated by H. R. Hutcheson (1944). See M. M. Rossi (3 vols., Florence, 1947) for enormously detailed account (in Italian) of life, writings, and intellectual background. (*CBEL*, I, 476.)

Philip Massinger (1583–1648). Last complete edition by William Gifford (1805, etc.). The Mermaid edition (introduction by Arthur Symons, 2 vols., 1887–89) prints ten plays, L. A. Sherman's (1912) only four. *A New Way to Pay Old Debts*, edited by A. H. Cruickshank (1926), has some notes. T. S. Eliot's brilliant essay in *The Sacred Wood* (1920) was originally a review of Cruickshank's modest study (1920), which has now been superseded by that of Thomas A. Dunn (1957). (*CBEL*, I, 630 f.)

The English Bible (Authorized Version, 1611). A. W.

Pollard's *Records of the English Bible* (1911) is the basic modern work. Pollard has also edited Tindale's earliest version (1926) and a facsimile of the Authorized Version (1911). *The English Hexapla* (1841, rev. 1872) prints the New Testament in the original Greek and in the Wycliffe, Tindale, Cranmer, Geneva, Rheims, and 1611 versions. The best general account is F. F. Bruce's *The English Bible* (1961). C. S. Lewis has an essay arguing against the literary influence of the Authorized Version in *They Asked for a Paper* (1962). (*CBEL*, I, 672 f.)

Francis Beaumont (1585?–1616) and John Fletcher (1579–1625). Collected plays: edited by A. H. Bullen and others (Variorum edition, with separate introductions and notes, 4 vols., 1904–12; only twenty plays, the edition was never completed); edited by A. Glover and A. R. Waller (10 vols., 1905–12; complete, but no notes). Selected plays: edited by J. St. Loe Strachey (Mermaid series, 2 vols., 1904; ten plays, no notes); edited by G. P. Baker (Everyman's Library, 1911). The most recent critical study is by Clifford Leech (1962). (*CBEL*, I, 632 f.)

William Drummond (1585–1649). Poetical Works (with *A Cypresse Grove*), edited by L. E. Kastner (2 vols., 1913; the definitive edition). Useful critical study by F. R. Fogle (1952). (*CBEL*, I, 444 f.)

John Ford (1586–1639). Collected plays, edited by W. Bang and H. de Vocht (2 vols., Louvain, 1908–27). The Mermaid selection gives five plays (introduction by Havelock Ellis, 1888), and there is a well-annotated edition of *The Broken Heart* by T. J. B. Spencer (1963). T. S. Eliot's essay is in his *Selected Essays* (1932). A good general account has been provided in French by Robert Davril (Paris, 1954), and there are sound short critical introductions by H. J. Oliver (1955) and Clifford Leech (1957). (*CBEL*, I, 637 f.)

Thomas Hobbes (1588–1679). *Leviathan* (1946; stimulating introduction by Michael Oakeshott). The critical writings appear in J. E. Spingarn's collection (Vol. II, 1908). There is a good account of Hobbes's aesthetic doctrine by C. D. Thorpe (1940). See also D. G. James, *The Life of Reason* (1949). Bibliography by Hugh Macdonald and Mary Hargreaves (1952). (*CBEL*, I, 871 f.)

George Wither (1588–1667). Works, reprinted by the Spenser Society (6 vols., 1871–82). Poetry, edited by Frank Sidgwick (2 vols., 1902; good biographical introduction). (*CBEL*, I, 446 f.)

William Browne (1590?–1645). Complete works, edited by W. Carew Hazlitt (2 vols., 1868–69). Poems, edited by Gordon Goodwin (2 vols., 1894). (*CBEL*, I, 449.)

Robert Herrick (1591–1674). Poems: edited by F. W. Moorman (1915); edited by L. C. Martin (1956; definitive edition); edited by J. Max Patrick (1963; complete, occasional footnotes). Concordance by Malcolm MacLeod (1936). (*CBEL*, I, 449 f.)

Henry King (1592–1669). Poems: edited by L. Mason (1914); edited by John Sparrow (1925). See L. Mason, *Transactions of Connecticut Academy*, XVIII (1913), and R. Berman, *Henry King and the Seventeenth Century* (1964). (*CBEL*, I, 450.)

George Herbert (1593–1633). Works, edited by F. E. Hutchinson (1941, rev. 1945; definitive edition). There are good critical studies by Rosemond Tuve (1952), Margaret Bottrall (1954), and J. H. Summers (1954). Modern criticism of Herbert begins in William Empson's brilliant if erratic *Seven Types of Ambiguity* (1930). T. S. Eliot's contribution to the British Council's Writers and Their Work series (1963) is rather conventional. Concordance by Cameron Mann (1927); bibliography by G. H. Palmer (1911). (*CBEL*, I, 451 f.)

Izaak Walton (1593–1683). *The Compleat Walton*, edited by Geoffrey Keynes (1929; no notes). For a detailed examination of Walton's lives, see D. Novarr (1958). (*CBEL*, I, 830 f.)

Thomas Carew (1595?–1640). Poems: edited by Rhodes Dunlap (1949; standard edition, but somewhat uncritical); unannotated in *Minor Poets* (ed. R. G. Howarth, 1931). Critical study by E. I. Selig (1958). (*CBEL*, I, 453.)

James Shirley (1596–1666). Only complete edition is still Gifford and Dyce (6 vols., 1833). Six plays in Mermaid edition (E. Gosse, 1888). See Arthur H. Nason (1915). (*CBEL*, I, 638 f.)

John Earle (1601?–1665). *Micro-cosmographie*, edited by H. Osborne (1933; many notes). (*CBEL*, I, 722.)

William Habington (1605–1654). Standard edition of poems by Kenneth Allott (1948). (*CBEL*, I, 453.)

Sir Thomas Browne (1605–1682). The only complete edition, by Geoffrey Keynes (6 vols., 1928–31, rev., 4 vols., 1964), is without notes; it includes Browne's letters. The scholarly edition by L. C. Martin (1963) omits *Vulgar Errors*. Of *Religio Medici* there are reliable editions by Jean-Jacques Denonain (1953 and 1959; important for text, no explanatory notes), V. Sanna (2 vols., 1958), and James Winny (1963; useful notes). The best critical studies are by William P. Dunn (1926, rev. 1950) and Joan Bennett (1962); for life see O. Leroy (1931), Jeremiah Finch (1950), and F. L. Huntley (1962). Bibliography by Geoffrey Keynes (1924, rev. 1957). (*CBEL*, I, 834 f.)

Sir William Davenant (1606–1668). Uncritical edition of plays by J. Maidment and W. H. Logan (5 vols., 1872–74). No modern edition of poems, but *Gondibert* preface is in *Seventeenth Century Critical Essays*, ed. J. E. Spingarn (Vol. II, 1908). Of the two modern studies (Alfred Harbage, 1935, and Arthur H. Nethercot, 1938) Nethercot's is somewhat the fuller. (*CBEL*, I, 453 f.)

Edmund Waller (1606–1687). Standard edition of poems by G. Thorn-Drury (2 vols., 1893). Critical edition in preparation by P. R. Wikelund. Good critical study by

A. W. Allison (1962). See also Johnson (*Lives of the Poets,* 1781). (*CBEL,* I, 455 f.)

Sir Richard Fanshawe (1608–1666). Good selection of shorter poems and translation edited by N. W. Bawcutt (1963). (*CBEL,* I, 644.)

Thomas Fuller (1608–1661). Modern edition of *Worthies of England* by J. Freeman (1952). (*CBEL,* I, 835 f.)

John Milton (1608–1674). The only complete Milton is the Columbia edition (general editor F. A. Patterson, 20 vols., 1931–40), which records the textual variants and has an excellent index (2 vols., 1940) but no introductions or explanatory notes; there are English translations of the Latin works, etc., as well as the original texts. For the prose, the Yale edition (each volume with a separate editor; 3 vols. of the 8 projected published 1953–62) is definitive, often indeed overelaborate. There is no equivalent for the poems so far, though a Yale variorum edition is promised. At the moment the best edition of the poems is Merritt Y. Hughes's one-volume *Complete Poems and Major Prose* (1957), which elaborates Hughes's earlier edition of the poems alone (2 vols., 1935–37). Hughes gives full but uncritical introductions and short footnotes, prose translations for the Latin poems (with the Latin), and over four hundred pages of the prose (including translations without the Latin of *Prolusions* and parts of *Christian Doctrine*). The detailed editions of the various poetical works by A. W. Verity (*The Cambridge Milton for Schools,* 11 vols., 1891–96, *Paradise Lost* rev. 1910), which absorbed the work of the earlier English editors, are still valuable if now often out of date. Of the unannotated editions, those of Helen Darbishire (2 vols., 1952–55, 1 vol. 1958) and B. A. Wright (1956) are of interest because the spelling is emended to conform to Milton's presumed intentions. H. F. Fletcher's facsimile edition (4 vols., 1943–48) prints photographic reproductions of all the early editions and manuscripts.

Minor poems. Facsimile of Trinity College MS. edited

by W. Aldis Wright (1899, and edited by F. A. Patterson 1933). 1645 *Poems,* edited by Cleanth Brooks and J. E. Hardy (1951; facsimile text with elaborate, often fanciful, critical interpretations). Sonnets, edited by J. S. Smart (1921). Shorter poems, edited by B. A. Wright (1938). *Paradise Lost:* Facsimile of MS. of Book I edited by Helen Darbishire (1931). *Samson Agonistes:* best edition is F. T. Prince's (1957). *Areopagitica:* edited by J. W. Hales (1878); edited by R. C. Jebb (1918). *Correspondence and Prolusions:* edited and translated by E. M. W. and P. B. Tillyard (1932). Prose selections: edited by Merritt Y. Hughes (1947; good short notes).

Biography and criticism. The Victorian life by David Masson (6 vols., 1859–80; rev. of first 3 vols. and index 1881–96) is useful for its mass of background information. It needs supplementing today by the exhaustive *Life Records of Milton,* edited by J. Milton French (5 vols., 1949–58). The illuminating and entertaining early lives have been edited by Helen Darbishire (1932). A sound modern biography is James H. Hanford's *John Milton, Englishman* (1949). Hanford's indispensable *Milton Handbook* (1926, rev. 1946) prints autobiographical passages, extracts from early lives, etc., and summarizes recent Milton literature. A more elaborate work of reference is D. H. Stevens's *Reference Guide to Milton* (1930; supplement to 1957 by C. Huckaby, 1960), which lists everything of any interest after 1800. The most recent manual is Marjorie Nicolson's *A Reader's Guide to Milton* (1964). James Thorpe's anthology of Milton criticism (1950) gives specimens from Addison, Johnson, and others down to Raleigh, Stoll, Ransom, Grierson, Charles Williams, and T. S. Eliot, but F. R. Leavis's brilliant depreciation in his *Revaluation* (1936) is omitted. The most interesting of the recent longer critical studies have been those of E. M. W. Tillyard (1930), C. S. Lewis, *A Preface to Paradise Lost* (1942), A. J. A. Waldock, *Paradise Lost and Its Critics* (1947; persuasive attack on Tillyard, Lewis, etc.), F. T. Prince (1954; Italian influences on style and verse), Robert M. Adams, *Ikon:*

Milton and the Modern Critics (1955; attacks the various specialists' theories), Kenneth Muir (1955; scholarly if indecisive), J. B. Broadbent (1960: a general study of *Paradise Lost*), William Empson, *Milton's God* (1961; perverse but stimulating), and Christopher Ricks (1963; style of *Paradise Lost*, most acute). The "baroque" approach is put to good account by Roy Daniells (*Milton, Mannerism, and Baroque*, 1963). *The Living Milton* (ed. Frank Kermode, 1960), a lively symposium by ten young English critics, provides an excellent introduction to the modern view of Milton. In addition there are many useful specialist studies, notably Charles G. Osgood's *Classical Mythology of Milton's English Poems* (1900, rev. 1925), Robert Bridges's *Milton's Prosody* (final rev. 1921), and W. R. Parker's analysis of the Greek influences in *Samson Agonistes* (1937). The best concordance is that by J. Bradshaw (1894); there is a geographical dictionary by A. H. Gilbert. (*CBEL*, I, 463 f.)

Sir John Suckling (1609–1642). Works, edited by A. Hamilton Thompson (1910; uncritical texts). Poems, edited by R. G. Howarth (1931, and in *Minor Poets of the Seventeenth Century*, 1953; no notes). (*CBEL*, I, 456.)

Sir Thomas Urquhart (1611–1660). Works, edited by T. Maitland, 1834. Translation of Rabelais, edited by Charles Whibley (3 vols., 1900). (*CBEL*, I, 836.)

Richard Crashaw (1612/13–1649). Standard edition of poems by L. C. Martin (1927, rev. 1957; useful notes). There is a first-class critical study of Crashaw by Austin Warren (*Richard Crashaw*, 1939); Ruth C. Wallerstein (1935) is learned but rather heavy going. (*CBEL*, I, 456 f.)

Jeremy Taylor (1613–1667). The authoritative study is by C. J. Stranks (1952). There is a pleasant anthology of Taylor's purple patches by Logan Pearsall Smith (1930).

Henry More (1614–1687). Selected poems: edited by M. H. Howard (1911; with Richard Ward's life of More); edited by Geoffrey Bullough (1931; notes and good introduction). Selected philosophical writings, edited by F. I. MacKinnon (1925). (*CBEL*, I, 700 f.)

Abraham Cowley (1618–1667). English writings, edited by A. R. Waller (2 vols., 1905–6; no introduction or notes). Essays: edited by J. R. Lumby (1887, rev. A. Tilley 1923); edited by A. B. Gough (1915). There is an elaborate French study of Cowley by Jean Loiseau (Paris, 1931) and a biography by Arthur H. Nethercot (1931); R. B. Hinman (1960) expounds Cowley's intellectual achievement. For Johnson's life see *Lives of the Poets*, edited by G. Birkbeck Hill (Vol. I, 1905). (*CBEL*, I, 458 f.)

Richard Lovelace (1618–1656/7). Standard edition of poems by C. H. Wilkinson (2 vols., 1925; rev. 1 vol. 1930). Unannotated edition in *Minor Poets of the Seventeenth Century*, edited by R. G. Howarth (1931). (*CBEL*, I, 460.)

Andrew Marvell (1621–1678). Standard edition of poems and letters by H. M. Margoliouth (2 vols., 1927, rev. 1952; some notes). Lyrics, edited by Hugh Macdonald (1952; short notes). Selected poems, edited with commentary by J. Winny (1962). There is a scholarly study in French by Pierre Legouis (Paris, 1928). The clever short critical interpretation by M. C. Bradbrook and M. G. Lloyd Thomas (1940) is somewhat inconclusive. (*CBEL*, I, 460 f.)

Henry Vaughan (1621–1695). Standard edition by L. C. Martin (2 vols., 1914, enlarged 1 vol. 1958; notes). Another good complete edition by French Fogle (1964). E. L. Marilla's edition of the secular poems (1958) has extensive notes, many of them irrelevant. There is an excellent life by F. E. Hutchinson (1947) and there are competent critical studies by Ross Garner (1959), E. C. Pettet (1960), and R. A. Durr (1962). Bibliography by E. L. Marilla (1948). (*CBEL*, I, 461 f.)

Thomas Stanley (1625–1678). Definitive edition of poems by Galbraith M. Crump (1962). (*CBEL*, I, 478.)

VI.   The Approach to Augustan Literature

1. A COMMON CULTURE

The complacency with which the English Augustans regarded their own achievements in poetry and the drama has not been shared by succeeding critics. "Dryden and Pope are not classics of our poetry, they are classics of our prose" (Matthew Arnold); "In the seventeenth century a dissociation of sensibility set in, from which we have never recovered" (T. S. Eliot). The disagreement with Johnson's view of Pope's metrics, for example—"to attempt any further improvement of versification will be dangerous. Art and diligence have now done their best, and what shall be added will be the effort of tedious toil and needless curiosity"—is almost total. But Augustan literature makes up in range and coherence what it lacks in glamour. In their several ways at least five of Dryden's non-literary contemporaries or near-contemporaries —Clarendon, Hobbes, Bunyan, Halifax, and Locke—are almost as good writers as he is. And the eighteenth century, if without supreme poets or dramatists, is after all that of our greatest philosopher (Hume), our greatest historian (Gibbon), our greatest political thinker (Burke), and our greatest biographer (Boswell). It was to an exceptional degree a *common* culture—one based on common assumptions, many of which were literary. And one of them was that the way to serve one's society, whatever one's speciality might be, was to write good English.

By the end of the eighteenth century it was generally agreed that the English Augustan age par excellence had been the reign of Queen Anne. Originally the analogy had been a political one. The English Civil War (which modern historians are now beginning to call the English Revolution) invited an obvious comparison with the last phase of republican Rome, and in these circumstances an English Augustus was not hard to find. To Waller, writing in 1655, he was Cromwell:

> As the vexed world, to find repose, at last
> Itself into Augustus' arms did cast;
> So England now does, with like toil oppressed,
> Her weary head upon your bosom rest.
>   ("A Panegyric to My Lord Protector")

In 1660, in Dryden's "Astraea Redux," the role is as naturally allotted to Charles II:

> O happy age! O times like those alone
> By fate reserv'd for great Augustus' throne!
> When the joint growth of arms and arts foreshew
> The world a monarch, and that monarch *you*.

But the new Augustus's exact identity was not the real point. The real point was the country's need for a governmental system which would ensure that a Civil War did not break out again. For reasons that are still not fully understood, the century-old economic inflation suddenly came to an end about 1650 and an English society could therefore be rebuilt on rational foundations. The new organizing concept was essentially that of equipoise—a balance of property (the land versus business), a balance of classes (the gentry versus the middling class and the mob), and a balance of Protestant sects (Anglicanism versus the Dissenters), all reflecting themselves, however imperfectly, in a prevailing dualism of which the two-party Parliament was only one aspect. "Common sense" (the ability to distinguish appearance from reality) is the period's key term at every level. Its opposite, "private sense" or "inspiration," had been the cause of the Civil War; common sense, the rational faculty shared by all human beings except babies and lunatics, was obviously preferable to the emotional and intellectual individualism of the first part of the century. Civil peace was the common concern of all.

The linguistic corollary of common sense was common usage. Here too the Augustan analogy was invoked. Just as the Latin spoken and written in Augustus's time had become the model of what all future Latin should be, so the Restoration heralded a conscious campaign to improve English as a medium of communication. The anonymous author of the extremely intelligent preface to *The Second Part of Mr. Waller's Poems* (1690)—he is thought to have been Francis Atterbury—wonders "whether in Charles II's reign English did not come to its full perfection; and whether it has not had its Augustan age as well as the Latin." This was, apparently, the first time the word *Augustan* had been used in English and it refers to the English language. Its extension to English literature was not made until 1712 when John Oldmixon asserted that Charles II's reign "probably may be the Augustan Age of English Poetry."[1] The sequence of senses is significant —from a political one to a linguistic one, and only then, and finally, from language to literature. The basis of English Augustanism remained political until well into the eighteenth century; it is no accident that the "neo-classic" Dryden, Swift, Pope, Fielding, and Johnson were Tories —or that the "pre-Romantic" Addison, Thomson, Gray, Collins, and Cowper were Whigs. The language, with the new emphasis on "correctness" and "perspicuity"—and so reflecting the ideals of Tory "common sense"—was only one remove from politics. And Johnson's great *Dictionary of the English Language* (1755) is full of Tory wisdom as well as of Tory prejudice. The literature, on the other hand, if two removes from politics, was only one remove from language; Whigs shared most of the same linguistic ideals as Tories, and despite the occasional intrusions of

[1] *Reflections on Dr. Swift's Letter to the Earl of Oxford about the English Tongue* (1712).

pre-Romanticism, Augustan literature is stylistically remarkably homogeneous.

One unifying element—it is, of course, implicit in the
Augustan myth—was the general acceptance of Rome as
the social model. Latin was far more important than
Greek, or indeed any other subject, in the education of
the ruling class, and for the budding writer a Latin classic
—especially Horace, Virgil, Ovid, and Juvenal among the
poets and Cicero among the writers of prose—was always
available as a criterion of excellence. The "imitation," a
form of free translation with the original allusions adapted
to modern circumstances, was one of the most success-
ful poetic inventions of the period; the Horatian imita-
tions of Rochester, Oldham, Dryden, Swift, and Pope, and
Johnson's two Juvenalian satires, in demonstrating the
creative possibilities of such parallels, also showed how
close the two cultures were in their essential features.
And the confidence the Roman Augustans had in their
civilizing mission was exactly that of their English imitators. "What was said of Rome adorned by Augustus,"
Johnson wrote in his life of Dryden, "may be applied
by an easy metaphor to English poetry embellished by
Dryden, *lateritiam invenit, marmoream reliquit,* he found
it brick, and he left it marble."

2. FIRST AID FOR THE MODERN READER

What then are the questions a modern reader must ask
himself when he is reading a later seventeenth- or
eighteenth-century poem, play, or novel?

The first question, to be answered more or less precisely according to circumstances, is the matter of context. Since Augustan literature is socially committed in a
way no other body of English literature has ever been,
the modern reader must be at least dimly aware of each
work's original cultural implications if he is to understand
what it is about. Most of the Augustan poems that get
into the anthologies—Dryden's "Alexander's Feast," for ex-

ample, or Pope's "Elegy to the Memory of an Unfortunate Lady," or Gray's "Ode on the Death of a Favourite
Cat"—owe their place there to their contextual detach-
ability. They are not the period's best poems, and by the
side of Marvell's or Wordsworth's lyrics they tend to have
a rather shabby or trivial look. Even considered as a tour
de force Dryden's "Secular Masque" is greatly superior
to "Alexander's Feast," but whereas that is a self-sufficient
and self-explanatory poem, "The Secular Masque," which
is essentially the seventeenth century's verdict on itself,
requires a reader who can transport himself back mentally
to the year 1700. Again, Pope's "Epistle to Miss Blount
on Her Leaving the Town after the Coronation" is a much
better poem than his "Elegy," but its full appreciation de-
pends on an easy familiarity with the London-versus-coun-
try tradition of Restoration comedy. (The geographical
ambivalence derived from the squirearchy's habit of
spending some six months every year in London or Westminster and the other six months on their country estates.) And Gray's "Favourite Cat," engaging though she
is, has none of the satiric power of his "On Lord Holland's
Seat Near Margate, Kent," which uses an outdated style
of landscape gardening to discredit with damning effect
a corrupt politician who has been "dropped":

> Art he invokes new horrors still to bring:
> Now mouldring fanes and battlements arise,
> Arches and turrets nodding to their fall,
> Unpeopled palaces delude his eyes,
> And mimick desolation covers all.

A second question that must always be asked the English Augustans is a stylistic one. As Donald Davie has
put it in his brilliant *Purity of Diction in English Verse*
(1952), a study which lays forever the old ghost of "poetic diction," the dominant impression created by Augustan poetry is "that words are thrusting at the poem and
being fended off from it, that however many poems these
poets wrote certain words would never be allowed into

the poems, except as a disastrous oversight." The Victorians dismissed this stylistic chastity of the eighteenth century as verbal prudery; the contrast with Shakespeare or even Browning was obvious and appeared final. But art is necessarily selective and the only question is the mode or level at which the selection is operating. Thus in drama or the dramatic monologue the dramatis persona's vocabulary is only limited—*has* only to be limited—by the "character" he is supposed to embody. But the typical Augustan, whatever his medium, aimed first of all at concision and concentration, a maximum verbal density in which every word is immediately recognized as necessary, and the reader was only left to fill out the verbal implications. "Last week I saw a woman flayed, and you will hardly believe how much it altered her person for the worse." By the side of this characteristic comment of Swift's (it is, of course, from *The Tale of a Tub*) one might put Johnson's tightly packed line from *The Vanity of Human Wishes* on the afflictions that a scholar has to expect:

Toil, envy, want, the patron, and the jail.

Two of Donald Davie's examples have carried the stylistic process a stage further:

(i)   So first when Phoebus met the Cyprian queen,
       And favour'd Rhodes beheld their passion crown'd,
       Unusual flowers enrich'd the painted green,
       And swift spontaneous roses blush'd around.
                                        (Shenstone)

(ii)   Urging at noon the slow boat in the reeds
       That wav'd their green uncertainty of shade.
                                        (Langhorne)

Shenstone and Langhorne are minor mid-eighteenth-century poets, but they are here exploiting with great skill the aesthetic elegances possible in the minor distortions of grammar which will also assist semantic concision.

Shenstone's flowers were not really unusual or spontaneous, it was their flowering that was; and Langhorne's boat was not slow but slow-moving, the uncertain shade not the reed's concern but the boatman's. Such effects have not been possible in more recent poetry, when the poet has all the words in the English dictionary at his beck and call and is expected to be as long-winded as he likes.

A third question for the modern reader to ask is the nature of the relationship between concreteness and abstraction in the Augustan style. In a literature such as that of the twentieth century, which is primarily concrete, an abstract word or concept is immediately noticed because it is so different from its surroundings. A single abstract noun in a poem by Hardy or Yeats, for example, will often carry as much weight as a whole stanza of detailed physical description. In Augustan literature the same principle is at work in reverse. The concrete images protrude because they are so rare. It follows that a mere minimum of concreteness is all that is needed to give vigor to a series of abstractions. Johnson's line had originally been:

> Toil, envy, want, the garret, and the gaol.

Since *gaol* is concrete, a second physical image is not essential; *patron* (displacing *garret*) can refer back simultaneously to the earlier abstracts, when it becomes equivalent to *patronage*, or forward to the concrete *gaol*, when it becomes a particular patron, such as the Earl of Chesterfield.

The principle is the explanation and justification of a favorite Augustan device that the nineteenth century found particularly abhorrent, the device of personification or prosopopoeia. In Gray's "Elegy"—especially in its earlier and more Augustan stanzas—the personifications crowd in thick and fast, often with only one concrete appurtenance (usually a verb) to differentiate the personification from a mere abstraction. But what effective use Gray makes of his personifications!

> Let not Ambition mock their useful toil,
>   Their homely joys, and destiny obscure;
> Nor Grandeur hear, with a disdainful smile,
>   The short and simple annals of the poor.

Against the background of generalities—*useful toil, homely joys*, etc.—the mocking of Ambition and the disdainful smile of Grandeur acquire an unusual particularity. Nor are the personifications mere collective nouns, synonyms of "the ambitious" or "the grand." "Grandeur" is in fact contrasted with "the poor," and by calling in the rhetorical figure to help him make his point, Gray nicely underlines the pretentiousness of the closed circle of the Augustan aristocracy. This quasi-sarcastic use of personification must be distinguished from its "pre-Romantic" or "picturesque" form, in which the poet—Pope in *The Temple of Fame*, Gray in the "Ode on a Distant Prospect of Eton College," and Collins almost everywhere (his *Odes* are on "Several Descriptive and Allegoric Subjects")—is deliberately competing with the allegoric portraits of popular Italian painters of the seventeenth century like Guido Reni. Picturesque poetry, as Lessing demonstrated in the masterly *Laokoön* (1766), is ultimately a contradiction in terms, and this latter mode of personification is often tasteless. But the specifically Augustan personifications simply exploit—at their best with great force and economy—a grammatical characteristic of the English language, viz., that a single noun, however abstract or general, must be followed by a verb in the third person singular. The present indicative tense, simply because it distinguishes between its singular and plural forms, imposes a degree of personification on the single abstract word. (Compare "war begins" with "hostilities commence.") Horace Walpole's comment on Gray's speech compared with the slovenly conversation of the London drawing rooms of the time was that "Mr. Gray was so circumspect in his usual language that it seemed unnatural, though it was only pure

English."[2] The case for Augustan personification could be put in precisely those terms; they may seem unnatural, but they are really pure English.

3. THE RETURN OF LOVE

Sir Lewis Namier, the master-historian in our time of the English eighteenth century, has used extracts from two letters to illustrate the difference between the House of Commons as it was in Queen Anne's reign and as it had become at the accession of George III. One is from the elder Pitt's grandfather, the wealthy Governor Pitt of Madras, to his son Robert, a letter written on January 16, 1706:

> If you are in Parliament, show yourself on all occasions a good Englishman and a faithful servant to your country. . . . Avoid faction . . . and vote according to your conscience and not for any sinister end whatever. I had rather see any child of mine want than have him get his bread by voting in the House of Commons.

Namier's comment on these admirable sentiments is:

> This was written after a century of Parliamentary contests over causes which had moved the consciences of men and for which they had "died on the scaffold and the field of battle." Fifty years later the nation was at one in all fundamental matters, and whenever that happy but uninspiring condition is reached, Parliamentary contests lose reality and unavoidably change into a fierce though bloodless struggle for places.

Namier then quotes his second letter—from Edward Gibbon—on what entering the House of Commons meant in

[2] The comment occurs in Walpole's "Thoughts on Comedy" (*Works*, Vol. II, 1798, p. 321).

his time: "It is to acquire a title the most glorious of any in a free country, and to employ the weight and consideration it gives in the service of one's friends." Namier's comment follows: "In 1706 it was 'faithful service to your country'; in 1760 'service of one's friends.' The community had become atomised and individualised. . . ."[3]

No doubt Namier has overstated the difference. Some public spirit remained in the House of Commons even in 1760 and political corruption was certainly not unknown in 1706. But the trend was what Namier describes, as the different literary climates of opinion in the earlier and later Augustan period amply corroborate. It was a transition from "The Age of Satire" to "The Age of Sentiment." Satire is the most public of the genres. In the hands of Samuel Butler, Dryden, and Rochester it corrected the public errors of public figures, and in passing into the prose dialogue of "genteel comedy" as practiced by Etherege, Wycherley, Congreve, and Vanbrugh it retained much of this public character. With a few unimportant exceptions the dramatis personae of Restoration comedy are not the portraits of identifiable individuals; instead the satire is directed via its butts and eccentrics at the whole concept of individualism, the presumed right of any one individual to be noticeably different from other individuals. It is a striking fact that the principal victim of the Restoration dramatists was love, the intensest and most intimate of the private emotions. Love as it emerges from *The Country Wife*, which I take to be the most characteristic of the Restoration comedies, turns out to be nothing but the sexual instinct. Indeed, between the private letters of Dorothy Osborne to William Temple and the songs of Blake and Burns love virtually disappears from English literature. It was the golden age of the bachelor writer: Cowley, Butler, Oldham, Etherege, Wycherley, Swift, Prior, Congreve, Gray, Pope, Gay, Col-

[3] *The Structure of Politics at the Accession of George III* (Vol. I, 1929), pp. 21, 23.

lins, Goldsmith, Cowper, and Gibbon, to say nothing of
Hobbes, Locke, and Hume, were all unmarried. (The
unromantic marriages of Addison and Johnson only prove
the rule.) Love only returned into literature, apologetically
and halfheartedly, via the middle-class reading public and
its special middle-class genre, the novel. The Age of Sentiment—which begins very tentatively with the sentimental
comedies of Cibber and Steele, *c.* 1700—was the literary
product of that lowering of the political temperature described by Namier. As public problems receded, the private
life—to which all Non-Conformists (Protestant and Catholic) were in any case restricted by law—began to loom
larger.

Of course, if sentimentalism had carried everything before it in the later eighteenth century, it would not be
possible to describe its literature as even a modified Augustanism. What distinguishes the period from the nineteenth century is the rear-guard resistance that "common
sense" continued to put up. The term *sentimental*, apparently the only critical term English criticism contributed at this time to the European stock, was itself a
victim almost immediately of a satiric upsurgence. The
details are not uninstructive. As used by Richardson and
his circle a *sentiment* was primarily a moral aphorism and
to be *sentimental* was an end in itself—to overflow with
emotional morality. "What, in your opinion," Lady Brad-
shaigh, an enthusiastic Richardsonian, wrote to Richardson in 1749, "is the meaning of the word *sentimental*, so
much in vogue among the polite. . . . Everything clever
and agreeable is comprehended in that word. . . . I am
frequently astonished to hear such a one is a *sentimental*
man; it was a *sentimental* party; I have been taking a
sentimental walk." (Unfortunately, Richardson's answer
has not survived.) But if some of "the polite" were using
the word in a favorable sense, others, including Horace
Walpole (with whom the word was a favorite), were
not. For these anti-Richardsonians, to be "sentimental"
was at best to be naïve and often to be merely overemo-

tional in a silly way. Considering the vogue both of the sentimental novels—though Sterne, whose *Sentimental Journey* (1768) gave the word its European currency, characteristically mixes a good deal of sex with the emotionalism—and of the sentimental comedies, it is surprising how soon the word acquired its modern pejorative sense. The *coup de grâce* was given in the later 1760s and 1770s by a group of dramatists—Goldsmith, Sheridan, George Colman, and Arthur Murphy—with that amiable "man of sentiment" Joseph Surface as the most effective discreditor of all.

Dr. Johnson, who refused to include the word *sentimental* in his *Dictionary*, is rightly considered the bastion of Augustanism in the later eighteenth century. A dialogue recorded by Boswell between himself and Johnson brings out neatly the roles of the two men in English literary history:

> I maintained that Horace was wrong in placing happiness in *nil admirari;* for that I thought admiration one of the most agreeable of all our feelings; and I regretted that I had lost much of my disposition to admire, which people generally do as they advance in life. JOHNSON. "Sir, as a man advances in life, he gets what is better than admiration—*judgment*, to estimate things at their true value."[4]

A man in love cannot estimate things at their true value.

[4] *Life of Johnson*, April 16, 1775.

VII. An Augustan Reading List, 1650–1800

1. Bibliographies, Literary Histories, and Anthologies

The second volume of *CBEL* is devoted to this period and should always be the student's first port of call. It lists *all* the separate publications of the principal writers (over a thousand), *all* the poetry miscellanies, newspapers, and magazines, and a great deal else, including innumerable books and articles *about* the period to *c.* 1935. The Supplement brings such secondary titles down to 1955. For work on the period since 1925 a somewhat fuller bibliography has appeared annually in *PQ* (1925–60 lists reissued with indexes by L. Landa et al., 4 vols., 1950–62), which includes expert comments by American specialists, those of R. S. C[rane] being especially instructive. Donald Wing's meticulous *Short-Title Catalogue, 1641–1700* (3 vols., 1945–51) lists every English publication within his terminal dates except periodicals. The eighteenth century has nothing comparable to Wing, though detailed bibliographies exist for some twenty of the principal authors.

Only one of *OHEL*'s three volumes projected for the period has so far appeared. This is Bonamy Dobrée's stylistically elegant but somewhat pedestrian *English Literature in the Earlier Eighteenth Century* (1959). The much shorter *The Restoration and Eighteenth Century* by George Sherburn—a part of Albert C. Baugh's *Literary History of England* (1948), though it is also obtainable separately—is much more successful, a model indeed of the literary handbook. And the even shorter *English Literature from Dryden to Burns* (1948) by A. D. McKillop can also be recommended. Although Louis I. Bredvold's brief treatment of the period in *A History of English Literature* (ed. Hardin Craig, 1950) is also a very competent sketch, the best literary history of the period really is still, of course, Johnson's *Lives of the Poets* (4 vols., 1781; standard edition by G. Birkbeck Hill, 3 vols., 1905; Yale critical edition in preparation by F. W. Hilles and others). Six recent miscellanies within the period—in honor respectively (in the order of their areas of interest) of Herbert Grierson (1938), Richard Foster Jones (1951), Arthur E. Case (1952), David Nichol Smith (1945), George Sherburn (1949), and Chauncey Brewster Tinker (1949)— provide literary history of a more specialist kind, though they also include interesting critical pieces by T. S. Eliot, C. S. Lewis, Maynard Mack, and others. James L. Clifford's collection *Eighteenth Century English Literature: Modern Essays in Criticism* (1959) assembles twenty-one recent articles, mainly from the American learned journals. It omits, however, T. S. Eliot's brilliant survey of mid-eighteenth-century poetry (originally the introduction to a 1930 reprint of *London* and *The Vanity of Human Wishes*), as well as Eliot's more commonplace essay on "Johnson as Critic and Poet" in *On Poetry and Poets* (1957). Two eminently readable critical surveys are George Saintsbury's *The Peace of the Augustans* (1916) and J. R. Sutherland's *A Preface to Eighteenth-Century Poetry* (1948), though the most acute recent criticism of eighteenth-century poetry is Donald Davie's *Purity of Diction in English Verse* (1952). Restoration comedy has had a stormy critical career since Charles Lamb's "Elia" essay ("On the Artificial Comedy of the Last Century"), and the case against it has been effectively re-formulated in modern terms in L. C. Knights's essay in his *Explorations* (1946). A less jaundiced view is provided by Norman H. Holland (*The First Modern Comedies*, 1959). A good book on the novel—primarily on Defoe, Richardson, and Fielding—is Ian Watt's *The Rise of the Novel*

(1957); A. D. McKillop's useful and sensible *The Early Masters of English Fiction* (1956) is more of a guide-book, as is inevitably Miss J. M. S. Tompkins's intelligent *The Popular Novel in England, 1770–1800* (1932).

Of the anthologies, much the most valuable is Joel E. Spingarn's *Critical Essays of the Seventeenth Century* (3 vols., 1908–9); Spingarn's introduction is still the authoritative analysis of Restoration criticism. The recent sequel *Eighteenth-Century Critical Essays*, edited by Scott Elledge (2 vols., 1961), though useful, is comparatively undistinguished. Alexander Chalmers's mighty *The Works of the English Poets from Chaucer to Cowper* (21 vols., 1810) is still indispensable for this period, in spite of the bad print and paper, because it includes the complete poetical works of so many of the minor English Augustans. Two intelligent shorter selections are Ronald S. Crane's *A Collection of English Poems, 1660–1800* (1932) and David Nichol Smith's *The Oxford Book of Eighteenth-Century Verse* (1926). Donald Davie's *The Late Augustans* (1958), which is limited to the longer poems, has an acute critical introduction. Chalmers also assembled the best of the eighteenth-century essay-periodicals in *The British Essayists* (45 vols., 1817). *British Dramatists from Dryden to Sheridan*, edited by G. H. Nettleton and A. E. Case (1939), which reprints twenty-five plays in critical texts with much useful background material, is decidedly the best of the drama collections, though Leigh Hunt's *Dramatists of the Restoration* (1840) is still handy, in spite of the minute type, because it assembles *all* the plays of Wycherley, Congreve, Vanbrugh, and Farquhar. The Augustan Reprint Society (now based in Los Angeles) issues facsimiles of out-of-the-way items in the period, each with a scholarly introduction (100 numbers, 1946–63); the series of more or less forgotten critical pieces are especially valuable. A definitive edition of the *Poems on Affairs of State* is coming from Yale (Vol. I, ed. G. de F. Lord, 1964).

2. SPECIAL SUBJECTS

MISCELLANEOUS

John Nichols: *Literary Anecdotes of the Eighteenth Century* (9 vols., 1812–15); *Illustrations of the Literary History of the Eighteenth Century* (8 vols., 1817–58). Ragbags of letters, publishers' ledgers, etc., often of great historical interest.

Isaac D'Israeli: *Calamities of Authors* (2 vols., 1812); *Quarrels of Authors* (3 vols., 1814). The expert on Grub Street.

Thomas Babington Macaulay: *Critical and Historical Essays* (3 vols., 1843). More than half on this period; originally reviews in the *Edinburgh Review*.

Leslie Stephen: *Hours in a Library* (3 sers., 1874–79, enlarged 3 vols., 1892, 1907); *History of English Thought in the Eighteenth Century* (2 vols., 1876); *Studies of a Biographer* (4 vols., 1898–1902); *English Literature and Society in the Eighteenth Century* (1904). The best Victorian criticism of the period.

Austin Dobson: *Eighteenth-Century Vignettes* (3 sers., 1892–96); *Side-Walk Studies* (1902); *Old Kensington Palace, and Other Papers* (1910); *At Prior Park, and Other Papers* (1912); *Rosalba's Journal, and Other Papers* (1915). All available now in World's Classics series. Short essays on minor literary figures, special aspects of eighteenth-century social life, etc., often of great brilliance.

POETRY AND CRITICISM

A. Bosker: *Literary Criticism in the Age of Johnson* (Groningen 1930, rev. 1953).

Samuel Monk: *The Sublime* (1935). Pre-Romantic critical theory.

Robert Aubin: *Topographical Poetry in England* (1937). Detailed survey of the loco-descriptive poems.

Hoxie N. Fairchild: *Religious Trends in English Poetry*

(5 vols., 1939–62; 1700–1920; 6 vols. planned). From an Anglo-Catholic standpoint.

W. J. Bate: *From Classic to Romantic* (1946).

John Arthos: *The Language of Natural Description in Eighteenth-Century Poetry* (1949).

Paul Fussell: *Theory of Prosody in Eighteenth-Century England* (1954).

Chester F. Chapin: *Personification in Eighteenth-Century English Poetry* (1955).

Geoffrey Tillotson: *Augustan Studies* (1961). Excellent on poetic diction.

K. G. Hamilton: *The Two Harmonies* (1963). Theories of poetry and prose in the seventeenth century (a very intelligent discussion).

DRAMA

Allardyce Nicoll: *A History of Restoration Drama, 1660–1700* (1923); *A History of Early Eighteenth-Century Drama, 1700–1750* (1925); *A History of Later Eighteenth-Century Drama, 1750–1800* (1927). Revised as Volumes I–III of *A History of English Drama* (1952). Critically naïve, but useful as a work of reference because of its completeness and the information on the theater.

Arthur Sherbo: *English Sentimental Drama* (1957).

W. Van Lennep, E. L. Avery, A. H. Scouten, G. W. Stone, and C. B. Hogan: *The London Stage 1660–1800.* In progress. Parts 2 (1700–29) and 3 (1729–47), 4 vols., 1960–61. Includes a calendar of performances, casts, box office receipts, contemporary comments, etc. Dugald MacMillan's *Drury Lane Calendar 1747–1776* (1938) provides similar material for the period of Garrick's management. For other periods or theaters, reference must still be made to John Genest's remarkably thorough *Some Account of the English Stage, from 1660 to 1830* (10 vols., 1832).

John Loftis: *Comedy and Society from Congreve to Fielding* (1960); *The Politics of Drama in Augustan England* (1963).

OTHER GENRES

Walter Graham: *The Beginnings of English Literary Periodicals, 1665–1715* (1926); *English Literary Periodicals* (1930).

Donald A. Stauffer: *English Biography before 1700* (1930); *The Art of Biography in the Eighteenth Century* (2 vols., 1941).

René Wellek: *The Rise of English Literary History* (1941).

POLITICAL AND SOCIAL BACKGROUND

Alexandre Beljame: *Le Public et les Hommes de Lettres en Angleterre, 1660–1744* (Paris, 1881; tr. English 1948).

Elizabeth W. Manwaring: *Italian Landscape in Eighteenth-Century England* (1925). Useful for the literary picturesque and landscape gardening.

Lewis Namier: *The Structure of Politics at the Accession of George III* (1929).

Herbert Butterfield: *The Whig Interpretation of History* (1931).

B. Sprague Allen: *Tides in English Taste* (1932). The minor arts and crafts during the eighteenth century.

A. S. Turberville (ed.): *Johnson's England* (2 vols., 1933). Separate chapters by different experts, including one on "Journalism."

Jean H. Hagstrum: *The Sister Arts* (1958; influence of painting on poetry from Dryden to Gray).

INTELLECTUAL BACKGROUND

Basil Willey: *The Seventeenth-Century Background* (1934); *The Eighteenth-Century Background* (1940).

K. Maclean: *John Locke and English Literature of the Eighteenth Century* (1936).

Marjorie Hope Nicolson: *The Microscope and English Imagination* (1935); *A World in the Moon* (1936);

Mountain Gloom and Mountain Glory (1959); *The Breaking of the Circle* (rev. ed. 1960).

Richard Foster Jones: *Ancients and Moderns* (1936).

Arthur O. Lovejoy: *Essays in the History of Ideas* (1948). Mainly in this period.

Maren-Sofie Røstvig: *The Happy Man: Studies in the Metamorphosis of a Classical Ideal, 1600–1700* (2 vols., 1954–58, Vol. I rev. 1962).

Martin Price: *To the Palace of Wisdom: Studies in Order and Energy from Dryden to Blake* (1963). Abstract and difficult to read, but a perceptive book.

3. THE PRINCIPAL WRITERS

(Arranged in chronological order of birth.)

Edmund Waller (1606–1687). See p. 87 above.

Edward Hyde, Earl of Clarendon (1609–1674). *History of the Rebellion,* edited by W. Dunn Macray (6 vols., 1888); selections, edited by G. Huehns (1955). Standard life by Henry Craik (2 vols., 1911). For critical appreciation see L. C. Knights, *Explorations* (1946). (*CBEL*, II, 864 f.)

Samuel Butler (1612–1680). Collected works, edited by A. R. Waller and René Lamar (3 vols., 1905–28; no notes). Zachary Grey's *Hudibras* (2 vols., 1774) has elaborate notes. For criticism see Johnson's *Lives of the Poets* (1781) and Edward A. Richards (1937). (*CBEL*, II, 260 f.)

Sir John Denham (1615–1669). Poems, definitive edition by T. H. Banks (1928). Johnson included Denham in *The Lives of the Poets* (1781). (*CBEL*, I, 457 f.)

John Evelyn (1620–1706). Diary, edited by E. S. de Beer (6 vols., 1955; complete and fully annotated). Further biographical material in W. G. Hiscock's *Evelyn and*

Mrs. Godolphin (1951) and *Evelyn and His Family Circle* (1955). (*CBEL*, II, 827 f.)

John Aubrey (1626–1697). *Brief Lives,* edited by Andrew Clark (2 vols., 1898); selections, edited by Anthony Powell (1949) and Oliver L. Dick (1949; from manuscripts). Also, edited by Oliver L. Dick, with a short preface by Edmund Wilson (1957). Powell's amusing *Aubrey and His Friends* has been revised (1963). (*CBEL*, II, 866 f.)

Sir Robert Howard (1626–1698). H. J. Oliver's life of Howard (1963) is a good, solid job.

John Bunyan (1628–1688). Works, edited by Henry Stebbing (4 vols., 1859–60). Critical editions of *Grace Abounding* by Roger Sharrock (1962) and of *Pilgrim's Progress* by J. B. Wharey (1928, rev. Roger Sharrock 1960). Standard life by John Brown (1885, rev. Frank Mott Harrison 1928). For criticism see the intelligent studies by Henri Talon (Paris, 1948; tr. English 1951) and Roger Sharrock (1954). Bibliography by F. M. Harrison (1932). (*CBEL*, II, 490 f.)

Charles Cotton (1630–1687). Poems, edited by John Buxton (1952). (*CBEL*, II, 261 f.)

John Dryden (1631–1700). Complete works, edited by Walter Scott (18 vols., 1808, rev. George Saintsbury 1882–93); elaborate critical edition in preparation by E. N. Hooker, H. T. Swedenberg, etc. (Vol. I, 1956). Poems: edited by George R. Noyes (1909, enlarged 1950; good notes); edited by James Kinsley (4 vols., 1958; better texts but notes less full than Noyes; texts only, 1962). Criticism: edited by W. P. Ker (2 vols., 1900); edited by George Watson (2 vols., 1961). Useful dictionary of Dryden's criticism by J. M. Aden (1963). Letters, edited by Charles E. Ward (1942). Detailed life by Charles E. Ward (1962). For criticism see Johnson's *Lives of the Poets* (1781), Mark Van Doren (1920), T. S. Eliot

(1924), and Louis I. Bredvold (1934; Dryden's "intellectual milieu"). Of the specialist works, William Frost's *Dryden and the Art of Translation* (1955) and Bernard Schilling's *Dryden and the Conservative Myth* (1961) are of critical interest. Valuable bibliography by Hugh Macdonald (1939); concordance by Guy Montgomery (1957). (*CBEL*, II, 262 f.)

John Locke (1632–1704). *Essay concerning Human Understanding*, edited by A. C. Fraser (2 vols., 1894). Educational writings, edited by J. W. Adamson (1912, rev. 1922). Critical edition of letters in preparation by E. S. de Beer. Standard life by Maurice Cranston (1952). For literary implications of the philosophy, see D. G. James (1949; with Hobbes and Bolingbroke). (*CBEL*, II, 940 f.)

George Savile, Marquis of Halifax (1633–1695). Complete works, edited by Walter Raleigh (1912; no notes). Standard life by H. C. Foxcroft (2 vols., 1898) includes the works. (*CBEL*, II, 570 f.)

Samuel Pepys (1633–1703). Diary, edited by Henry B. Wheatley (10 vols., 1893–99). Complete new transcription by F. McD. C. Turner promised shortly. Letters, edited by J. R. Tanner (3 vols., 1926–29); further letters, edited by R. G. Howarth (1932) and Helen T. Heath (1955; "The Family Circle"). Lives by J. R. Tanner (1925), Arthur Bryant (3 vols., 1933–38), and J. H. Wilson (1959). (*CBEL*, II, 831 f.)

Sir George Etherege (1635–1691). Plays, edited by H. F. B. Brett-Smith (2 vols., 1927; good notes). Poems, edited by James Thorpe (1963; excellent notes). *Letterbook*, edited by Sybil Rosenfeld (1928). Sound critical study by Dale Underwood (1957). (*CBEL*, II, 410.)

Thomas Traherne (1637/9–1674). Works, definitive edition by H. M. Margoliouth (2 vols., 1958). Gladys

I. Wade's life of Traherne (1944, rev. 1946), though detailed, is somewhat fanciful. (*CBEL*, I, 462 f.)

Sir Charles Sedley (1639–1701). Poetical and dramatic works, edited by V. de Sola Pinto (2 vols., 1928). Standard life also by Pinto (1927). (*CBEL*, II, 275.)

Aphra Behn, née Amis (1640–1689). Works, edited by Montague Summers (6 vols., 1915). (*CBEL*, II, 417 f.)

Thomas Rymer (1641–1713). Definitive edition of critical works by Curt A. Zimansky (1956; excellent introduction and notes). (*CBEL*, II, 875.)

William Wycherley (1640–1716). Works, edited by Montague Summers (4 vols., 1924). For a popular life, see Willard Connely (1930). (*CBEL*, II, 410 f.)

Thomas Shadwell (1642?–1692). Complete works, edited by Montague Summers (5 vols., 1927). Standard life by Albert S. Borgman (1928). (*CBEL*, II, 411 f.)

Charles Sackville, Earl of Dorset (1643–1706). See the scholarly study by Brice Harris (1940). (*CBEL*, II, 280.)

John Wilmot, Earl of Rochester (1647–1680). Collected works, edited by John Hayward, 1926. Poems: edited by V. de Sola Pinto (1953, rev. 1964; uncritical text, short notes). Critical edition in preparation by D. M. Vieth has been preceded by his *Attribution in Restoration Poetry* (1963), a special study of Rochester's text. Edition of the letters to Savile by J. H. Wilson (1941). See also Wilson's *Restoration Court Wits* (1948). Life by V. de Sola Pinto (1935, rev. 1962) is readable if unscholarly. The basic facts and documents are given by Johannes Prinz (Leipzig, 1927). Johnson's brief account in *The Lives of the Poets* (1781) is still the best critical discussion. (*CBEL*, II, 276 f.)

Nathaniel Lee (1649?–1692). Standard edition by T. B. Stroup and A. L. Cooke (2 vols., 1954–55). Good life in

Roswell G. Ham's *Otway and Lee* (1931). (*CBEL*, II, 412 f.)

Thomas Otway (1652–1685). Standard edition by J. C. Ghosh (2 vols., 1932). Standard life by Roswell G. Ham (1931; with Lee). Stage history of *The Orphan* and *Venice Preserv'd* in Alice M. Taylor's *Next to Shakespeare* (1950). Critical analysis in Bonamy Dobrée's *Restoration Tragedy* (1929) is somewhat perfunctory. (*CBEL*, II, 413 f.)

John Dennis (1657–1734). Critical works, edited with detailed commentary by E. N. Hooker (2 vols., 1939–43). Standard life by H. G. Paul (1911). (*CBEL*, II, 571 f.)

Daniel Defoe (1660–1731). *Novels and Selected Writings* (14 vols., Oxford, 1927–28; 2 vols. of non-fiction, no notes, etc.); prose fiction edited by G. A. Aitken (16 vols., 1895) is less reliable textually but has pleasant illustrations by J. B. Yeats. *The Review*, edited by A. W. Secord (22 vols., 1938; index, 1948); *A Tour thro' Great Britain*, edited by G. D. H. Cole (2 vols., 1927); letters, edited by George H. Healey (1955). Good short life by James Sutherland (1937, rev. 1950); the most detailed biography is by John Robert Moore (1958). Paul Dottin's *De Foe et ses romans* (3 vols., Paris, 1924; tr. English 1929) is a thorough study, if less perceptive than Ian Watt's account in *The Rise of the Novel* (1957). (*CBEL*, II, 495 f.)

Matthew Prior (1664–1721). Definitive edition of all literary works by H. Bunker Wright and Monroe K. Spears (2 vols., 1959), who are also preparing an edition of the letters. A competent life by Charles K. Eves (1939) has superseded Johnson's in *The Lives of the Poets* (1781), though that retains its interest as literary criticism. (*CBEL*, II, 289 f.)

Sir John Vanbrugh (1664–1726). Complete works,

edited by Bonamy Dobrée and Geoffrey Webb (4 vols., 1927–28), though superior to A. E. H. Swaen's Mermaid edition (1896) leaves much to be desired. Laurence Whistler's biography (1938) is better on the architect than the dramatist. (*CBEL*, II, 414.)

Anne Finch, Countess of Winchelsea, née Kingsmill (1666–1720). Good edition of poems by Myra Reynolds (1903). (*CBEL*, II, 333.)

John Arbuthnot (1667–1735). Incomplete edition of works by George A. Aitken (1892); *The History of John Bull*, edited by Herman Teerink (Amsterdam, 1925); *Memoirs of Martin Scriblerus* (with Pope), edited by C. Kerby-Miller (1950). Standard life by Lester M. Beattie (1935). (*CBEL*, II, 576 f.)

Jonathan Swift (1667–1745). Temple Scott's edition of the prose (12 vols., 1897–1908) has now been superseded by Herbert Davis's (14 vols., 1939–59; index in preparation), which has excellent introductions to each item but unfortunately no explanatory notes. Its only omission is the *Journal to Stella* (standard edition by Harold Williams, 2 vols., 1948). Williams has also brought out exemplary editions of the poems (3 vols., 1937, rev. 1958) and of Swift's letters (5 vols., 1963). Joseph Horrell's edition of the poems (2 vols., 1958) is an inexpensive alternative to Williams. (Both are rather underannotated.) There is a fully annotated edition of *A Tale of a Tub* and *The Battle of the Books* by A. C. Guthkelch and D. Nichol Smith (1920, rev. 1958), and of *The Drapier's Letters* by Herbert Davis (1935). The most elaborate if not the best edition of *Gulliver's Travels* is by R. A. Greenberg (1961), which also includes eighty-nine pages of twentieth-century criticism; Martin Price's edition (1963) has a good introduction. The biographies of Johnson (in *Lives of the Poets*, 1781) and Scott (in his edition of Swift's *Works*, 19 vols., 1814) retain an interest, but the definitive life is likely to be that by Irvin Ehrenpreis (Vol. I, 1962).

Ricardo Quintana's *The Mind and Art of Swift* (1936, rev. 1953) is a sound general introduction, as is also Kathleen Williams's *Swift and the Age of Compromise* (1959), though the best single critical essay is probably F. R. Leavis's "The Irony of Swift" (in his *The Common Pursuit*, 1952). Herbert Davis's miscellaneous writings on Swift have been assembled in a useful paperback (1964). There are many modern specialist studies, e.g. those by Maurice Johnson (1950; on the verse), John M. Bullitt (1953; satiric technique), Martin Price (1953; rhetoric), and Philip Harth (1961); Arthur E. Case's *Four Essays on Gulliver's Travels* (1945) fills in the contemporary background, and Ronald S. Crane has an especially acute study of the Voyage to the Houyhnhnms in *Reason and the Imagination,* edited by J. A. Mazzeo (1962). John Traugott's *Discussions of Swift* (1962) assembles some of the best shorter critiques. Bibliography by H. Teerink (Hague, 1937). (*CBEL*, II, 581 f.)

William Congreve (1670–1729). Complete works: edited by Montague Summers (4 vols., 1923); edited by Bonamy Dobrée (2 vols., 1925–28). Critical edition in preparation by Herbert Davis. John C. Hodges has edited new letters and documents (1964). Hodges's *Congreve the Man* (1941) is detailed but omits Congreve's literary career. Chapters on Congreve in the various surveys of Restoration comedy—e.g. those of John Palmer (1913), Bonamy Dobrée (1924), Thomas H. Fujimara (1952)— are all rather thin. (*CBEL*, II, 414 f.)

Bernard Mandeville (1670–1733). *The Fable of the Bees,* edited by F. B. Kaye (2 vols., 1924). A model edition of this philosophical classic. (*CBEL*, II, 599 f.)

Anthony Ashley Cooper, 3rd Earl of Shaftesbury (1671–1713). *Characteristics of Men, Manners, Opinions, Times,* edited by J. M. Robertson (2 vols., 1900); *Second Characters,* edited by Benjamin Rand (1914). Rand also printed a philosophical fragment and unpublished letters, etc. (1900). Shaftesbury's literary theories are lucidly expounded in R. L. Brett's study (1951). (*CBEL*, II, 948.)

Joseph Addison (1672–1719). Only 2 volumes of A. C. Guthkelch's projected critical edition were completed (1914); there is, however, a scholarly edition of the letters by Walter Graham (1941). For *The Tatler* and *The Spectator*, see under Steele below. The most recent life— by Peter Smithers (1954)—is primarily on Addison's political career. Bonamy Dobrée has an intelligent depreciation in his *Essays in Biography* (1925), but the classic accounts by Johnson (in *Lives of the Poets*, 1781) and Macaulay (in *Critical and Historical Essays*, 1843) are still unsurpassed. (*CBEL*, II, 601 f.)

Sir Richard Steele (1672–1729). George A. Aitken's edition of *The Tatler* (4 vols., 1898–99) is convenient but less detailed than that by John Nichols and others (6 vols., 1786). *The Spectator* has been edited by Donald F. Bond in exemplary detail (5 vols., 1964). Robert J. Allen's unpretentious selection from both (1957) makes a handy introduction. Rae Blanchard has definitively edited *The Christian Hero*, the minor periodicals (except *The Theatre*, ed. John Loftis, 1962), the tracts, and the occasional verse in a series of separate volumes (1932–55), as well as Steele's correspondence (1941). For the plays the perfunctory Mermaid edition by George A. Aitken (1894) is still the only collection. Aitken's life of Steele (2 vols., 1889), on the other hand, was a sound and solid job, to which John Loftis's *Steele and Drury Lane* (1952) and Calhoun Winton's reinvestigation of Steele's early career (1964) are useful supplements. (*CBEL*, II, 608 f.)

Henry St. John, Viscount Bolingbroke (1678–1751). The nearest thing to a standard edition is the Philadelphia edition of 1841 (4 vols.). *Letters on the Spirit of Patriotism, on the Idea of a Patriot King, and on the State of the Parties* has been edited by Arthur Hassall (1912). Three of the *Letters on the Study and Use of History* were edited by G. M. Trevelyan (1933). Standard life by Walter Sichel (2 vols., 1901–2); D. G. James analyzes the philosophy in some detail in *The Life of Reason* (1949). (*CBEL,* II, 612 f.)

George Farquhar (1678–1707). Complete works, edited (with some notes) by Charles A. Stonehill (2 vols., 1930). William Archer's Mermaid edition (1906), a reprint of the four plays, has an intelligent introduction. (*CBEL,* II, 416 f.)

Edward Young (1683–1765). No modern edition except of *Conjectures on Original Composition* (ed. Edith J. Morley, 1918). Henry C. Shelley's *Life and Letters* (1914) is somewhat perfunctory; a more scholarly performance is C. V. Wicker's *Edward Young and the Fear of Death* (1952). George Eliot's essay on Young (in her *Essays and Leaves from a Notebook,* 1884) is of considerable interest. (*CBEL,* II, 290 f.)

George Berkeley (1685–1753). Complete works, edited by A. A. Luce and T. E. Jessop (9 vols., 1948–57). Luce's biography (1949) is now the standard life. Recent work on Berkeley has been entirely on the philosophy. (*CBEL,* II, 944 f.)

John Gay (1685–1732). Poetical works, edited by G. L. Faber (1926), includes all the poems and several of the plays; unfortunately there are no explanatory notes. William E. Schultz's detailed study of *The Beggar's Opera* (1923) has been partly superseded by E. M. Gagey's *Ballad Opera* (1937); William Empson has an ingenious essay on it in *Some Versions of Pastoral* (1935). The standard life is by W. H. Irving (1940); Sven M. Armens has recently analyzed Gay's social philosophy (1954). (*CBEL,* II, 292 f.)

William Law (1686–1761). *Selected Mystical Writings,* edited by Stephen Hobhouse (1938, rev. 1948); *A Serious Call* has been edited by Norman Sykes (1955). Henri

Talon's *Law: a Study in Literary Craftsmanship* (1948) can be recommended. (*CBEL,* II, 858.)

Allan Ramsay (1686–1758). Works, edited by Burns Martin and John W. Oliver (2 vols., 1951–53). Martin is also the author of the standard biography and bibliography of Ramsay (both 1931). (*CBEL,* II, 969 f.)

Henry Carey (1687?–1743). *Poems,* edited by F. T. Wood (1930), is only a selection. F. W. Bateson has a chapter on the plays in his *English Comic Drama, 1700–1750* (1929). (*CBEL,* II, 433 f.)

Alexander Pope (1688–1744). Poems, edited by John Butt and others (6 vols., 1939–62, and abbreviated 1 vol., 1963; this Twickenham edition includes all Pope's verse except the Homer translations, which are to follow shortly, ed. Maynard Mack, in 4 vols.). This is now the standard edition and supersedes the one by William Elwin and W. J. Courthope (10 vols., 1871–89) except for some of the prose. The incomplete *Prose Works,* edited by Norman Ault (Vol. I, 1935) includes several dubious ascriptions. The definitive edition of Pope's letters is by George Sherburn (5 vols., 1956), who is also the author of the standard biography (to 1729), *The Early Career of Alexander Pope* (1934). Both are models of perceptive scholarship. A definitive edition of Joseph Spence's *Anecdotes of Pope and Others* (ed. S. W. Singer, 1820) is expected shortly from J. M. Osborn. The two best recent critical studies are probably Geoffrey Tillotson's *On the Poetry of Pope* (1938, rev. 1950) and Aubrey L. Williams's *Pope's Dunciad* (1955), though Johnson's life (in *The Lives of the Poets,* 1781) and Joseph Warton's *Essay on the Writings and Genius of Pope* (2 vols., 1756–82) are still indispensable reading. Rufus A. Blanchard's *Discussions of Alexander Pope* (1960) is a useful critical anthology (from Swift to Maynard Mack). Bibliography by R. H. Griffith (2 vols., 1922–27); concordance by S. A. Abbott (1875; excludes translations). (*CBEL,* II, 294 f.)

Lady Mary Wortley Montague, née Pierrepont (1689–1762). Standard life by Robert Halsband (1956). (*CBEL*, II, 834 f.)

Samuel Richardson (1689–1761). Novels (18 vols., Oxford, 1929–31; no notes or editorial matter). *Pamela*, edited by George Saintsbury (2 vols., 1914); *Clarissa*, edited by J. Butt (4 vols., 1961); *Sir Charles Grandison*, edited by George Saintsbury (1895). Correspondence, edited by Anna L. Barbauld (6 vols., 1804). The best general account is Alan D. McKillop's *Richardson, Printer and Novelist* (1936). William M. Sale's bibliography (1936) and his study of Richardson's printing activities (1950) are detailed and definitive. The best critical discussion is probably that in Ian Watt's *The Rise of the Novel* (1957). There is a detailed analysis of *Richardson's Characters* (1963) by Morris Golden. (*CBEL*, II, 514 f.)

Joseph Butler (1692–1752). See Ernest Mossner, *Bishop Joseph Butler* (1936). (*CBEL*, II, 946.)

Philip Dormer Stanhope, Earl of Chesterfield (1694–1773). Letters, edited by Bonamy Dobrée (6 vols., 1932). Some of Dobrée's omissions were edited by Sidney L. Gulick (1937). (*CBEL*, II, 835 f.)

Lord John Hervey (1696–1743). *Memoirs of the Reign of George II*, edited by Romney Sedgwick (3 vols., 1931). (*CBEL*, II, 879.)

John Dyer (1699–1758). Poems, edited by Hugh I'Anson Fausset (in *Minor Poets of the Eighteenth Century*, 1930). Definitive edition of *Grongar Hill* by Richard C. Boys (1941). The life by Johnson (in *Lives of the Poets*, 1871) is still valuable. (*CBEL*, II, 315.)

James Thomson (1700–1748). Complete poetical works, edited by J. Logie Robertson (1908; gives textural variants of *Seasons* but no explanatory notes). *The Castle of Indolence,* etc., edited by Alan D. McKillop (1961; good notes). McKillop's *Background of Thomson's Seasons* (1942) is a valuable scholarly study. The best general account is by Douglas Grant (1951), which must, however, be supplemented by McKillop's *Letters and Documents* (1958); Johnson's life (in *Lives of the Poets,* 1781) retains its critical interest. For an attempt to relate *The Seasons* to its critical context, see Ralph Cohen, *The Art of Discrimination* (1964). (*CBEL,* II, 305 f.)

Henry Fielding (1707–1754). Complete works, edited by W. E. Henley and others (16 vols., 1903; no notes but nearly complete); novels, edited by George Saintsbury (12 vols., 1893; sensible introductions). There are scholarly modern editions of *Tom Thumb* (ed. James T. Hillhouse, 1918), *Shamela* (ed. Richard W. Baker, 1953), *The Covent Garden Journal* (ed. G. E. Jensen, 1915), and *The Journal of a Voyage to Lisbon* (ed. H. E. Pagliaro, 1963). The best biography is that of Wilbur L. Cross (3 vols., 1918), though it must now be supplemented by H. R. Miller's scholarly commentary on the minor works (1961). What is probably the best full-length critical study is Andrew Wright's *Fielding: Mask and Feast* (1964). Ronald S. Crane has an acute study of the plot of *Tom Jones* in his *Critics and Criticism* (1952), a serious omission in the otherwise useful paperback *Fielding: A Collection of Critical Essays,* edited by Ronald Paulson (1962). Maurice Johnson's *Fielding's Art of Fiction* (1962) is more "explication" than criticism. (*CBEL,* II, 517 f.)

Samuel Johnson (1709–1784). Yale edition by Allen T. Hazen and Herman W. Liebert, et al. (Vol. I, 1958), will reprint the complete works with full annotation. Standard edition of poems by D. Nichol Smith and E. L. McAdam (1941), revised by McAdam and George Milne as Volume III of the Yale edition (1965?). Standard edition of letters by R. W. Chapman (3 vols., 1952). *Prefaces and Dedications,* edited by Allen T. Hazen (1937). Useful selections (without annotation) by Mona Wilson (1950), R. W. Chapman (1955), and E. L. McAdam and George Milne (1964); *Johnson on Shakespeare,* edited by W. K. Wimsatt (1960; good selection). Standard edition of Boswell's life by G. Birkbeck Hill (superbly revised by L. F. Powell, 6 vols., 1934–50; Vol. V includes *Tour to the Hebrides*). James L. Clifford's *Young Sam Johnson* (1955) covers authoritatively the years where Boswell is weakest. Walter Raleigh's *Six Essays in Johnson* (1910) is still the most attractive introduction to Johnson. There are now longer competent general studies by Joseph W. Krutch (1944, primarily biographical) and Walter J. Bate (1955). The most important recent contributions to Johnson criticism have been W. K. Wimsatt's discussions of the prose style (1941) and of the "philosophical" (scientific) words in *The Rambler* (1948). Jean H. Hagstrum has also expounded Johnson's critical doctrines effectively (1952), and J. E. Brown's *Critical Opinions of Samuel Johnson* (1926), an anthology arranged as a dictionary, is a useful critical tool. *New Light on Dr. Johnson* (ed. F. W. Hilles, 1960) contains several excellent special studies, critical and biographical, as well as a good deal of chaff. Several recent specialist studies (for details see J. L. Clifford, *Johnsonian Studies*, 1951; supplement to 1960 in *Johnsonian Studies*, ed. M. Wahba, Cairo, 1962) have been of a high quality. Bibliography by W. P. Courtney and D. Nichol Smith (1915, rev. 1925). (*CBEL*, II, 613 f.)

David Hume (1711–1776). Philosophical works, edited by T. H. Green and T. H. Grose (4 vols., 1874–75). Letters, edited by J. Y. T. Greig (2 vols., 1932); *New Letters,* edited by Raymond Klibansky and Ernest C. Mossner (1954). Standard life by Ernest C. Mossner (1954). (*CBEL*, II, 949 f.)

Laurence Sterne (1713–1768). Works, good edition by Wilbur L. Cross (12 vols., 1904). Useful selection by Douglas Grant (1950). Letters, standard edition by Lewis

P. Curtis (1935). Critical edition of *Tristram Shandy* by James A. Work (1940). There is a clever critical study by John Traugott (1954); a more thorough work is Henri Fluchère's elaborate but verbose survey (Paris, 1961; in French). A. D. McKillop gives a good critical introduction in *Early Masters of English Fiction* (1956). For the sermons, see the scholarly discussion by L. van der H. Hammond) (1948). The life by Wilbur L. Cross (1909, rev. 1929) is detailed and readable, and it has a good bibliography. (*CBEL*, II, 521 f.)

William Shenstone (1714–1763). Letters, edited by Marjorie Williams (1939) and Duncan Mallam (1939); these are two independent editions, each including letters omitted in the other. There is a pleasant study by A. R. Humphreys (1937). Life by Marjorie Williams (1935). See also Johnson's *Lives of the Poets* (1781). (*CBEL*, II, 307 f.)

Thomas Gray (1716–1771). Works, edited by Edmund Gosse (4 vols., 1884; incomplete and inadequate annotation but useful for miscellaneous prose included). Critical edition in preparation by H. W. Starr. Poems: edited by Duncan C. Tovey (1898; good notes); edited by A. L. Poole (1917, rev. Frederick Page 1937; best text but no notes). Correspondence, definitive edition by Paget Toynbee and Leonard Whibley (3 vols., 1935); W. S. Lewis has edited letters to Walpole, in latter's *Correspondence*, (Vols. XIII, XIV, 1948). Good short life by R. W. Ketton-Cremer (1955), though it needs supplementing by W. Powell Jones's *Thomas Gray, Scholar* (1937). For criticism see especially Johnson's *Lives of the Poets* (1781), Matthew Arnold's *Essays in Criticism*, Ser. 2 (1888), and Geoffrey Tillotson's *Augustan Studies* (1961). Concordance by A. S. Cook (1908); bibliography by C. S. Northup (1917), with supplement (1917–51) by H. W. Starr (1953). (*CBEL*, II, 333 f.)

Horace Walpole, Earl of Orford (1717–1797). Works,

edited by Mary Berry, etc. (9 vols., 1798–1825). Letters: edited by Mrs. Paget Toynbee (16 vols., 1903–5; Supplement, edited by Paget Toynbee, 3 vols., 1918–25); definitive edition by W. S. Lewis, et al. (in progress, Vol. I, 1937; fully annotated). *The Castle of Otranto*, edited by Oswald Doughty (1929). Biographies by R. W. Ketton-Cremer (1940) and W. S. Lewis (1961). Bibliography by A. T. Hazen (1948). (*CBEL*, II, 836 f.)

Gilbert White (1720–1793). Writings, edited by H. J. Massingham (2 vols., 1938, incomplete). Journals, edited by Walter Johnson (1931). *Life and Letters* by Rashleigh Holt-White (2 vols., 1901). (*CBEL*, II, 841.)

Mark Akenside (1721–1770). See study by Charles T. Houpt (1944). (*CBEL*, II, 350 f.)

William Collins (1721–1759). The best annotated edition is that by W. C. Bronson (1898). *Drafts and Fragments of Verse*, edited by J. S. Cunningham (1956). For criticism see Johnson (*Lives of the Poets*, 1781), H. W. Garrod (1928), and E. G. Ainsworth (1937). (*CBEL*, II, 335 f.)

Tobias Smollett (1721–1771). Novels: edited by George Saintsbury (12 vols., 1895; good introductions); 11 vols., Oxford, 1925–26 (plain texts). Letters, standard edition by Edward S. Noyes (1926). For life see Louis L. Martz (1942; only "later career") and Lewis M. Knapp (1949; ponderous but thorough). (*CBEL*, II, 523 f.)

"Junius" (1769–1772). Letters, edited by C. W. Everett (1927, with full discussion of problem of authorship). Alvar Ellegård's *Who Was Junius?* (1962) confirms statistically the authorship of Sir Philip Francis (1740–1818). (*CBEL*, II, 630 f.)

Christopher Smart (1722–1771). Collected poems, edited by Norman Callan (2 vols., 1949; not quite complete). Selected poems, edited by Robert Brittain (1950). *Jubilate*

Agno, edited by W. H. Bond (1954; good notes). For life and criticism, see E. G. Ainsworth and Claude E. Jones (1943). (*CBEL,* II, 338 f.)

Sir Joshua Reynolds (1723–1792). For Reynolds's literary career, see F. W. Hilles (1936), who has also edited the letters (1929). (*CBEL,* II, 629 f.)

Edmund Burke (1729–1797). Works, edited by W. Willis and F. W. Raffety (6 vols., 1906–7; no notes, etc.). *Sublime and the Beautiful,* standard edition by J. T. Boulton (1958). Letters, standard edition by Thomas W. Copeland (in progress; Vol. I, 1958). Early notebook, edited by H. V. F. Somerset (1957). Short selections: edited by A. M. D. Hughes (1924); edited by L. I. Bredvold and R. G. Ross (1960). For life see Philip Magnus (1939) and Thomas W. Copeland (1949; six important essays). Bibliography by W. B. Todd (1964). (*CBEL,* II, 632 f.)

Thomas Percy (1729–1811). *Reliques of Ancient English Poetry,* edited by H. B. Wheatley (3 vols., 1876–77). Letters, standard edition by D. Nichol Smith, Cleanth Brooks, et al. (in progress; 6 vols., 1944–61). (*CBEL,* II, 78 f.)

Oliver Goldsmith (1730?–1774). Works, critical edition by Arthur Friedman (5 vols., c. 1965). Poems, edited by Austin Dobson (1906; complete, with notes). *New Essays,* edited by Ronald S. Crane (1927; uncollected pieces; good notes, etc.). Letters, edited by Katharine C. Balderston (1928). Most detailed life still that by James Prior (2 vols., 1837), though this has been partly superseded by Ralph M. Wardle (1957). Concordance by W. D. Paden and C. K. Hyder (1940). (*CBEL,* II, 636 f.)

Charles Churchill (1732–1764). Poems, definitive edition by Douglas Grant (1956). Correspondence with

Wilkes, edited by Edward H. Weatherly (1954). For life see Wallace C. Brown (1953). (*CBEL*, II, 339 f.)

William Cowper (1731–1800). Poems, edited by Humphrey Milford (1905, rev. 1934; good text but no notes). Letters, edited by T. Wright (4 vols., 1904; short notes). Critical edition of letters in preparation by Neilson C. Hannay. Good lives by Maurice J. Quinlan (1953) and Charles Ryskamp (1959; to 1768). Bibliography by N. H. Russell (1963), and of Cowper criticism 1895 to 1959 by Lodwick Hartley (1960). Concordance by John Neve (1887). (*CBEL*, II, 341 f.)

James MacPherson (1736–1796). *Works of Ossian*, edited by O. L. Jiriczek (3 vols., Heidelberg, 1940). Life and letters by Thomas Bailey Saunders (1894). See also Derick S. Thomson, *The Gaelic Sources of Macpherson's Ossian* (1952). (*CBEL*, II, 343 f.)

Edward Gibbon (1737–1794). *Decline and Fall of the Roman Empire*, edited by J. B. Bury (7 vols., 1896–1900, rev. 1926–29). Autobiography: edited by John Murray (1896; with manuscript drafts); edited by G. Birkbeck Hill (1900; final version only). Journals: English edition by D. M. Low (1929); French edition by G. A. Bonnard (3 parts; Lausanne, 1945, and London, 1961). Letters, edited by J. E. Norton (3 vols., 1956; definitive edition). For criticism see G. M. Young (1932, rev. 1947) and Harold L. Bond (1960). Bibliography by J. E. Norton (1940). (*CBEL*, II, 882 f.)

James Boswell (1740–1795). *Life of Johnson*, edited by G. Birkbeck Hill (6 vols., 1887, rev. L. F. Powell, 1934–50; includes *Tour to the Hebrides*). The best separate edition of the *Tour* is that of C. H. Bennett and F. A. Pottle (1963). *Private Papers*, edited by Geoffrey Scott and Frederick A. Pottle (18 vols., 1928–34; "trade" edition in progress, various editors). *Letters*, edited by C. B. Tinker (2 vols., 1924). See Tinker's *Young Boswell*

(1922) and Pottle's *Literary Career of Boswell* (1929). (*CBEL*, II, 650 f.)

Robert Fergusson (1751–1774). Scots poems, edited by Bruce Dickins (1925). Complete poems, edited by M. P. McDiarmid (Scottish Text Society, 2 vols., 1954–). Unpublished poems, edited by William E. Gillis (1955). For biography and criticism see the bicentenary essays edited by Sydney Goodsir Smith (1952). (*CBEL*, II, 990 f.)

Richard Brinsley Sheridan (1751–1816). Plays and poems, edited by R. Crompton Rhodes (3 vols., 1928; long introductions but no notes). Plays only, edited by G. H. Nettleton (1906, with notes), and in *Dramatists from Dryden to Sheridan*, edited by A. E. Case and G. H. Nettleton (1939; good notes and discussion for *Rivals, School for Scandal*, and *Critic*). The *Rivals*, edited (from Larpent MS.) by Richard L. Purdy (1935). Critical edition of letters in preparation by Cecil Price. Standard life by Walter Sichel (2 vols., 1909). (*CBEL*, II, 454 f.)

Frances Burney, later d'Arblay (1752–1840). *Evelina*, exemplary edition by F. D. MacKinnon (1930). Selection from diary and letters edited by Muriel Masefield (1931). See thorough study by Joyce Hemlow (1958). (*CBEL*, II, 527 f.)

Thomas Chatterton (1752–1770). Poems, edited by Sidney Lee (2 vols., 1906–9; minimum annotation); *Rowley Poems* edited by S. E. Hare (1911). Standard life by E. H. W. Meyerstein (1930). Letters to Walpole in W. S. Lewis's edition of Walpole's *Correspondence* (Vol. XVI, 1951). (*CBEL*, II, 344 f.)

George Crabbe (1754–1832). Uncritical editions of poems by A. W. Ward (3 vols., 1905–7) and A. J. and R. M. Carlyle (1908). Life by his son has been reprinted with introductions by E. M. Forster (1932) and Edmund Blunden (1947). For criticism see René Huchon

(Paris, 1906, tr. English 1907; very thorough) and Lilian Haddakin (1955). (*CBEL*, II, 345 f.)

William Blake (1757–1827). Complete works, edited by Geoffrey Keynes (3 vols., 1925, without notes; 1 vol. 1927; rev. to include all variant readings and marginalia, but still without explanatory notes, 1957). Critical editions: poems, edited by John Sampson (2 vols., 1905, rev. with omission of long poems, 1913); complete poetical works, edited by Harold Bloom and David V. Erdman (1964; better text than Keynes). Selected poems, edited by F. W. Bateson (1957; full explanatory notes) and Stanley Gardner (1962; with notes); *Vala*, edited by H. M. Margoliouth (1956; good notes) and facsimile edition by G. E. Bentley (1963; full commentary). Facsimile of Rossetti Notebook, edited by Geoffrey Keynes (1935). Letters, edited by Keynes (1956). Concordance by David V. Erdman et al. (1964: complete prose as well as verse). For life see Alexander Gilchrist (2 vols., 1863; edited by Ruthven Todd, 1942) and Mona Wilson (1927, rev. 1948). Best recent general critical studies are those by S. Foster Damon (1924), Mark Schorer (1946), Northrop Frye (1947), David V. Erdman (1954), and Harold Bloom (1963). J. G. Davies's *Theology of William Blake* (1948) is also to be recommended (short, coherent, comprehensible). T. S. Eliot's brilliant essay was originally published in *The Sacred Wood* (1920). The 1953 *Census* of Blake's illuminated books by Keynes and Edwin Wolf supersedes Keynes's 1921 *Bibliography*. A detailed bibliography of writings on Blake is in preparation by G. E. Bentley and M. K. Nurmi. (*CBEL*, II, 347 f.)

Robert Burns (1759–1796). Poems: critical edition by W. E. Henley and Thomas F. Henderson (4 vols., 1896–97); edited by C. S. Dougall (1927; complete, short notes). Good short selection and introduction by G. S. Fraser (1960). Letters, edited by J. De Lancey Ferguson (2 vols., 1931). The fullest life is by Franklin B. Snyder (1932). For criticism see Franklin B. Snyder (1936),

David Daiches (1952), and Thomas Crawford (1960; the best general account). Maurice Lindsay's *Burns Encyclopaedia* (1959) is a useful work of reference. J. G. Lockhart's classic life has been edited for Everyman's Library by J. Kinsley (1959). The standard bibliography is by J. W. Egerer (1964). (*CBEL*, II, 973 f.)

William Beckford (1759–1844). *Vathek*, edited by Guy Chapman (2 vols., 1929; French original and Samuel Henley's English version). *The Vision* and *Liber Veritatis*, edited by Guy Chapman (1930). Travel journals: edited by Chapman (2 vols., 1928); edited by Boyd Alexander (1954). Detailed critical study of *Vathek* by André Parreaux (Paris, 1960; in French). For life see Chapman (1937, rev. 1952) and Alexander (1962). (*CBEL*, II, 528 f.)

VIII.   The Approach to Romanticism

1. THE SUBJECTIVE INDIVIDUAL

T. S. Eliot's most recent statement on the mid-seven-
teenth-century "dissociation of sensibility" has a method-
ological relevance beyond its immediate context:

> All one can say is, that something like this did hap-
> pen; that it had something to do with the Civil War;
> that it would even be unwise to say it was caused by
> the Civil War, but that it is a consequence of the same
> causes which brought about the Civil War; that we
> must seek the causes in Europe, not in England alone;
> and for what these causes were, we may dig and dig
> until we get to a depth at which words and concepts
> fail us.[1]

This is surely the proper way to approach any literary
period or phase. Literature after all, as Leslie Stephen
once put it, is only "a particular function of the whole
social organism."[2] Without the society there could not be
a literature. Politics is another and similar function. (So
too *pace* the Marxists is economics.) And in Europe at
any rate the social organism's frontiers are always likely
to be wider than those of the single nation-state. It is true
Stephen might not have had much patience with Eliot's
final claim, with its Jungian intimations of a collective
unconscious shared by all colors and all classes. But Eliot

---

[1] *On Poetry and Poets* (1957), p. 153. The passage occurs in
a lecture on Milton originally delivered in 1947.

[2] *English Literature and Society in the Eighteenth Century*
(1904), p. 13.

has been careful not to pursue that prickly subject either in this passage or elsewhere.

The Eliot formula works particularly well with Romanticism. Something like Romanticism did happen and it must have had something to do with the French Revolution; it was not exactly caused by the French Revolution, but it was presumably a consequence of the same causes; and it was a European, and not just an English or German, phenomenon. Without invoking Jung we may also agree that many discussions of Romanticism have almost reached the point where "words and concepts fail." Indeed, according to Jerome Hamilton Buckley in his informative survey *The Victorian Temper* (1951), "romanticism has already passed into the realm of the unknowable." At any rate, such snap definitions as Pater's "the addition of strangeness to beauty," or Watts-Dunton's "the Renascence of Wonder," or W. H. Auden's recent equation of Romanticism with "self-consciousness," suggestive though they may perhaps be, will not do now. Whatever the Romantic phenomenon may or may not be, it is not reducible to a definition three or four words long.

Our awareness of our plight goes back to 1923. In that year Arthur O. Lovejoy, an American philosopher who was a pioneer and specialist in the history of literary ideas, read an epoch-making paper to the Modern Language Association of America, "On the Discrimination of Romanticisms,"[3] which reached the scathing conclusion that "the word 'romantic' has come to mean so many things that, by itself, it means nothing":

> It has ceased to perform the function of a verbal sign. When a man is asked, as I have had the honour of being asked, to discuss Romanticism, it is impossible to know what ideas or tendencies he is to talk about,

[3] It will be found in Lovejoy's *Essays on the History of Ideas* (1948), pp. 228–53.

when they are supposed to have flourished, or in
whom they are supposed to be chiefly exemplified.[4]

Lovejoy proved his point by a long series of contradictory
examples from Romanticism's various friends and ene-
mies, in the United States, England, France, and Ger-
many, from Joseph Warton's *The Enthusiast* (1744) to
Irving Babbitt's *Rousseau and Romanticism* (1919). Altogether, "On the Discrimination of Romanticisms" was
both a brilliant and an intimidating performance. Recently, however, its blankly negative conclusions have
been skillfully disputed by René Wellek, of Prague and
Yale, in two definitive articles on "The Concept of 'Romanticism' in Literary History"[5] which trace the history
of the word and its analogues in great detail and also
demonstrate, more or less convincingly, the logical inter-
connection of the various senses that the term has had.
Lovejoy had been to some extent the victim of his own
atomistic method of reducing the history of thought to a
card-index of what he called "unit-ideas." According to
Wellek, however, Romanticism is not to be defined as a
single idea, or even a single complex of ideas, so much
as a loose conceptual congeries organized around three
dominant terms: Imagination, Nature, Symbol (or Myth).
And on the whole Wellek seems to prove his point, though
he does admit that English Romanticism—especially that
of Keats and Byron—is a good deal less "romantic" than
the German and French brands. The key figure in England was of course, Coleridge, who was the main trans-
mitter of German Romanticism (especially Schelling's and
A. W. Schlegel's); as literary theorists, if not as poets,
Wordsworth and Shelley are Coleridge's pupils and contribute only minor variations of their own. Blake's
hodge-podge of Platonism and alchemical mysticism has
an interesting twist in his insistence that Nature is not

[4] Ibid., p. 232.
[5] *Comparative Literature,* I (Winter and Spring 1949).

good but evil.[6] But in general the later Blake fits neatly
enough into the Wellek scheme.

In one important respect, however, Wellek's account
of Romanticism—which, it should be added, is generally
accepted today—is as negative as Lovejoy's: it fails com-
pletely to relate Romantic literature to the contemporary
social organism. By restricting the terms of reference to
literature—essentially poetry and the novel (Scott and
Balzac are for Wellek *the* Romantic novelists)—the new
sophisticated version of Romanticism has not only been
compelled to drop the connections with the French Revolution, which used to be the staple theme of the literary
textbooks, but also to turn a blind eye to the Industrial
Revolution, which was clearly its economic counterpart.
Such abstractions as Imagination, Nature, and Symbol are
almost meaningless except in some more concrete human
context. Who did the imagining and on behalf of whom?
If natural objects did become symbolic at the end of the
eighteenth century, what human realities did these myths
communicate? An even more inclusive formula seems
to be needed.

The French Revolution was not the cause of Romanticism; nor was the Industrial Revolution. All three, on
the contrary, were the concurrent consequences of a single cause, a sudden mutation, as it were, in the European
social organism, for which the best available label seems
to be Individualism. In a sense English society reverted
to its condition before the Civil War, and once again
"private sense" seemed to have lost all contact with public
or common sense. But the evasion and relaxation of social pressures which recommenced toward the middle of

6 Thus Blake's marginal comment on a fragment of *The Prelude* that Wordsworth published separately as "Influence of
Natural Objects in Calling Forth and Strengthening the Imagination in Boyhood and Early Youth" sets two of the elements
in Wellek's triad in emphatic opposition: "Natural objects always did and now do weaken, deaden and obliterate Imagination in me."

the eighteenth century and reached its climax about 1850 was all-pervasive, insinuating itself into each and every stratum and institution in the kingdom, as Renaissance egotism had never done. The hierarchical society of the Middle Ages was far from extinct when Charles I and Laud tried to revive it; when Disraeli and his Young England movement proposed in the 1840s to resurrect the stratified society of Augustan England the proposal was so unreal that its proclamation seems to us now just a sort of high-spirited political amateur theatricals.

An individualist asks of each function of the social organism "What does it mean to *me?*" This was Goethe's final criterion and one which the Victorian intellectuals learned from him. Goethe's test became the criterion that early nineteenth-century individualism implicitly applied to every function of the social organism. The literature that maximized private satisfactions was *ipso facto* the best literature on exactly the same principle that proved *laissez faire* capitalism the best economic system and Utilitarianism the best social philosophy. In this wider individualist context "Creative" Imagination, "Organic" Nature, and Symbol or Myth take on a new significance. The Creative Imagination of the poet or novelist supplied the Romantic reader with the material out of which he could elaborate or explore his own inner subjective world. The greater its subjective possibilities, then, the more satisfying the aesthetic material would be. In the terminology of English Romanticism the essential quality is "intensity," a favorite word of Hazlitt, Shelley, and Keats as well as of the Pre-Raphaelites. Like the pre-Romantic "sublime"— but without the classical and Miltonic paraphernalia that eighteenth-century sublimity needed for its production— "intensity" is achieved at the point of "fusion" or "evaporation" of "discordant" ideas and "disagreeable" emotions. The most specific account of the process is that provided by Coleridge in Chapter XIV of *Biographia Literaria,* but Coleridge omitted from his definition of the imagination the role of the unconscious mind in it—presumably to

save the theory from the charge of irrationalism. Shelley
had no such scruples in his account of "Inspiration" in
The Defence of Poetry, and Eneas Swetland Dallas, whose
interesting *The Gay Science* (1866) is the most philosophical of the Victorian poetics, actually makes the "Under-
soul" or unconscious mind the key to his whole system.
Ironically it is Coleridge's own dream-poem "Kubla Khan"
that is now enthroned as the most romantic of all the
English Romantic poems. Indeed on less formal occasions than *Biographia Literaria,* Coleridge himself made
no bones about the ability to create unconsciously being
"the genius in the man of genius."

"Nature," for the Romantic, was always to some extent
the projection on to non-human phenomena of the individual's own subconscious fantasies. In Coleridge's beautiful
ode "Dejection" the connection between Nature and
Imagination is made in so many words. It is the human
observer who animates the natural scene:

> O Lady! we receive but what we give,
> And in our life alone does Nature live. . . .

In the absence of such empathy—which Ruskin, whose
literary theory was of a less Romantic complexion than
his native temperament, was soon to dismiss as "The
Pathetic Fallacy"—Coleridge could only "see" and not
"feel," because his "shaping spirit of Imagination" had
become suspended.

Nature was a mirror in which the Imagination saw itself reflected. Since the Imagination was private and
a-social if not anti-social, the Nature it found itself looking
at was necessarily wild nature—that of tigers not cows;
of nightingales, skylarks, and albatrosses not cocks and
hens; of stars, clouds, mountains, and oceans not lamps,
smoke, houses, or reservoirs. And since the Imagination
cannot formulate logical propositions, its message to the
Romantic reader had to be oblique. The images of wild
nature, and their relationship to the human poet, carried
with them when all went well obscure symbolic signifi-

cances of universal interest. Coleridge's account of the process is to be found in an appendix to *The Statesman's Manual* (1816):

> I seem to myself to behold in the quiet objects on which I am gazing, more than an arbitrary illustration, more than a mere *simile,* the work of my own fancy. I feel an awe, as if there were before my eyes the same power as that of the reason— . . . a symbol established in the truth of things. I feel it alike, whether I contemplate a single tree or flower, or meditate on vegetation throughout the world. . . .

An earlier note by Coleridge—it is dated "Saturday Night," April 14, 1805—is an even franker statement of the subjective basis of the Symbol:

> In looking at objects of Nature while I am thinking, as at yonder moon dim-glimmering thro' the dewy window-pane, I seem rather to be seeking, as it were *asking,* a symbolical language for something within me that already and forever exists, than observing any thing new. Even when that latter is the case, yet still I have always an obscure feeling, as if that phaenomenon were the dim Awaking of a forgotten or hidden Truth of my inner nature.—It is still interesting as a Word, a Symbol!

But what the symbols *meant,* in cognitive terms, it was difficult even for Coleridge to say. One symbol could sometimes be elucidated by another. Indeed, interpretation by metaphor—Iago is *explained* (by Hazlitt) by comparing him to a boy killing flies—was a favorite Romantic critical procedure. (It is rampant not only in Hazlitt but also in Carlyle, Swinburne, and Pater and his school, and even, surprisingly, in Arnold and Leslie Stephen.)

2. "Diversitarianism"

English Romanticism did not add much that can be called systematic or co-ordinated to the sum of human wisdom. The "symbolical language" was a device for asking questions and not one for recording answers. In "The Tiger," characteristically, the word that Blake uses most often is the interrogative *what;* it recurs fourteen times, whereas even *the,* the next most frequent word, is only used thirteen times. And the "Ode to a Nightingale," another of the crucial documents in English Romanticism, also ends on a question:

> Was it a vision, or a waking dream?
> Fled is that music:—do I wake or sleep?

It is the question that Romanticism inevitably poses. How valid in the end is the subjective criterion ("vision," "Beauty," "intensity")? Is the symbolic music perhaps no more than a daydream—or perhaps "a psychological curiosity" (as Coleridge himself described "Kubla Khan" in the prefatory note that he prefixed to it in 1816)? Was nineteenth-century Individualism as a whole simply a temporary reaction against its eighteenth-century suppression?

The Victorians at any rate did not think so. Even such enlightened Victorians as Walter Bagehot and John Stuart Mill had no doubt that "progress" was being made in the nineteenth century. In *On Liberty* (1859)—which is with Newman's *Grammar of Assent* (1870) one of the intellectual peaks of the century—Mill's position is unequivocal. In earlier periods "the element of spontaneity and individuality" may have been "in excess" with "the social principle" having "a hard struggle with it," but "society has now fairly got the better of individuality; and the danger which threatens human nature is not the excess, but the deficiency, of personal impulses and preferences." To the modern eye Mill's alarm may seem unnecessary. The "originality" for which he was pleading was in fact burgeoning all round him as never before, and it is precisely "the social principle" that seems to us to have been neglected in Early Victorian England. The two trends have been called "universality" and "diversitarianism" by Lovejoy in an important paper on "Optimism and Romanticism" (1927) which is something of a retreat from the skepticism of "On the Discrimination of Romanticisms." Lovejoy's "universality" represents the eighteenth-century ideal of "conforming as nearly as possible to a standard conceived as universal, static, uncomplicated, uniform for every rational being." But with the coming of Romanticism "it came to be believed that in many, if not all, phases of human activity, not only are there diverse excellences, but that diversity itself is of the essence of excellence." Lovejoy's list of nineteenth-century "diversitarian" tendencies is worth quoting *in extenso:*

> . . . the immense multiplication of *genres* and of verse-forms; the admission of the aesthetic legitimacy of the *genre mixte;* the naturalization in art of the "grotesque"; the quest for local colour; the endeavour to reconstruct in imagination the *distinctive* inner life of people remote in space or in cultural condition; the *étalage du moi;* the demand for particularized fidelity in landscape-description; the revulsion against simplicity; the distrust of universal formulas in politics; the aesthetic antipathy to standardization; the apotheosis of the "concrete universal" in metaphysics; sentimentalism about "the glory of the imperfect"; the cultivation of personal, national and racial idiosyncrasy; the general high valuation (wholly foreign to most earlier periods) of originality, and the usually futile and absurd self-conscious pursuit of that attribute.[7]

The one omission from Lovejoy's catalogue is Romantic emotionalism—that indulgence in feeling for its own sake which Wordsworth made the basis of poetry ("the overflow of powerful feelings") and which flourished in the "Gothic" melodrama and the sentimental novel. But since

[7] *PMLA,* XLII (1927). The essay has been reprinted in *Eighteenth Century English Literature,* edited by J. L. Clifford (1959).

the gamut of human feeling is coextensive with the range of human experience, unbridled emotionalism is potentially at least as "diversitarian" as any of the doctrines listed by Lovejoy. It is true the human heart can also be a unifying element—as Wordsworth assumed it *must* be—but that was not its role in the literary masterpieces of this period, which are as emotionally variegated and unprecedented as those of the Renaissance, though in quite a new way. (Faust is not Doctor Faustus; "Caliban upon Setebos" is not the comment on *The Tempest* that it appears to claim to be.)

3. The Reading Public

Romanticism is also in a final analysis a new class, the middle-class intelligentsia, in the process of discovering its identity. The medium of discovery was linguistic. Though the social origins of the English Romantics—from the peasants like John Clare and James Hogg and the autodidacts like Dickens and George Eliot to aristocrats like Shelley and Byron—were decidedly mixed, as writers they spoke a single language: that of the university-educated intellectual. In the "diversitarian" chaos the degree of stylistic uniformity is remarkable. No doubt Blake and Keats both *spoke* English with a cockney accent, but what they wrote was "good English," the best English possible at the time, an English far less "vulgar" in fact than that of either a patrician like Byron or a Prime Minister like Disraeli.

What is especially noticeable in the first- and second-generation Romantics—as distinct from the Brownings, Pater, and Meredith—is the naturalness of the writing, the absence of strain. Such spontaneity is only possible when communication is immediate and effective between writer and reader. The writer must know that he will be read and who he will be read by. It is true that the early audiences both of the Romantic poets and of such novelists as Jane Austen and the Brontës were often small numerically. But few though the Wordsworthians and their like were initially, they were intelligent and enthusiastic. (*Lyrical Ballads* included among its original devotees De Quincey and John Wilson, afterward "Christopher North" of *Blackwood's*, as well as Lamb and Hazlitt.) And with one or two lonely exceptions the audiences grew and grew. Indeed, the growth of the reading public —*all* the reading publics, Romantic, frivolous, working-class—was one of the principal cultural achievements of the century. Even if the term is restricted to book readers, and not merely to the literate or the readers of newspapers, the proportion of the total population constituting the reading public multiplied dramatically. At the time of Addison and Steele's *Spectator* the serious readers are estimated at less than 1 per cent of the population. If Burke's estimate is correct, the number of book readers had only risen to 80,000 about 1790; that is, to 1.3 per cent of the population. In 1812, however, according to Francis Jeffrey, there were at least 200,000 persons reading "for amusement or instruction, among the middling classes" and a further 20,000 "in the higher classes"—a total of 220,000 readers or about 2 per cent of the population. In 1844 Jeffrey raised his earlier estimates to 300,-000 and 30,000 respectively and by then a considerable number of serious working-class readers must certainly be added—a grand total of at least 500,000 or about 3 per cent of the population.

The estimates may not be very reliable, but what other evidence there is is to the same general effect. Thus in the 1820s the *Penny Magazine* sold some 200,000 copies— mainly, however, because of its illustrations. In 1855, on the other hand, the *London Journal* had a circulation, mainly among lower-middle-class readers, of 510,000, and the penny novels of G. W. M. Reynolds in the 1850s and 1860s are said to have had "millions of readers." That seems to suggest a book-reading public of at least 10 per cent of the population in 1860. An enormous increase in the number of readers in the prosperous period that began in 1851 is indicated by the fact that in 1865 there were no less than 1271 newspapers and 554 periodicals published in the United Kingdom. The best-seller of the mid-century, curiously enough, was a ballad on the execution of the criminals Rush and Manning, of which two and a half million copies were printed![8]

The term *reading public* seems to have been coined at this time, apparently by Coleridge. It appears in both *The Statesman's Manual* (1816) and *Biographia Literaria* (1817) and caught on immediately. Hazlitt was one who adopted it, though he disliked Coleridge's censorious attitude to the new readers, and Peacock makes the Coleridgian Mr. Flosky in *Nightmare Abbey* (1818) use the phrase several times ("a *reading public* that is growing too wise for its betters," etc.). Coleridge's distinction between the uncritical *reading public* and the critical *clerisy* (another coinage of his that has had less success with posterity) was as fanciful as Wordsworth's between *the people* (the country folk) and *the public* (the urban middle class), but both indicate an awareness, however prejudiced, of the momentous shift in what might be called the contemporary balance of cultural power. With the rapid growth during the Napoleonic Wars of the middle class in wealth and influence, new interests and values were making themselves felt. An aristocracy of intellect was beginning to supersede the older aristocracy of birth. The intellectual is the real hero of Carlyle's *Heroes and Hero-Worship* (1841), just as it is the creative "few" who are "the salt of the earth" in Mill's *On Liberty*. The cultural revolution of the nineteenth century occurred when men were gathered together in small numbers. It is the char-

[8] Some of these statistics are culled from R. K. Webb, *The British Working Class Reader 1790–1848* (1955), and Alvar Ellegård, *The Readership of the Periodical Press in Mid-Victorian Britain* (Gothenburg, 1957). Louis James's *Fiction for the Working Man, 1830–1850* (1963) gives details about the sensational or sentimental novels written especially for the new readers.

acteristic of the nineteenth-century intellectual that he flourished most in small groups and *cénacles*. You will find him in the Clapham Sect or among the Benthamites, amid the Wordsworthians or the Cambridge "Apostles," in the neighborhood of Carlyle or of Newman, among the Pre-Raphaelite Brethren or the followers of T. H. Green or the poets of the "Cheshire Cheese"—not in the political parties or the London clubs or any ecclesiastical organization, High, Low, or Broad.

The sudden growth in population during the Romantic period can be compared with the economic inflation of the Renaissance in its cultural consequences. Between 1791 (the year in which Blake wrote most of the *Songs of Experience*) and 1832 (the year of Scott's, Goethe's, Crabbe's, and Bentham's deaths) the population of England and Wales doubled—from approximately 8 million to some 16 million. The enormous decrease in the death rate (the birth rate did not change) in these forty years was dramatically different from the slow climb from a 4 million population *c.* 1550 to 5 million *c.* 1660 and 6 million *c.* 1750, and it must have helped to create an atmosphere of "buoyancy" and "exhilaration" similar to that engendered, according to Keynes, by the profit inflations of the sixteenth century and with the same consequential abundance of "great writers and artists." Life was showing itself the master of Death. And it was, of course, in the middle classes in particular that the sensational population increases occurred. (The crucial factor apparently was the improvement in sanitation—the scientific product of the Puritan cleanliness that came next to godliness.) Moreover, as with the Renaissance inflation, almost nobody at the time was able to explain the causes of the phenomenon.

Some of the crucial Romantic premises—that the external world is organic, that the unconscious mind is more likely to be right than the conscious mind, that it is important to be "earnest" (like Carlyle and Dr. Arnold)[9]—are implicit in this ignorance. Indeed, the parallel between the role of Fortune at the Renaissance and of Inspiration in the nineteenth century is exact. The main difference is that Fortune was conceived to be external to man, a kind or aspect of the Divine, whereas Inspiration was internal, the Divine element in man. A passage in "Characteristics" (1831), the essay which embodies the quintessence of Carlylean wisdom, takes the religious issue to what was to be its Victorian conclusion:

> Of Literature, and its deep-seated, wide-spread melodies, why speak? Literature is but a branch of Religion, and always participates in its character: however, in our time, it is the only branch that still shows any greenness; and, as some think, must one day become the main stem.

Here, almost in so many words, is Matthew Arnold's notorious prophecy—made in "The Study of Poetry" (1880) —that "most of what now passes with us for religion and philosophy will be replaced by poetry." By an ironic coincidence, most of what passed for poetry to Arnold has in fact been replaced by the novel.[10]

[9] "The word 'earnest' has got spoilt. It was used over and over again till it got to sound like cant, and then people began to laugh at it" (P. G. Hamerton, *Autobiography*, 1897, p. 447, reporting a comment made by Richmond Seeley in 1878). Wilde's comedy was not produced until 1895. The first protest against the Rugbeian abuse of the word is in the *Edinburgh Review* article (1858; by James FitzJames Stephen) on *Tom Brown's Schooldays*. According to Bagehot it was Carlyle who popularized the word, more or less displacing "serious." Matthew Arnold only uses the word in his earlier poems.

[10] The English novel was one of Arnold's critical blind spots. The satiric catalogue of typical philistine literature in the Preface to *Essays in Criticism* (1865) includes—along with Bentham's *Deontology, The Wide, Wide World,* and Beecher's *Sermons*—Dickens's *Little Dorrit!*

4. THE RETREAT FROM ROMANTICISM

In a recent article in the *Journal of Aesthetics,* Romanticism was defined, correctly, as "the tendency to break the confines, the rules, the limits, to go beyond that which has been crystallized".[11] As opposed to the Classic, then, with its trend to a norm or mean, the Romantic is essentially antinomian and extremist. Like nationalism and capitalism, its political and economic counterparts, Romanticism's instinct is to absorb or enslave whatever it may encounter other than itself. The eighteenth century had been an age that relied on checks and balances, not only in constitution-building and foreign policy, but equally in its favorite verse form (the heroic couplet) and its prose style (the balanced clause). With the coming of Romanticism the Augustan balance of opposites is succeeded in Coleridge's formula by what he called the "fusion" of discordant elements. The Ego, instead of being in equipoise with the Non-Ego, now tries to assimilate all phenomena external to itself, as the nation-state asserts its identity by conquering its neighbors. A similar refusal to compromise operated in science and in religion. As between these two rival absolutes science would not allow the truths of religion even a metaphoric validity, to which religion, in the person of Newman, reacted by raising atoms to angels—a "beautiful prospect" was the product of angelic robes, and every flower, herb, and pebble "some powerful being who was hidden behind the visible things he was inspecting."[12]

Nevertheless, in spite of these appearances to the contrary, nineteenth-century individualism did contain within itself its own limiting principle. An individual cannot rebel unless there is a society of which he has been a member to rebel against. You cannot break confines, rules, and lim-

[11] Herbert M. Schueller, "Romanticism Reconsidered," *Journal of Aesthetics and Art Criticism,* XX (1962), 360.
[12] *Apologia Pro Vita Sua,* ed. Wilfrid Ward (1913), p. 129.

its unless they have been previously crystallized. Subjectivism implies and indeed requires an objective universe on which, to use one of Wordsworth's favorite metaphors for expressing the relationship, it can "feed."[13]

And so, as the Victorian intellectual woke up from the Romantic dream in which he had spent his adolescence, he began to feel a new respect for "things." A concept of Realism was implicit in the concept of Romanticism. Beauty must also be in some sense truth. Lascelles Abercrombie in his persuasive critical study *Romanticism* (1926) has argued that Realism is always the antithesis or polar opposite of Romanticism. But it would be better to say that the two ideals complement each other. Considered simply as literary doctrine, Realism is merely the consequence or corrective of Romanticism. To be a Realist you must first have been a Romantic;[14] to be a good Realist you must still be a Romantic—a little disillusioned no doubt, preferably perhaps a little embittered, but a Romantic at heart. If the formula applies to Flaubert and Zola, will it not also apply to Thomas Hardy and Rudyard Kipling?

In the mid-Victorian retreat from Romanticism the crucial document is Matthew Arnold's "The Function of Criticism at the Present Time," the brilliant and often profound essay which leads off his *Essays in Criticism* (1865), having been delivered as the Professor of Poetry's statutory lecture at Oxford the preceding October. Arnold begins "The Function of Criticism" by reinvoking a principle that he had defined in the second lecture *On Trans-*

---

[13] See F. W. Bateson, *Wordsworth: A Re-Interpretation* (1954), p. 182.

[14] The earliest examples of "realism" cited by the *OED* are by Emerson (1856) and Ruskin (1857). See Harry Levin, "What Is Realism?", *Comparative Literature*, III (1951), 193–99. According to Wellek, *Comparative Literature*, I (1949), 15, "romanticism" enters the language in 1823 in a review by Stendhal of his own *Racine et Shakespeare*. It was not used again until 1831 when Carlyle introduces the term in an article on Schiller.

lating Homer (1861). On that occasion the oddities of
the version of the *Iliad* by Francis Newman, the Cardi-
nal's agnostic brother, had been the point of exasperated
departure:

> Our present literature, which is very far, certainly,
> from having the spirit and power of Elizabethan
> genius, yet has in its own way these faults, eccen-
> tricity and arbitrariness, quite as much as the Eliza-
> bethan literature ever had. They are the cause that,
> while upon none, perhaps of the modern literatures
> has so great a sum of force been expended as upon
> the English literature, at the present hour this litera-
> ture, regarded not as an object of mere literary in-
> terest but as a living intellectual instrument, ranks
> only third in European effect and importance among
> the literatures of Europe; it ranks after the litera-
> tures of France and Germany. Of these two litera-
> tures, as of the intellect of Europe in general, the
> main effort, for now many years, has been a *critical*
> effort; the endeavour, in all branches of knowledge
> —theology, philosophy, history, art, science—to see the
> object as in itself it really is. But, owing to the pres-
> ence in English literature of this eccentric and ar-
> bitrary spirit, owing to the strong tendency of English
> writers to bring to the consideration of their object
> some individual fancy, the last thing for which one
> would come to English literature is just that very
> thing which now Europe most desires—*criticism*.

For Arnold, criticism—which he opposes to "individual
fancy"—is the intellectual discipline of seeing the object
as it really is. Though it includes literary criticism, the
discipline which he advocates is wider than literature,
which is to him only one of the many forms or modes of
"knowledge." If Arnold's "really" implies Realism it is at
the more abstract, almost metaphysical, level of the
word's etymology (*res* = thing or "object"). Appearance, in other words, must be distinguished from reality.

As Arnold, a competent Greek scholar, must have known, the word κρίνειν meant to "separate" or "sort out" before it meant to "judge."

But what is Arnold's reality? To the mid-Victorian mind as to the Romantic's, phenomena were essentially "diversitarian." Indeed the greater the diversity, the more there was for the "esemplastic" (Coleridge's word) imagination to unify. But the Romantic temptation had been to simplify and speed up the process by imposing on phenomena a premature unity. Thus Ruskin's gospel of patient particularity, as he elaborated it in volume after volume of *Modern Painters*, was intended to save Romanticism from itself. Ruskin's insistence that "every great man paints what he sees or did see, his greatness being indeed little else than his intense sense of fact,"[15] connects with Arnold's demand that the object shall be *seen* as it really is. Proper seeing ensures a correct record of the object; the achievement is cognition, a form of knowledge. It is in some such context therefore that Arnold's notorious judgment on the English Romantics in "The Function of Criticism" needs to be read. What Arnold said was that they "did not know enough." Wordsworth, Byron, Shelley, and Coleridge—the four writers of "the first quarter of the century" whom Arnold picks out for reluctant reprehension—were deficient in knowledge, in objectivity. They were the victims, that is, of their own subjectivism.

Arnold's prescription for the reform of English literature was a simple one: creative writing was to give place temporarily to literary criticism. He was bold enough even to specify a date when the critical reform would make it possible for creative writing—now less eccentric and less arbitrary—to be resumed. "Perhaps in fifty years . . ." If calculated from the autumn of 1864, when Arnold was writing the essay, the prophetic fifty years would terminate in the autumn of 1914. Not exactly an

[15] *Pre-Raphaelitism* (1851), p. 41 of Everyman's Library reprint (1906).

auspicious date! But if Arnold's fifty years are accepted, as they reasonably may be, as a round figure, his prophecy or prescription has not proved far out. The period immediately preceding World War I was in fact one of English literature's most productive periods. It was the period after all of *Man and Superman* (1903), of *The Old Wives' Tale* (1908), of *Sons and Lovers* (1913), of Joyce's *Dubliners* (1914), and of Yeats's *Responsibilities* (1914), as well as of the early writings of E. M. Forster, Virginia Woolf, T. S. Eliot, and Robert Graves.

The mid-Victorian concern with the relationship of "thing" to "eye," of "seeing" the "object" with more care and precision than the Romantics were in the habit of doing, found its literary expression in the descriptive passages of Tennyson, Ruskin, Pater, Hopkins (whose tutor at one time at Oxford had been Pater himself), Arthur Symons, and even Max Beerbohm. What is missing only too often in these descriptions is the human element. The eye that sees each minute detail in the landscape does not succeed in seeing human figures in it. The contribution of the great Edwardians was precisely to restore human beings and human societies to literature. And this humanization was effected by a radical departure from the Arnoldian doctrine. Insight, imaginative sympathy, was now the means (not just "seeing"), and the human object seen into was real in a profounder sense than Ruskin's rocks. The model or analogy is no longer the reality of the physical sciences, as it had implicitly been for Arnold, but of the social sciences, especially of psychology. A better prescription than Arnold's can be found in Mill's account of Bentham who, according to Mill, was totally deficient in the imagination

which enables us, by a voluntary effort, to conceive the absent as if it were present, the imaginary as if it were real, and to clothe it in the feelings which, if it were indeed real, it would bring along with it. This is the power by which one human being enters into the mind of another. This power constitutes the poet, in so far as he does anything but melodiously utter his own actual feelings. It constitutes the dramatist entirely.[16]

The essential progress in twentieth-century English literature over the nineteenth century, so far as there has been a progress, has been by virtue of its superior power to enter into the mind of another. In distinction from Coleridge's Primary and Secondary Imaginations, the psychological insight that Joyce and Lawrence possessed supremely, and the other Edwardians in their various degrees, might be called the Tertiary Imagination. For Coleridge the Primary Imagination was "the living power and prime agent of human perception." What Coleridge did not distinguish was the difference between our modes of perception of non-human and human phenomena. A wife is not "seen" in the same way as a cloud, because psychological otherness differs *toto coelo* from physical otherness. A fellow human being is "valued"—sympathetically or antipathetically—almost the moment physical contact, through the eyes, ears, or other senses, is made, whereas rocks and stars and trees are only "registered." In the figures of Bloom and Paul Morel's mother, to take two typical instances, the Romantic amalgamation of fancy and landscape has been reversed. Instead, a human nature external to the author, and different from him and from all non-human nature, has been constructed verbally. The human flesh has become words.

[16] *Mill on Bentham and Coleridge,* ed. F. R. Leavis (1950), p. 61.

IX. A Reading List, 1800–1960

1. BIBLIOGRAPHIES

Volume III of *CBEL* (1940) devotes its 1100 double-column pages entirely to the nineteenth century. With its Supplement (1957) it covers almost every aspect of the period including the Anglo–Irish, Anglo–Indian, English–Canadian, English–South African, Australian, and New Zealand literatures. Unfortunately it is not free from errors. (The second edition will start with this volume.) A more modest affair is the bibliography (of over 200 pages) attached to *The Victorians and After, 1830–1914* by Edith Batho and Bonamy Dobrée (1938). For the major authors the Modern Language Association of America has recently sponsored a "Review of Research" in nineteenth-century English literature, of which 3 volumes have so far appeared—*The English Romantic Poets* (ed. T. S. Raysor, 1950, rev. 1956), *The Victorian Poets* (ed. F. J. Faverty, 1956), and *The English Romantic Poets and Essayists* (ed. C. W. and L. H. Houtchens, 1958). The last item covers Blake, Southey, Campbell, Moore, and Landor, who had been excluded from Volume I (which was restricted to Wordsworth, Coleridge, Byron, Shelley, Keats), as well as Lamb, Hazlitt, Scott, Leigh Hunt, and De Quincey. The Victorian volume covers Tennyson, the Brownings, FitzGerald, Clough, Arnold, Swinburne, the Rossettis, Morris, Hopkins, and fourteen "Later Victorian Poets" (from Meredith to A. E. Housman). *The Victorian Novelists* (ed. Lionel Stevenson) is announced. Each section is by a separate scholar, but the method—a list of recent editions, books, and articles with appropriate comments—is uniform. An anti-critical bias diminishes the value of the series. Lewis Leary's *Contemporary Literary Scholarship* (1958) is less comprehensive, but the chapters on "The Romantic Movement" (by R. H. Fogle) and "The Victorian Period" (by L. Stevenson) are useful for authors outside the scope of the MLA series.

Current work on the period is recorded annually with remarkable thoroughness in two annual bibliographies— "The Romantic Movement" (*ELH*, 1937–49; transferred to *PQ*, 1950–   ), and "Victorian Bibliography" (*MP*, 1933–57; transferred to *Victorian Studies*, 1958–   ). The Victorian bibliographies, 1932–44, were reissued by W. D. Templeman (1945), and those for 1945–54 by A. Wright (1956); both have a general index. Some of the more important works receive brief comments, but these cannot compare with the searching critiques in the 1660– 1800 annual bibliographies in *PQ*—which should always be consulted for books or articles straddling both centuries. The actual reviews in *Victorian Studies* are excellent and numerous.

The aspiring literary detective, however unbibliographical, should not miss *An Enquiry into the Nature of Certain Nineteenth-Century Pamphlets* by John Carter and Graham Pollard (1934), which has demonstrated that Thomas J. Wise, the most pretentious of all recent bibliophiles and bibliographers, was a large-scale forger of Victorian first editions.

2. LITERARY HISTORIES, SURVEYS, AND CRITICISM

Apart from George Saintsbury's *History of Nineteenth Century Literature* (1896)—still worth reading, though now out of date[1]—and Joseph W. Beach's judicious survey

---

[1] Saintsbury's best criticism of Romantic and Victorian literature is to be found in his *Essays in English Literature, 1780– 1860* (2 series, 1890–95; shrewd, well-informed appreciations of some twenty more or less minor figures) and *Corrected Impressions* (1895; the principal Victorians). Both collections are reprinted in his *Collected Essays and Papers* (4 vols., 1923–24). Within his limits—he is essentially a "practical" critic—Saintsbury is unsurpassed.

of the nineteenth century in the Hardin Craig *History of English Literature* (1950), which is now obtainable separately, there is no good general account of the literature of the century as a whole. Oliver Elton's two *Surveys* —1780–1830 (2 vols., 1912), 1830–80 (2 vols., 1920)— are not what they appear to be, since Elton's method is to take each writer separately without any connecting framework. But Elton wrote well and had more literary sense than most of his successors. An intelligent introduction to the period is Louis Cazamian's volume in the Legouis–Cazamian *Histoire de la littérature anglaise* (1924; English tr. 2 vols., 1926–27, rev. 1948), though this actually begins at 1660. Cazamian was an especially good critic of the novel. The *OHEL* Volume IX (1789–1815) by W. L. Renwick (1963) is disappointing apart from the Scotch sections; Volume X (1815–32) by Ian Jack (1963) is a very much better survey, if critically undistinguished. The Victorian volumes have still to appear.

Four unassuming handbooks can be commended. They are C. H. Herford's *Age of Wordsworth* (1897; includes brief sketches of many minor authors), Ernest Bernbaum's *Guide through the Romantic Movement* (1930, rev. 1948; has good critical bibliographies), J. D. Cooke and Lionel Stevenson's *English Literature of the Victorian Period* (1949; more modern in tone), and the similar but slightly more up to date *Companion to Victorian Literature* by T. M. Parrott and R. B. Martin (1955).

Of the many critical surveys the two with the widest range are H. V. Routh's *Towards the Twentieth Century: Essays in the Spiritual History of the Nineteenth* (1937) and the less solemn and very well-informed *The Victorian Temper* by J. H. Buckley (1951). Useful surveys of somewhat narrower scope are Holbrook Jackson's *The Eighteen-Nineties* (1914), B. Ifor Evans's *English Poetry in the Later Nineteenth Century* (1933), Graham Hough's *The Last Romantics* (1949), Douglas Bush's *Mythology and the Romantic Tradition in English Poetry* (1937), Walter E. Houghton's *Victorian Frame of Mind, 1830–*

1870 (1957), Albert Gérard's *L'Idée romantique de la poésie en Angleterre* (Paris, 1958), and Allan Rodway's *The Romantic Conflict* (1963; interesting sociological interpretation).

Some of the best criticism of the great Romantics is to be found in A. C. Bradley's *Oxford Lectures on Poetry* (1909), F. R. Leavis's *Revaluation* (1936), and G. Wilson Knights's *The Star-lit Dome* (1941). A scholarly supplement is C. P. Brand's *Italy and the English Romantics* (1957). The Victorian novel has been discussed, from very different critical points of view, by David Cecil (*Early Victorian Novelists*, 1934, rev. 1958), F. R. Leavis (*The Great Tradition*, 1948), and Kathleen Tillotson (*Novels of the Eighteen-Forties*, 1954; especially informative on economic background). For the minor novelists Michael Sadleir's bibliographical explorations—notably *Nineteenth-Century Fiction* (2 vols., 1951)—are indispensable. Basil Willey's *Nineteenth-Century Studies* (1949) and *More Nineteenth-Century Studies* (1956) and John Holloway's *The Victorian Sage* (1953) are conscientious, if somewhat heavy-going, attempts to grapple with the Victorian "thinkers" (Carlyle, both Newmans, George Eliot, etc.); a more lighthearted and still relevant excursion into this area was made by G. K. Chesterton in *The Victorian Age in Literature* (1913). See also Raymond Williams's *Culture and Society, 1780–1950* (1958) for the displacement of religion by "culture" in England. For the literary criticism there is M. H. Abrams's brilliantly lucid survey *The Mirror and the Lamp* (1953), Geoffrey Tillotson's well-informed but rather inconclusive *Criticism and the Nineteenth Century* (1951), Vol. II of René Wellek's indispensable *History of Modern Criticism* (1955), Frank Kermode's ingenious reinterpretation *Romantic Image* (1957), and Richard Stang's *Theory of the Novel, 1850–1870* (1959; mainly from articles and reviews). Some good modern essays on the principal novelists have been assembled by R. C. Rathburn and M. Steinmann (1959); A. Wright has a similar collection on Victorian literature in general (1961).

Of the numerous specialist studies within the period, three deserve special mention: *The Romantic Agony* by Mario Praz (1933, rev. 1952; tr. from Italian; on the morbid excesses of the century), René Wellek's *Kant in England, 1793–1838* (1931), and Josephine Miles's statistical investigations, especially *The Vocabulary of Poetry* (1946). A book that is much respected, if not often read right through, is J. W. Beach's *Concept of Nature in Nineteenth-Century Poetry* (1936).

The critical reader will also find it profitable to look into recent accounts of the great magazines, such as G. L. Nesbitt on the *Westminster* (1930), Miriam Thrall on *Fraser's* (1934), J. Bauer on the *London* (Copenhagen 1953), and H. and H. C. Shine on the *Quarterly* under Gifford (1949).

3. ANTHOLOGIES

A. H. Miles's *Poets and Poetry of the Century* (10 vols., 1891–97, rev. 12 vols., 1905–7) is still indispensable— especially for the minor poets (some three hundred in all). The editors Miles enlisted for the separate introductions to each poet's work were among the best critics writing at the time. (The selection from Hopkins, tactfully introduced by Bridges, were the first Hopkins poems to get into print.) Of the more recent collections the best are certainly the American college texts (with explanatory notes, bibliographies, etc.), such as E. Bernbaum's *Anthology of Romanticism* (5 vols., 1929–30, rev. 1948), O. J. Campbell, J. F. A. Pyre, and B. Weaver's *Poetry and Criticism of the Romantic Movement* (1932), G. B. Woods's *Poetry of the Victorian Movement* (1930, rev. with J. H. Buckley, 1955; over fifty poets included), and E. L. Beck and R. H. Snow's *Victorian and Later English Poets* (1934; silly prefatory essay by James Stephens, but includes some thirty poets generously represented with ample notes). The new *Oxford Book of Nineteenth Century Verse* (ed. John Hayward, 1964) is an excellent selection with reliable texts but unfortunately no notes; the eccentric *Oxford Book of Modern Verse* (ed. W. B. Yeats, 1936), which begins *c.* 1885, has an illuminating and entertaining introduction. Of the more specialized anthologies three are of general interest—Walter Jerrold and R. M. Leonard's *Century of Parody and Imitation* (1913; good notes); Charles Williams's *Book of Victorian Narrative Verse* (1927), and D. Davidson's *British Poetry of the Eighteen-Nineties* (1937).

Similar selections from the prose are R. Withington and C. Van Winkle, *Eminent British Writers of the Nineteenth Century: Prose* (1934), C. F. Macintyre and M. Ewing, *English Prose of the Romantic Period* (1938), C. F. Harrold and W. D. Templeman, *English Prose of the Victorian Era* (1938; exceptionally well edited), Carl R. Woodring, *Prose of the Romantic Period* (1961; twenty-nine authors included), and William E. Buckler, *Prose of the Victorian Period* (1958).

There is a useful collection of nineteenth-century critical essays by E. D. Jones (1916; seventeen critics represented, but without notes or introduction). Some of the best-known reviews have been assembled by R. Brimley Johnson (1914); for the pre-Victorians, John Wain's *Contemporary Reviews of Romantic Poetry* (1953) supplements E. Stevenson's *Early Reviews of Great Writers, 1786–1832* (1890).

4. THE TWENTIETH CENTURY

There are few bibliographies of post-1900 English literature. The useful lists compiled by J. M. Manly and Edith M. Rickert as *Contemporary British Literature* (1921, rev. 1928) were expanded (and contracted) by Fred B. Millett in 1935 to cover 232 authors. A twentieth-century Supplement to *CBEL* is in preparation; and a number of authors have achieved their own bibliographies

—notably Max Beerbohm, Hilaire Belloc, Rupert Brooke, Norman Douglas, T. S. Eliot, John Galsworthy, James Joyce, D. H. Lawrence, Katherine Mansfield, John Masefield, Somerset Maugham, Frederick Rolfe, Siegfried Sassoon, Dylan Thomas, Edward Thomas, and Virginia Woolf. Although not primarily bibliographies, two volumes in the "Introduction to English Literature" series have select lists of writings by and about each author included—the 1830–1914 volume by Edith C. Batho and Bonamy Dobrée (1938, rev. 1950) and the post-1914 volume by Edwin Muir (1939; rewritten by David Daiches, 1958). Similar in scope is *Contemporary English Literature* by Mark Longaker and Edwin C. Bolles (1953).

Much the best critical survey of the English literature of this century is G. S. Fraser's *The Modern Writer and His World* (1953, rev. and enlarged 1964), which manages to be thorough, fair, and perceptive at the same time. Apart from Fraser there are one or two competent handbooks, such as Carl and Mark Van Doren's *American and British Literature since 1890* (1925, rev. 1939), William Y. Tindall's *Forces in Modern British Literature, 1880–1946* (1947; lively but eccentric), B. Ifor Evans's *English Literature between the Wars* (1948), and H. V. Routh's *English Literature and Ideas in the Twentieth Century* (1948; better on the ideas than on the literature). The final *OHEL* volume by J. I. M. Stewart (Vol. XII, 1963) is virtually limited to Hardy, James, Shaw, Conrad, Kipling, Yeats, Joyce, and Lawrence.

The books with a more limited range make better reading. F. R. Leavis's *New Bearings in English Poetry* (1930), Frank Swinnerton's *The Georgian Literary Scene* (1935, rev. 1950), and George Orwell's *Inside the Whale* (1940) are already minor classics. Graham Hough's recent *Image and Experience* (1960) is a similar critical postscript, hostile but persuasive, on Imagism and its offshoots. Other surveys that can be recommended are: H. P. Collins, *Modern Poetry* (1925), Una M. Ellis-Fermor, *The Irish Dramatic Movement* (1939, rev. 1954),

J. Isaacs, *The Assessment of Twentieth-Century Literature* (1951), J. K. Johnstone, *The Bloomsbury Group* (1954; Forster, Strachey, Virginia Woolf, etc.), Sean O'Faolain, *The Vanishing Hero* (1956; Joyce to Waugh), and Walter Allen, *Tradition and Dream* (1964; the post-1920 novelists).

For those who can spare the time, much the best introduction to modern literature is via the literary journals. Those especially meriting exploration are perhaps *The English Review* (Ford Madox Ford), *The Egoist* (Ezra Pound and T. S. Eliot), *The Criterion* (T. S. Eliot), *Life and Letters* (Desmond MacCarthy), *The Calendar* (Edgell Rickword), *Scrutiny* (F. R. Leavis and L. C. Knights, 2nd ed. 20 vols., 1963), *New Verse* (Geoffrey Grigson), *Horizon* (Cyril Connolly), *New Writing* (John Lehmann), and *Essays in Criticism* (F. W. Bateson).

5. PRINCIPAL AUTHORS

(In chronological order of birth. The *CBEL* references are to *The Cambridge Bibliography of English Literature* [ed. F. W. Bateson, 4 vols., 1940] and its Supplement [ed. G. Watson, 1957], which has the same pagination as the parent work.)

William Cobbett (1762–1835): *The Life and Adventures of Peter Porcupine*, edited by G. D. H. Cole (1927); *The Opinions of Cobbett*, edited by G. D. H. and M. Cole (1944; extracts from the *Political Register*, 1802–35); *Rural Rides*, edited by G. D. H. and M. Cole (3 vols., 1930; includes Scotch tours and letters from Ireland). *Selections*, edited by A. M. D. Hughes (1923; short representative extracts with good notes). G. D. H. Cole's *Life of Cobbett* (1924, rev. 1947) is the standard biography. G. K. Chesterton's study (1925) is lively. There is a helpful bibliography by M. L. Pearl (1953). (*CBEL*, III, 629 f.)

Maria Edgeworth (1767–1849). The uncritical Long-ford edition (10 vols., 1893) includes all the fiction; *Tales*, edited by Austin Dobson (1903). *Castle Rackrent* and *The Absentee* are available in Everyman's Library (1910). Official *Life and Letters*, by A. J. C. Hare (2 vols., 1894). There is a good critical appreciation by P. H. Newby (1950) and a life by Isabel C. Clarke (1950); Elizabeth Inglis-Jones has recently used unpublished letters to good effect in a lively, if unscholarly, study (*The Great Maria,* 1959). (*CBEL*, III, 366 f.)

James Hogg (1770–1835). *The Private Memoirs of a Justified Sinner:* edited by T. E. Welby (1924); introduction by André Gide (1947). The standard life is by Edith C. Batho (*The Ettrick Shepherd*, 1922). See also *The Life and Letters*, edited by A. L. Strout (Vol. I, 1947). (*CBEL*, III, 164 f.)

William Wordsworth (1770–1850). Best edition of poems by E. de Selincourt and Helen Darbishire (5 vols., 1940–49); this is complete (with many new poems from manuscript) and fully annotated, but excludes *The Prelude*, which was edited separately by de Selincourt with 1805 and 1850 versions on opposite pages (rev. Darbishire 1959, also 1805 text alone 1933). Of the single-volume editions, T. Hutchinson's (1904, rev. E. de Selincourt 1936) is complete and reliable textually but has no notes; Arthur Beatty's *Representative Poems* (1937) omits only the trivia and is well annotated, though the introduction is often inaccurate. Competent editions (most now largely superseded by de Selincourt–Darbishire) of separate works include: *Lyrical Ballads: 1798*, edited by T. Hutchinson (1898, rev. 1920); *1800*, edited by G. Sampson (1903); *1798–1805*, edited by R. L. Brett and A. R. Jones (1963). *Poems in Two Volumes*, edited by H. Darbishire (1915; useful notes). *The White Doe of Rylstone*, edited by A. P. Comparetti (1939; very thorough). *Ecclesiastical Sonnets*, edited by A. F. Potts (1922). Of the numerous shorter selections a good modern one, intelligently annotated, is that by R. Sharrock (1958).

A definitive edition of the prose is in preparation by W. J. B. Owen and others; Owen's edition of the Preface to *Lyrical Ballads* (Copenhagen, 1957) is excellent. The *Convention of Cintra* has been edited by A. V. Dicey (1915) and the *Guide to the Lakes* by E. de Selincourt (1906) and W. M. Marchant (1951). The letters, including those of Dorothy Wordsworth, were edited by E. de Selincourt (6 vols., 1935–39). M. L. Peacock has assembled Wordsworth's various critical dicta alphabetically under Topics and Authors (1950).

The standard life (to 1803) is that by Mary C. Moorman (1957; a second volume is promised). After 1803, reference must still be made to G. M. Harper's less detailed work (2 vols., 1916, revised and abridged 1929) and to Edith C. Batho's *The Later Wordsworth* (1933). A minor biographical masterpiece is Emile Legouis's *Wordsworth and Annette Vallon* (1922).

A bibliographical guide through the jungles of Wordsworthian criticism has been compiled by J. V. Logan (1947; supplement to 1959 by E. F. Henley, 1960), and E. Bernbaum's chapter in *The English Romantic Poets: a Review of Research* (ed. T. M. Raysor, 1950) fulfills the same function on a more modest scale. Scholarly criticism of Wordsworth begins with Emile Legouis, *La jeunesse de Wordsworth* (Paris, 1896, tr. 1897; essentially a biographical commentary on *The Prelude*). Walter Raleigh's *Wordsworth* (1903) is still a good general critical introduction; the reappraisals of H. W. Garrod (1923, rev. 1927), Herbert Read (1930; often inaccurate), Lascelles Abercrombie (1952), F. W. Bateson (1954, rev. 1956), John Jones (1954), C. C. Clarke (1962), and D. D. Perkins (1964: on Wordsworth's "sincerity"), are more critically ambitious. Two specialist studies of considerable importance are R. D. Havens's *The Mind of a Poet* (1941; analysis of Wordsworth's thinking) and F. M. Todd's survey of Wordsworth's political evolution (1957). There is a good concordance by Lane Cooper (1911). (*CBEL*, III, 165 f.)

Sir Walter Scott (1771–1832). No critical edition of novels; last complete reprint 24 volumes, 1914. *Poetical Works,* edited by J. Logie Robertson (1904; complete but without notes). Fullest edition of miscellaneous prose, 30 volumes, 1869–71, is uncritical. *Journal,* edited by J. G. Tait (3 vols., 1939–46). *Letters,* edited by H. J. C. Grierson (12 vols., 1932–37; well annotated). Lockhart's brilliant *Memoirs* (2 vols., 1837–38) are still unsuperseded but they must now be supplemented by Grierson's strictly factual life (1938). John Buchan's biography (1932) is more in the modern manner. A first-rate critical study has not yet been devoted to Scott, but Edwin Muir's *Scott and Scotland* (1936) is often suggestive. Donald Davie's *The Heyday of Sir Walter Scott* (1961) has a brilliant chapter on *Waverley* but is mainly concerned with Scott's imitators—from Pushkin to Lever. Of the shorter critiques one of the best is by C. S. Lewis in *They Asked for a Paper* (1962). J. T. Hillhouse's *The Waverley Novels and Their Critics* (1936) is a mine of useful information; an expert assessment of other specialist studies was contributed by Hillhouse to *The English Romantic Poets and Essayists: a Review of Research and Criticism* (ed. C. W. and L. H. Houtchens, 1958). J. C. Corson's bibliography (1943) lists books and articles on Scott, 1797–1940. (*CBEL,* III, 369 f.)

Sydney Smith (1771–1845). *Selected Writings,* edited by W. H. Auden (1956). Letters, edited by Nowell C. Smith (2 vols., 1953). (*CBEL,* III, 679 f.)

Samuel Taylor Coleridge (1772–1834). Complete poetical works, edited by E. H. Coleridge (2 vols., 1912, also 1 vol. without plays; critical texts but no explanatory notes). Selected poems and prose edited by Stephen Potter (1933, enlarged 1950). Editions of separate works: *Ancient Mariner* (R. P. Warren, 1946; fanciful but ingenious), *Biographia Literaria* (J. Shawcross, 2 vols., 1907; G. Watson, 1956), *Shakespearean Criticism* (T. M. Raysor, 2 vols., 1930, rev. 1960), *Miscellaneous Criticism*

(T. M. Raysor, 1936), *Philosophical Lectures* (K. Coburn, 1949). A definitive edition of the complete works, in 20 volumes, is in preparation under the general editorship of Kathleen Coburn. Notebooks: complete text edited by K. Coburn (11 vols., 1957–); selections, edited by E. H. Coleridge (1895, as *Anima Poetae*), edited by K. Coburn (1951, as *Inquiring Spirit*). Letters: edited by E. H. Coleridge (2 vols., 1895); edited by E. L. Griggs (6 vols., 1956– ; complete but underannotated). There is no really good life, though Lawrence Hanson (1938) is sound on the young Coleridge, and E. K. Chambers (1938, rev. 1950) at least assembles most of the facts. The best general introduction is probably Humphry House's short study (1953). J. L. Lowes's brilliant *The Road to Xanadu* (1927; on sources of "Ancient Mariner" and "Kubla Khan") has been partly superseded by Elisabeth Schneider's *Coleridge, Opium, and "Kubla Khan"* (1954) and J. B. Beer's *Coleridge the Visionary* (1959). Another reliable introduction is *The Idea of Coleridge's Criticism* (1962) by R. H. Fogle. I. A. Richards's *Coleridge on Imagination* (1934, rev. 1950), though well worth reading, is more about Richards than about Coleridge and needs correcting by John H. Muirhead, *Coleridge as Philosopher* (1930). The chapter in René Wellek's *History of Modern Criticism* (Vol. II, 1955) is useful for the German sources. There is a good concordance by Eugenia Logan (1940). For an expert recent assessment of the many specialist studies, see T. M. Raysor and R. Wellek's chapter in *The English Romantic Poets: a Review of Research* (ed. Raysor, 1950, rev. 1956). Bibliography by T. J. Wise (1913; Supplement 1919). (*CBEL*, III, 172 f.)

Robert Southey (1774–1843). Poems, edited by M. H. Fitzgerald (1909; incomplete). Selected letters, edited by M. H. Fitzgerald (1912). There is a good modern life by Jack Simmons (1945), and the non-literary aspects have been covered by Geoffrey Carnall (1960). Kenneth Curry writes on Southey in *The English Romantic Poets and Essayists: a Review of Criticism and Research* (ed. C. W. and L. H. Houtchens, 1958). (*CBEL*, III, 180 f.)

Jane Austen (1775–1817). Standard edition by R. W. Chapman (6 vols., 1923–54; the six novels with the juvenilia and fragments, all superbly annotated). Chapman has also edited the letters (2 vols., 1932; selection 1955) and the Victorian *Memoir* by J. E. Austen-Leigh (1926). Chapman's *Jane Austen: Facts and Problems* (1948) assembles all the biographical material, and his *Jane Austen: a Critical Bibliography* (1955) is a skillful guidebook through the Austen literature, including reviews and critical discussions. The most substantial critiques at the moment are those by Mary Lascelles (1939; sensitive, detailed, but inconclusive), Marvin Mudrick (1952; on the irony), Andrew H. Wright (1953, rev. 1961; a Jamesian "Study in Structure"), Howard Babb (1962; clever analysis of dialogue), and Robert Liddell (1963; thorough but conventional). Of the shorter essays Lionel Trilling's "Mansfield Park" piece in his *Opposing Self* (1955) is perhaps the most interesting. This and other modern critical essays have now been assembled by Ian Watt (1963), who also provides a useful survey of the growth of Jane Austen's reputation. (*CBEL*, III, 381 f.)

Charles Lamb (1775–1834). Standard edition by E. V. Lucas (7 vols., 1903–5, 6 vols., 1912; virtually complete but underannotated). Letters, edited by E. V. Lucas (3 vols., 1935; includes Mary Lamb's letters). A selection from Lamb's criticism has been edited by E. M. W. Tillyard (1923). The standard life—by E. V. Lucas (1905, rev. 1921)—is supplemented in Edmund Blunden's *Lamb and His Contemporaries*. Books and articles about Lamb —none of much critical interest—are sifted by G. L. Barnett in *The English Romantic Poets and Essayists: a Review of Research and Criticism* (ed. C. W. and L. H. Houtchens, 1958). (*CBEL*, III, 631 f.)

Walter Savage Landor (1775–1864). Standard edition by T. E. Welby and S. Wheeler (16 vols., 1927–36; all the English prose and verse, with some annotation); Wheeler's edition of the poems is also issued separately (3 vols., 1937). Selections from the poems by Geoffrey Grigson (1964) and from *Imaginary Conversations* (1915; good introduction by E. de Selincourt). The pleasant official life by John Forster (2 vols., 1869) has been superseded factually by R. H. Super (1954), critically by M. Elwin (1941, rev. 1958). See also R. H. Super in *The English Romantic Poets and Essayists: a Review of Research and Criticism* (ed. C. W. and L. H. Houtchens, 1958), and Super's *The Publication of Landor's Works* (1954). (*CBEL*, III, 637 f.)

Thomas Campbell (1777–1844). Complete poetical works, edited by J. L. Robertson (1907; no notes). What little has been written about Campbell is surveyed authoritatively by H. H. Jordan in *The English Romantic Poets and Essayists: a Review of Research and Criticism* (ed. C. W. and L. H. Houtchens, 1958). (*CBEL*, III, 183 f.)

William Hazlitt (1778–1830). Standard edition by P. P. Howe (21 vols., 1930–34; complete but underannotated). Good selection of essays by Geoffrey Keynes (1930; no notes), who has also published the standard bibliography (1931). P. P. Howe's short but well-informed life (1922, rev. 1947) has now been superseded by the more elaborate biography of Herschel Baker (1962), which is especially good on the more literary aspects. A proper critical assessment of Hazlitt has yet to be written. For a survey of the attempts to date, see Elisabeth Schneider (author of *The Aesthetics of Hazlitt*, 1933) in the Houtchens *Review of Research and Criticism* (1958). Bibliography by Geoffrey Keynes (1931). (*CBEL*, III, 640 f.)

John Galt (1779–1839). Works, edited by D. S. Meldrum and W. Roughead (10 vols., 1936). See the study by Jennie W. Aberdein (1936) and Erik Frykman's *Galt's Scottish Stories* (Upsala, 1959). (*CBEL*, III, 394 f.)

Thomas Moore (1779–1852). Poems, edited by A. D. Godley (1910; complete but without notes). Collected letters edited by W. S. Dowden (1964). Standard life by H. Mumford Jones (1937). See H. H. Jordan in the Houtchens *Review of Research and Criticism* (1958). (*CBEL*, III, 184 f.)

Leigh Hunt (1784–1859). Poems, edited by H. Milford (1923; complete, some notes). L. H. and C. W. Houtchens have brought out fully annotated collections of Hunt's literary criticism (1957; with a long essay by C. de W. Thorpe on Hunt as man of letters), dramatic criticism (1949), and political and occasional essays (1962; long introduction by Carl R. Woodring). *Autobiography*, edited by J. E. Morpurgo (1948). Blunden's attractive biography (1930) has been partly superseded by Louis Landré's (2 vols., Paris, 1935–36; in French and very thorough). For other discussions of Hunt see the Houtchens *Review of Research and Criticism* (1958). (*CBEL*, III, 643 f.)

Thomas De Quincey (1785–1859). *Collected Writings*, edited by D. Masson (14 vols., 1889–90; no notes); *Uncollected Writings*, edited by J. Hogg (2 vols., 1892); letters and fragments, edited by A. H. Japp (4 vols., 1891). E. Sackville-West's edition of the *Opium Eater* (1950) includes selections from *Autobiographic Sketches;* M. Elwin's edition (1956) is of both texts and includes related pieces. Sackville-West's edition of *Recollections of the Lake Poets* (1948) is of its original unabridged text. S. K. Proctor's *De Quincey's Theory of Literature* (1943) has been followed by J. E. Jordan's more discursive *De Quincey, Literary Critic* (1953). The life by H. A. Eaton (1936) is more reliable factually than Sackville-West's agreeable sketch (1936). For later work on De Quincey see J. E. Jordan in the Houtchens *Review of Research and Criticism* (1958). (*CBEL*, III, 648 f.)

Thomas Love Peacock (1785–1866). Standard edition by H. F. B. Brett-Smith and C. E. Jones (10 vols., 1924–34; complete but no notes, includes a good life of Peacock by Brett-Smith). The fullest life so far is by Carl Van Doren (1911). David Garnett's edition of the novels (3 vols., 1948) has short notes. The uncritical 1895–97 edition (5 vols.) has racy introductions by George Saintsbury, and J. B. Priestley has written a pleasant general appreciation of Peacock (1927); for a more scholarly view see the essay by H. House in his *All in Due Time* (1955). (*CBEL*, III, 384 f.)

George Gordon Byron, Baron Byron (1788–1824). Standard edition by E. H. Coleridge and R. E. Prothero (13 vols., 1898–1904; well annotated, includes all the letters available at the time). Complete poems edited by E. H. Coleridge (1905; good short notes). Of the selections the best, because of the extensive notes, are L. I. Bredvold's *Don Juan and Other Satiric Poems* (1935) and the complementary volume by S. C. Chew (*Childe Harold's Pilgrimage and Other Romantic Poems*, 1936); there is also a helpful paperback edition of *Don Juan* by L. A. Marchand (1959; excellent notes). The definitive life is that by Marchand (3 vols., 1957), though some additional material is to be found in Doris Langley Moore's rather slovenly *The Late Lord Byron* (1961). Of the earlier biographies Ethel Colburn Mayne's *Byron* (1912; sensitive and acute), Harold Nicolson's Stracheyan *Byron: the Last Journey* (1924), Charles du Bos's *Byron et le besoin de la fatalité* (1929, tr. E. C. Mayne 1932; psychological analysis), and Iris Origo's *Byron: the Last Attachment* (1949; the Teresa Guiccioli affair with all the original letters) continue of great interest. Three short general studies—by E. J. Lovell (1949), Paul West (1960), and Andrew Rutherford (1961)—can be recommended. S. C. Chew—the author of *Byron in England: His Fame and*

After-Fame (1924; a very useful book)—surveys the Byron editions and commentaries in the Raysor *Review of Research* (1950, rev. 1956). Two important recent publications are the critical edition of *Don Juan* by T. G. Steffan and W. W. Pratt (4 vols., 1957) and W. W. Robson's *Byron as Poet* (British Academy Lecture, 1957; an acute criticism of the poems simply as poems). The best of the shorter critical pieces have been assembled by Paul West (1964). There is a concordance by F. S. Ellis (1892). For annual check-list of Byron studies, see under Shelley below. Bibliography by T. J. Wise (2 vols., 1932–33). (*CBEL*, III, 187 f.)

Percy Bysshe Shelley (1792–1822). The Julian edition by R. Ingpen and W. E. Peck (10 vols., 1926–30) is complete, but texts are unreliable and with insufficient annotation; includes all the letters then available. The best one-volume edition of the poems is still that by T. Hutchinson (1904; includes everything in print but no explanatory notes), and there is a useful edition of the 1820 poems by A. M. D. Hughes (rev. 1957). The selection by G. M. Matthews (1964) has good notes and texts, including some poems not previously printed. John Shawcross's edition of *Shelley's Literary and Philosophical Remains* (1909) is also unsuperseded. Of more recent editions, that of *Prometheus Unbound* by L. J. Zillman (1959) is much the most elaborate. Standard edition of the letters (also including many *to* Shelley) by F. L. Jones (2 vols., 1964). The standard life is that by N. I. White (2 vols., 1940, rev. 1947), which must now be supplemented by K. N. Cameron's brilliant *The Young Shelley: Genesis of a Radical* (1950), which is, however, as much concerned with the works as with the man. Edmund Blunden's shorter life (1946) is also first-class within its limits. Carl Grabo's studies of science in the poems (1930, 1935, 1936), C. H. Baker's *Shelley's Major Poetry* (1948), and Neville Rogers's *Shelley at Work* (1956; learned but inaccurate) are more for the scholar than for the general reader. P. H.

Butter's *Shelley's Idols of the Cave* (1954) is stimulating, however, on the imagery. In *The Unextinguished Hearth* (1938), White assembled the most significant comments on Shelley and his poetry. Later criticism has failed to take up the challenge of Shelley's poetic inferiority issued by Arnold, Eliot, and F. R. Leavis (see his *Revaluation,* 1936); a partial exception is the level-headed, if critically unambitious, appreciation of Desmond King-Hele (1960). For summaries of recent work see Bennett Weaver in the Raysor *Review of Research* (1950, rev. 1956). There is a Shelley concordance compiled by F. S. Ellis (1892). The *Keats–Shelley Journal* (founded 1952) lists current writings on Shelley with specialized articles on the whole Shelley circle, including Byron. (*CBEL*, III, 212 f.)

John Clare (1793–1864). Poems, edited by J. W. Tibble (2 vols., 1935; glossary but no notes); selections with good introductions by G. Grigson (1950) and J. Reeves (1954). *Poems of Madness,* edited by G. Grigson (1949; many new poems). Eric Robinson and Geoffrey Summerfield have edited (with notes) *The Shepherd's Calendar* and *The Later Poems* (both 1964 and from manuscripts). Prose, edited by J. W. and Anne Tibble (1951). Letters, edited by J. W. and Anne Tibble (1951). The Tibbles are also the authors of the standard life of Clare (1932, rev. 1956). The contemporary life by Frederick Martin (1865) has been edited by Eric Robinson and Geoffrey Summerfield with new material, etc. (1964). (*CBEL*, III, 218 f.)

Thomas Carlyle (1795–1881). Standard edition by H. D. Traill (30 vols., 1896–99; complete but no notes). Editions of separate works: *Sartor Resartus,* C. F. Harrold (1937); *The French Revolution,* J. H. Rose (3 vols., 1902); *Past and Present,* A. M. D. Hughes (1918); *Frederick the Great,* abridged by A. M. D. Hughes (1916). Generous selection by Julian Symons (1956; no notes); good Carlyle anthology by G. M. Trevelyan

(1953). Apart from Froude's life (4 vols., 1882–84) and
the elongated biographical pieties of D. A. Wilson (6
vols., 1923–34), there is a sound book by Emery Neff
(1932) and C. F. Harrold's valuable *Carlyle and German Thought, 1819–34* (1934). The life of Jane Welsh
Carlyle by L. and E. Hanson (1952) includes much new
material. A specialist study of great merit is Hill Shine's
Carlyle's Early Reading, to 1834 (1953), and Grace J.
Calder has traced the process of composition of *Past and
Present* (1949). Bibliography by I. W. Dyer (1928).
(*CBEL*, III, 652 f.)

John Keats (1795–1821). Complete works, edited by
H. B. Forman (5 vols., 1900–1, revised and enlarged by
M. B. Forman, 8 vols., 1938; especially useful for Keats's
marginalia and for the miscellaneous Keatsiana in the
notes). Best text of poems H. W. Garrod's edition (1939,
rev. 1958), fullest explanatory annotation E. de Selincourt's edition (1905); J. Middleton Murry's edition (2
vols., 1929, rev. 1 vol. 1949) prints the poems in chronological order of composition. The best annotated selection
is that by C. D. Thorpe (1935). The Hyder E. Rollins
edition of Keats's letters (2 vols., 1958; excellent annotation) supersedes M. B. Forman (2 vols., 1931, final rev.
1952); Lionel Trilling's selection from the letters (1951)
has notes and a brilliant introduction. *The Keats Circle*,
edited by H. E. Rollins (2 vols., 1948) assembles much
early Keatsiana, some of it important. Of the numerous
biographies the best are those of Sidney Colvin (1917;
judicious and well organized), Amy Lowell (1925; much
new information but often fanciful), Dorothy Hewlett
(1937, enlarged 1950; up to date and readable but rather
naïve critically), John Gittings (1954; restricted to one
year, 1819; great fun, but often unconvincing), and Aileen
Ward (1963; intelligent psychologizing). G. H. Ford's
Keats and the Victorians (1944) is a masterly account of
the growth of Keats's reputation. Other distinguished
critical studies are those by J. M. Murry (especially

Keats and Shakespeare, 1925), H. W. Garrod (1926),
C. D. Thorpe, *The Mind of Keats* (1926), C. L. Finney
(1936; poem by poem discussion of sources, technique,
attitudes), W. J. Bate (1945; detailed analysis of style and
prosody; and general study, 1964), and E. R. Wasserman
(1953; minute analyses of five poems). Earlier lives and
criticism are listed and summarized in J. R. MacGillivray,
Keats: a Bibliography and Reference Guide (1949). See
also C. D. Thorpe's useful section in the Raysor *Review
of Research* (1950, rev. 1956). There is a Keats concordance compiled by D. L. Baldwin et al. (1917); the *Keats–
Shelley Journal* (founded 1952) lists current work on
Keats. (*CBEL*, III, 220 f.)

Thomas Hood (1799–1845). Poetical works, edited
by Walter Jerrold (1906); letters, edited by L. A. Marchand (1945). The standard life is by Walter Jerrold
(1907). In 1930 Jerrold picked out items from *Hood's
Own* to form *Hood and Lamb*. There is a very competent
study by J. C. Reid (1963); BCB by Laurence Brander.
(*CBEL*, III, 224 f.)

Thomas Babington Macaulay, Baron Macaulay (1800–
1859). Works (9 vols., 1905–7; complete but without
notes). *Lays of Ancient Rome*, edited by G. M. Trevelyan
(1928); *Critical and Historical Essays*, edited by F. C.
Montague (3 vols., 1903); *History of England*, edited by
T. F. Henderson (5 vols. [1908]). Good selection by
G. M. Young (1952). The standard life is still G. O.
Trevelyan's *Life and Letters* (2 vols., 1876); Arthur
Bryant's *Macaulay* (1932) is a pleasant unpretentious
sketch which needs supplementing by the stodgier study
by R. C. Beatty (1938). (*CBEL*, III, 683 f.)

William Barnes (1801?–1886). Collected poems, edited by Bernard Jones (2 vols., 1962; complete but unscholarly in presentation). Thomas Hardy's selection from
Barnes's poems (1908) is much slimmer than Geoffrey

Grigson's (1950; good critical introduction). Life by Giles Dugdale (1953). (*CBEL*, III, 278 f.)

John Henry Newman (1801–1890). *The Idea of a University*, edited by C. F. Harrold (1947); *Apologia pro Vita Sua*, edited by W. Ward (1913; critical text), also edited by Harrold (1947) and Basil Willey (1964); *A Grammar of Assent*, edited by Harrold (1947). Harrold —who is the author of the best modern study (1945)— has also edited several of the theological works (1948–49). Generous selection from both the prose and poetry by Geoffrey Tillotson (1957). The definitive edition of Newman's letters and diaries by C. S. Dessain has begun with Vol. XI (1961). The standard life is by Wilfrid Ward (2 vols., 1912). Meriol Trevor's two-volume biography— *Pillar of the Cloud* (1962) and *Light in Winter* (1963) —is the most recent life. W. E. Houghton has analyzed the literary aspects of the *Apologia* in a good book (1945). (*CBEL*, III, 686 f.)

Thomas Lovell Beddoes (1803–1849). Standard edition by H. W. Donner (1935; also with omissions 1950). The only modern study is also by Donner (1935). (*CBEL*, III, 248 f.)

George Borrow (1803–1881). Standard edition by Clement Shorter (16 vols., 1923–24; complete, with much from manuscripts, but next to no notes). There is a thorough and sensible French study by René Fréchet (Paris, 1956). Official life by W. I. Knapp (2 vols., 1899; includes letters). See also Shorter's *Borrow and His Circle* (1913). Bibliography by T. J. Wise (1914). (*CBEL*, III, 421 f.)

Benjamin Disraeli, Earl of Beaconsfield (1804–1881). *Novels and Tales*, edited by P. Guedella (12 vols., 1926–27; separate introductions but no notes). The standard life is by W. F. Moneypenny and G. E. Buckle (6 vols., 1910–20). See also B. R. Jerman, *The Young Disraeli* (1960). The most recent critical discussion of the novels

is in John Holloway's *The Victorian Sage* (1953). (*CBEL,*
III, 423 f.)

Elizabeth Barrett Browning (1806–1861). Standard edition by Charlotte Porter and Helen A. Clarke (6 vols.,
1900). Single-volume editions of poetical works: F. G.
Kenyon (1897), H. W. Preston (1900), and 1904 (Oxford Standard Authors series). Letters, edited by F. G.
Kenyon (2 vols., 1897); letters to Robert Browning, Hen-
rietta Barrett, Haydon, Horne, and John Boyd have also
been printed separately. Latest life is by G. B. Taplin
(1957); there is a comprehensive study of the poetry by
Alethea Hayter (1962). A. M. Terhune summarizes the
literature in the Faverty *Guide to Research* (1956).
(*CBEL,* III, 249 f.)

John Stuart Mill (1806–1873). Of the definitive edition
in twenty volumes promised by Toronto University only
two (early letters, ed. F. Mineka, 1963) have appeared.
F. R. Leavis has reprinted the Bentham and Coleridge
essays from *Dissertations and Discussions* with a good introduction (1950). *Autobiography,* edited by R. Howson
(1924; first edition of complete text). Bernard Wishy
has compiled a useful selection from Mill called *Preface
to Liberty* (1959). The latest life by M. St. J. Packe
(1954) is first-class. See also Thomas Woods, *Poetry and
Philosophy in Mill* (1961). (*CBEL,* III, 871.)

Edward FitzGerald (1809–1883). Standard edition by
W. A. Wright (7 vols., 1902–3; includes letters) omits
some pieces in G. Bentham's edition (7 vols., 1902–3).
The selection by Joanna Richardson (1962) prints all
the essential items. Best editions of *Rubáiyát* by N. H.
Dole (2 vols., 1896) and C. J. Weber (1958; gives textual
minutiae). See also A. J. Arberry's *Romance of the Rubáiyát* (1958; prints FitzGerald's first edition with excellent
notes). The fullest life is by A. M. Terhune (1947), who
promises a collected edition of FitzGerald's letters. A. C.
Benson's book (1905) is still the only general discussion

of FitzGerald's *œuvre*. For an assessment of the literature, see Terhune's section in the Faverty *Guide to Research* (1956). (*CBEL*, III, 251 f.)

Alfred Tennyson, Baron Tennyson (1809–1892). Standard edition by Hallam Tennyson (1913; notes by Tennyson himself; virtually identical Eversley edition, 9 vols., 1907–8). Poems omitted from Hallam Tennyson's edition will be found in the edition by W. J. Rolfe (1898; short notes, but omits Tennyson's final volume) and in that in Oxford Standard Authors series (1953; no notes but includes most of suppressed poems). J. Churton Collins's editions of the early poems (1901) and *The Princess, In Memoriam, Maud* (1902) give original versions, notes, etc. Annotated edition of the 1842 collection by A. M. D. Hughes (1914). Selection by W. H. Auden (1946; no notes) has an interesting introduction. Christopher Ricks is preparing a complete edition with full explanatory notes.

Hallam Tennyson's omnium-gatherum *Memoir* (2 vols., 1897) has been usefully supplemented by Charles Tennyson's franker biography (1949). There is a competent poem-by-poem commentary by Morton Luce (1895), and one for *In Memoriam* by A. C. Bradley (1901, rev. 1930). J. H. Buckley's *Tennyson: the Growth of a Poet* (1960) utilizes much new material (early drafts and fragments) but is rather uncritical. An intriguing biographical interpretation of *Maud* by R. W. Rader (1964) breaks new ground, but the best criticism will be found in Harold Nicolson's *Tennyson* (1923), P. F. Baum's *Tennyson Sixty Years After* (1948), and E. D. H. Johnson's *The Alien Vision* (1952). John Killham has reprinted sixteen shorter modern essays on Tennyson (1960; Leo Spitzer to T. S. Eliot). There is a concordance by A. E. Baker (1914; supplement 1931). Bibliography by T. J. Wise (2 vols., 1908). (*CBEL*, III, 253 f.)

Elizabeth Gaskell (1810–1865). Novels and tales: edited by A. W. Ward (8 vols., 1906; separate introductions, with full life in Vol. I); edited by Clement Shorter (11 vols., 1906–19; uncritical but complete). Annette B. Hopkins's biography (1952) is thorough and sympathetic. David Cecil discusses Mrs. Gaskell in his *Early Victorian Novelists* (1934) and there is a good essay on *Mary Barton* in Kathleen Tillotson's *Novels of the Eighteen-Forties* (1954). (*CBEL*, II, 427 f.)

William Makepeace Thackeray (1811–1863). The nearest thing to a complete Thackeray is the uncritical Oxford edition by George Saintsbury (17 vols., 1908; brilliant critical introductions reprinted 1931 as *A Consideration of Thackeray*). The edition of *Vanity Fair* by J. W. Beach (1950) is now superseded by Geoffrey and Kathleen Tillotson's (1963; detailed introduction and notes, Thackeray's own illustrations). *The Letters and Private Papers*, edited by Gordon N. Ray (4 vols., 1945–46), is complete and definitive, and all earlier biographies are now surpassed by Ray's masterly life (2 parts, 1955–58). Of several notable recent critical studies—John Dodd (1941), Lionel Stevenson (1943), Lambert Ennis (1950), J. Y. T. Greig (1950), Gordon N. Ray (1952; on relationship between novels and Thackeray's personal life)—the best is perhaps that by Geoffrey Tillotson (1954). (*CBEL*, III, 429 f.)

Robert Browning (1812–1889). Works (collected): edited by Charlotte Porter and Helen A. Clarke (12 vols., 1910; many notes, often irrelevant); edited by F. G. Kenyon (10 vols., 1912; no notes but useful introductory comments to many poems). Best one-volume edition by A. Birrell (1915; virtually complete). Good annotated selections by W. C. De Vane (1933) and Walter Graham (1934). De Vane's *Browning Handbook* (1935, rev. 1955) is an indispensable tool, giving each poem's genesis, sources, history, etc. The standard life is by H. W. Griffin and H. C. Minchin (1910), though Betty Miller's recent psychological interpretation (1952) makes much livelier reading. Critical discussions of some distinction will be

found in the studies by F. G. R. Duckworth (1931),
W. O. Raymond (1950); E. D. H. Johnson (1952), and
R. Langbaum (1958; on the dramatic monologue as
genre). A. K. Cook's *Commentary* (1920) on *The Ring
and the Book* is an indispensable aid. The Browning
bibliography by C. S. Northup, L. N. Broughton, and R.
Pearsall (1953) is a complete census of printed editions,
manuscripts, and letters, as well as of writings on
Browning. Broughton and B. F. Stelter also compiled the
concordance (2 vols., 1924). For a summary of recent
work on Browning, see De Vane's chapter in the Faverty
Guide to Research (1956). (*CBEL*, III, 258 f.)

Charles Dickens (1812–1870). Works (collected, all
without notes): Nonesuch Dickens, edited by A. Waugh,
W. Dexter, etc. (23 vols., 1937–38); Oxford Illustrated
Dickens (21 vols., 1947–58). A critical edition of all
Dickens's novels is being prepared by John Butt and
Kathleen Tillotson. There have been some good recent
editions of single novels: *Great Expectations,* edited by
E. Davis (1949); *Hard Times,* edited by W. W. Watt
(1958); *Bleak House,* edited by M. D. Zabel (1956);
David Copperfield, edited by G. H. Ford (1958); *A
Tale of Two Cities,* edited by M. D. Zabel (1958). The
elaborate Pilgrim edition of Dickens's correspondence by
Graham Storey and others (Vol. I, 1963) supersedes
Walter Dexter's 3 volumes (1938) in the Nonesuch
Dickens. K. J. Fielding has edited the *Speeches* (1960).
The fullest life of Dickens is that by Edgar Johnson (2
vols., 1952), but John Forster's official life (1872, ed.
J. W. T. Ley, 1928) still makes excellent reading. The
more perceptive critics include George Gissing (1898),
G. K. Chesterton (1906), George Orwell (*Inside the
Whale,* 1940), and Edmund Wilson (*The Wound and
the Bow,* 1941); there is also a first-class *Critical Introduction* by K. J. Fielding (1958), a brilliant if eccentric
study by J. H. Miller (1958), and a stimulating critical
miscellany on Dickens edited by John Gross (1962;

W. Empson, Angus Wilson, etc.). The *Dickens Critics* (eds. G. H. Ford and L. Lane, 1962) is a convenient reprint of classics of Dickens criticism from Poe to Trilling. Three scholarly studies must also be mentioned: Humphry House, *The Dickens World* (1941), G. H. Ford, *Dickens and His Readers* (1955), John Butt and Kathleen Tillotson, *Dickens at Work* (1952; a study of the manuscripts and revisions). Two excellent background books—both by Philip Collins—are *Dickens and Crime* (1962) and *Dickens and Education* (1963). (*CBEL*, III, 435 f.)

Edward Lear (1812–1888). *Complete Nonsense*, edited by Holbrook Jackson (1947). Letters, edited by Lady [C.] Strachey (2 series, 1907–11). Selected journals by H. Van Thal (1952). There is a general account of Lear by A. Davidson (1938); for critical analysis see Elizabeth Sewell, *The Field of Nonsense* (1952). (*CBEL*, III, 567.)

Anthony Trollope (1815–1882). Barchester novels, edited by M. Sadleir (14 vols., 1929); Oxford Trollope, edited by Sadleir and F. Page (15 vols., 1948–54). *Doctor Thorne* (1959; good introduction by Elizabeth Bowen). Autobiography: edited by M. Sadleir (1923); edited by B. A. Booth (1947); edited by F. Page (1950; part of Oxford Trollope). Letters, edited by B. A. Booth (1951). A useful *Guide to Trollope* by W. G. and J. T. Gerould (1948) supplies the essential information. The most elaborate commentary is that by Michael Sadleir (1927, rev. 1945). There is a sound critical study by A. O. J. Cockshut (1955). Bibliography by Sadleir (1928, rev. 1936). (*CBEL*, III, 457 f.)

Charlotte Brontë (1816–1855). Standard edition by T. J. Wise and J. A. Symington (8 vols., 1932–38; also includes the unpublished writings of Emily, Anne, and Branwell Brontë). *Legends of Angria*, edited by Fannie E. Ratchford and W. C. De Vane (1933). The best modern biography is probably Lawrence and Elizabeth Hanson's *The Four Brontës* (1949). See also Fannie E. Ratchford's *The Brontës' Web of Childhood* (1941) on the juvenilia. Brontë bibliography by T. J. Wise (1917). (*CBEL*, III, 461 f.)

Emily Brontë (1818–1848). Complete poems, edited by C. W. Hatfield (1941). Two paperback editions of *Wuthering Heights* have good introductions—those of Mark Schorer (1950) and V. S. Pritchett (1956). See also Fannie E. Ratchford's *Gondal's Queen* (1955), and under Charlotte Brontë above. Mary Visick's *The Genesis of Wuthering Heights* (1958) is important for specialists. (*CBEL*, III, 462 f.)

Arthur Hugh Clough (1819–1861). Standard edition of poems by H. F. Lowry, A. L. P. Norrington, and F. L. Mulhauser (1951; critical text with early drafts, but no explanatory notes). Correspondence, edited by F. L. Mulhauser (2 vols., 1957; restricted to about half the extant letters). The latest life by Lady Chorley (1962), if tiresomely psychological, is more readable than that by Goldie Levy (1938). James I. Osborne's study (1920) relating the poems to Clough's personality has now been superseded by Walter E. Houghton's able and scholarly study (1963). See also H. F. Lowry's admirable edition of Matthew Arnold's letters to Clough (1932). A. M. Terhune summarizes recent articles on Clough in the Faverty *Guide to Research* (1956). (*CBEL*, III, 264 f.)

"George Eliot" (Mary Ann Evans, 1819–1880). Works (collected), illustrated copyright edition (21 vols. [1908–11]; uncritical). *Adam Bede*, edited by Gordon S. Haight (1948); *Middlemarch*, edited by Haight (1956; excellent notes). Letters, edited by Haight (7 vols., 1954–56; definitive edition). The various essays and reviews have been collected by T. C. Pinney (1963). The life by Lawrence and Elizabeth Hanson (1952) is competent and readable, though not always reliable. There are able critical studies by Joan Bennett (1948), F. R. Leavis (in *The Great*

Tradition, 1948), Barbara Hardy (1959), Jerome Thale (1959), and W. J. Harvey (1962); Jerome Beaty has recently investigated *Middlemarch from Notebook to Novel* (1960). There is a *George Eliot Dictionary* by Isadore G. Mudge and M. E. Sears (1924). (*CBEL,* III, 465 f.)

Charles Kingsley (1819–1875). The judicious biographical study by Margaret F. Thorp (1937) has a good bibliography; *The Dust of Combat* by Robert B. Martin (1959) is much slighter, if perhaps more readable. (*CBEL,* III, 487 f.)

John Ruskin (1819–1900). Definitive edition by E. T. Cook and A. Wedderburn (39 vols., 1903–12; complete works with full and strictly relevant annotation; includes many letters); diaries, edited by Joan Evans and J. H. Whitehouse (3 vols., 1956–59); *Praeterita,* edited by K. Clark (1949). *Ruskin as a Literary Critic,* edited by A. H. R. Bell (1928), is a useful selection; more general is Peter Quennell's (1952). An elaborate biography has been begun by Helen G. Volgoen (Vol. I, 1956), but for most purposes Derrick Leon's (1949) and Joan Evans's (1954) single-volume lives suffice. Henry Ladd's *The Victorian Morality of Art* (1932) is an intelligent introduction to Ruskin's thinking. The most recent general study is John Rosenberg's *The Darkening Glass* (1962). (*CBEL,* III, 691 f.)

Matthew Arnold (1822–1888). Standard edition (15 vols., 1903–4) is incomplete and textually unreliable. The critical edition of the poems by C. B. Tinker and H. F. Lowry (1950) has no explanatory notes and is to be used with their densely factual *Commentary* (1940). Kenneth Allott's edition of the poems (including manuscript fragments) in chronological order (1965) has detailed explanatory notes. Some uncollected essays and reviews have been edited by Fraser Neiman (1960); R. H. Super is now bringing out a model edition of all the prose (4 vols.

issued 1960–64). The *Note-Books* edited by H. F.
Lowry, K. Young, and W. H. Dunn (1952) are re-
stricted to the literary entries. *Letters,* edited by G. W. E.
Russell (2 vols., 1895; revised for Volumes XIII–XV of
Works, 1904) must now be supplemented by H. F.
Lowry's exemplary edition of the remarkable letters to
Clough (1932).

The life by E. K. Chambers (1947), a mere efficient
recitation of the available facts, is decidedly inferior to
the "psychological" interpretation by Louis Bonnerot
(1942; in French). Of the general studies, Lionel Trilling's (1939) is probably the best, though E. K. Brown's
slighter *Arnold: a Study in Conflict* (1948) is shrewd and
well-written. H. W. Garrod's *Poetry and the Criticism of
Life* (1931) discusses Arnold's critical principles wittily if
rather superficially. The poems are discussed in Edward
D. H. Johnson's refreshing *Alien Vision* (1952). Of the
specialist studies, F. E. Faverty's *Arnold the Ethnologist*
(1951) is outstanding. Faverty summarizes the shorter
essays and articles on Arnold in his *Guide to Research*
(1956). There is a concordance by Stephen M. Parrish
(1959). Bibliography by T. B. Smart (1892; rev. in the
Works, Vol. XV, 1904). (*CBEL,* III, 265 f.)

Coventry Patmore (1823–1896). Complete poems edited by Frederick Page (1949; no explanatory notes);
selected poems, edited by Derek Patmore (1931, rev.
1949; no notes). *Essay on English Metrical Law,* edited
by Mary A. Roth (1961; with detailed commentary).
The official life by Basil Champneys (2 vols., 1900) has
been superseded by Derek Patmore's *Life and Times*
(1949) and E. J. Oliver's short and stylish biography
(1956). The best critical study is that by Frederick Page
(1933), the fullest that by J. C. Reid (1957); Osbert
Burdett's book (1921) is still of some interest. Lionel
Stevenson has a section on Patmore in the Faverty *Guide
to Research* (1956). (*CBEL,* III, 270 f.)

Wilkie Collins (1824–1889). No collected edition of the novels; *The Moonstone* (1928) has an introduction by T. S. Eliot. There are two recent lives of Collins—by Kenneth Robinson (1951) and N. P. Davis (1956). (*CBEL*, III, 480 f.)

Walter Bagehot (1826–1877). *Biographical and Literary Studies*, edited by G. Sampson (2 vols., 1911; Everyman's Library). *The English Constitution*, edited by R. H. S. Crossman (1963). Modern studies by William Irvine (1939), Alastair Buchan (1959), and N. St. John-Stevas (1959). (*CBEL*, III, 707 f.)

George Meredith (1828–1909). Memorial edition (27 vols., 1909–11) is complete but unannotated (passages later omitted, etc., with bibliography in Vol. XXVII). A better bibliography was compiled by M. B. Forman, 1922 (Supplement 1924), which also lists every scrap *about* Meredith. *Beauchamp's Career* has been edited by G. M. Young (1950) and *The Egoist* by Lord Dunsany (1947). Standard edition of poems by G. M. Trevelyan (1912); selected poems, edited by Graham Hough (1962; short but well done). The best life is that by Lionel Stevenson (1953), and the most thorough general study that by René Galland (1923; in French, stops at 1878). Galland has also assembled extensive extracts from the early reviews (Paris, 1923). There is no first-rate criticism. G. M. Trevelyan's study of the poetry (1906) retains its value; there are recent critiques of the novels by Siegfried Sassoon (1948) and Walter F. Wright (1953). Norman Kelvin's *Troubled Eden* (1961) includes the poems as well. (*CBEL*, III, 467 f.)

Dante Gabriel Rossetti (1828–1882). Works, edited by W. M. Rossetti (1911; in chronological order of composition). Poems, edited by Oswald Doughty (1957; complete). Elaborate editions of *The House of Life* (1928), *Poems, Ballads, and Sonnets* (1937), and *The Blessed Damozel* (1937) by P. F. Baum. Baum also supervised the important *List of Manuscripts in Duke University Library with Unpublished Verse and Prose* (1931). The letters in W. M. Rossetti's *Memoir* (2 vols., 1895) need to be supplemented by the separate collections—to William Allingham (1897), F. S. Ellis (1927), Fanny Cornforth (1940), etc. A. C. Benson's short life (1904) has merit but has been superseded by Oswald Doughty's frank and well-informed *A Victorian Romantic* (1949). For other books and the articles, Howard Mumford Jones's chapter in the Faverty *Guide to Research* (1956) may be consulted. (*CBEL*, III, 271 f.)

Christina Georgina Rossetti (1830–1894). Complete poems, edited by W. M. Rossetti (1904; in chronological order of composition with notes; some manuscript poems omitted). The two best lives are those of Mackenzie Bell (1898) and Mary F. Sandars (1930). There are critical studies by Dorothy M. Stuart (1930) and Fredegond Shove (1931) and a detailed and persuasive biographical interpretation by Lona M. Packer (1964). See also H. M. Jones under D. G. Rossetti above. (*CBEL*, III, 273 f.)

"Mark Rutherford" (William Hale White, 1831–1913). No critical edition of the novels. There are studies by Wilfrid Stone (1954) and Irvin Stock (1956), and a good life by Catherine M. Maclean (1955). (*CBEL*, III, 559 f.)

"Lewis Carroll" (Charles Lutwidge Dodgson, 1832–1898). Complete works, introduction by Alexander Woollcott (1939); another edition (1949). Diaries, edited by R. L. Green (2 vols., 1954). In addition to the official life by S. D. Collingwood (1898), there is a competent modern biography by R. L. Green (1949). The bibliographical *Handbook* by S. H. Williams and F. Madan, revised by R. L. Green (1962), is a mine of information. (*CBEL*, III, 513 f.)

Leslie Stephen (1832–1904). No collected edition; see p. 107 above for the principal critical writings. S. O. A. Ullmann has reprinted a number of uncollected essays from various periodicals (*Men, Books, and Mountains,* 1956). The official *Life and Letters* by F. W. Maitland (1906) was very well done, and there is a brilliant, provocative, biographical study by Noel Annan (1951). (*CBEL,* III, 727 f.)

William Morris (1834–1896). Collected works, edited by May Morris (24 vols., 1910–15); a good selection by G. D. H. Cole (1934). J. W. Mackail's intelligent official life (2 vols., 1899) now needs supplementing both by May Morris's biography (2 vols., 1939) and by the solidly factual Marxist account of Edward P. Thompson (1955). A reliable general study is Margaret B. Grennan's *William Morris, Medievalist and Revolutionary* (1945). (*CBEL,* III, 314 f.)

James Thomson (1834–1882). Collected poems: edited by Bertram Dobell (2 vols., 1895; preliminary memoir enlarged as *The Laureate of Pessimism,* 1910); edited by Terence L. Connolly (1932, rev. 1941; useful notes). Selected poems: edited by G. H. Gerould (1927), Edmund Blunden (1932), and Anne Ridler (1963; very thorough with good use made of manuscripts). *Biographical and Critical Studies,* edited by B. Dobell (1896). *Literary Criticism,* edited by T. L. Connolly (1948; more essays and reviews 1959). H. S. Salt's life (1898, rev. 1914) is still useful. For criticism see Pierre Danchin's elaborate study (Paris, 1959; in French). Emogene B. Walker's *James Thomson* (1950) is a general account embodying much new material. (*CBEL,* III, 316 f.)

Samuel Butler (1835–1902). Works, edited by H. F. Jones and A. T. Bartholomew (20 vols., 1923–26); selection edited by G. D. H. Cole (1950). Notebooks, edited by G. Keynes and B. Hill (1951). In addition to Henry Festing Jones's official memoir (2 vols., 1919) and the elaborate French thesis by J. B. Fort (Paris, 1934), there is an acute short study by P. N. Furbank (1948), which is partly a reply to Malcolm Muggeridge's debunking *The Earnest Atheist* (1936). Stanley B. Harkness's bibliography (1955) lists everything by and about Butler with an essay on his fame. (*CBEL*, III, 728 f.)

Sir William Schwenk Gilbert (1836–1911). No critical edition. There is a good life by Sidney Dark and Rowland Grey (1923). See also W. A. Darlington, *The World of Gilbert and Sullivan* (1950). Bibliography by Townley Searle (1931). (*CBEL*, III, 610 f.)

Algernon Charles Swinburne (1837–1909). Complete works, edited by E. Gosse and T. J. Wise (20 vols., 1925–27; Bonchurch edition, some new matter but textually unreliable and with no notes). Annotated selected poems, edited by C. K. Hyder and L. Chase (1937). Letters, edited by C. Y. Lang (6 vols., 1960–62; definitive edition). Although Edmund Gosse's *Life of Swinburne* (1917, rev. 1927 as Vol. XIX of Bonchurch edition) makes pleasant reading, it is greatly inferior to G. Lafourcade's extremely thorough *La jeunesse de Swinburne* (2 vols., Paris, 1928) and his English "Literary Biography" (1932). The most successful critical studies to date are those of Harold Nicolson (1926), T. Earle Welby (1926), and S. C. Chew (1929; more scholarly). C. K. Hyder's *Swinburne's Literary Career and Fame* (1933) is a useful work of erudition; Hyder summarizes other books and articles in Faverty's *Guide to Research* (1956). Bibliography by T. J. Wise (2 vols., 1919–20). (*CBEL*, III, 317 f.)

Walter Pater (1839–1894). Collected works, 9 vols., 1900–1 (uncritical). *Marius the Epicurean*, edited by O. Burdett (1934). A. C. Benson's engaging little book (1906) needs supplementing biographically by Thomas Wright's rather ponderous life (2 vols., 1907). A.-J. Farmer's short study of *Appreciations* (Grenoble, 1931) and the thorough but verbose general survey in French by Germain d'Hangest (2 vols., Paris, 1961) are for specialists. (*CBEL*, III, 731 f.)

Thomas Hardy (1840–1928). Collected works, 23 vols., 1912–13 (uncritical). Collected poems (1932). Notebooks, edited by Evelyn Hardy (1955). *Far from the Madding Crowd,* edited by C. J. Weber (1959); *Tess of the d'Urbervilles,* edited by F. B. Pinion (1959). The official biography (*Early Life,* 1928; *Later Years,* 1930), nominally by his widow, was really written by Hardy himself. The standard life, however, is Carl J. Weber's *Hardy of Wessex* (1940); Weber has also edited Hardy's letters to his first wife (1963). Much biographical and other matter is accumulated in R. L. Purdy's indispensable bibliographical commentary (1954). The most illuminating of the critical studies are perhaps those of Lascelles Abercrombie (1912), W. R. Rutland (1938), David Cecil (1943), and A. J. Guérard (1949). There is a competent discussion of the poetry by S. L. Hynes (1961), and John Paterson has recently described *The Making of "The Return of the Native"* (1960). A representative collection of recent critical essays on Hardy has been edited by A. J. Guérard (1963). (*CBEL,* III, 516 f.)

Charles Montagu Doughty (1843–1926). Edition of *Arabia Deserta* by T. E. Lawrence (2 vols., 1921); abridgement by Edward Garnett (1931). The only life of Doughty is the official one by D. G. Hogarth (1928); there is a sensible pioneering critical study by Barker Fairley (1927). (*CBEL,* III, 338 f.)

Robert Bridges (1844–1930). Poetical works (6 vols., 1898–1905); shorter poems, edited by M. M. Bridges (1931); poetical works excluding the eight dramas (1936). Collected essays (30 parts, 1927–36). There is a slim but well-annotated selection from the prose and verse by John Sparrow (1955). The nearest thing to a biography is Jean-Georges Ritz's account of the Bridges–Hopkins friendship (1960). The best critical study of Bridges is by Albert Guérard (1942); Nowell C. Smith's *Notes on the Testament of Beauty* (1932, rev. 1940) identifies sources, quotations, etc. Bibliography by G. L. McKay (1933). (*CBEL*, III, 323 f.)

Gerard Manley Hopkins (1844–1889). Poems: edited by Robert Bridges (1918; some notes, important critical "Preface to Notes"), revised by Charles Williams (1930; adds some more poems), revised by W. H. Gardner (1948; complete re-editing with many new pieces added as well as more notes). *Note-books and Papers,* edited by Humphry House (1937; some notes), revised by Graham Storey (1959; greatly enlarged and improved); *Sermons and Devotional Writings,* edited by Christopher Devlin (1959). Letters: to Bridges (ed. C. C. Abbott, 1935, rev. 1955); to R. W. Dixon (ed. Abbott, 1935, rev. 1955); other letters (ed. Abbott 1937, rev. 1956). Selected prose and verse: edited by W. H. Gardner (1953; good notes); edited by John Pick (1953; much more prose than in Gardner).

The standard biographical-critical study is by W. H. Gardner (2 vols., 1944–49, Vol. I rev. 1948). John Pick's critical study (1942), a collection of articles from the *Kenyon Review* (1944), a Jesuit collection (ed. N. Weyand, 1949) entitled *Immortal Diamond,* and the elaborate account of "inscape" by W. A. M. Peters (1948) must also be consulted. Jean-Georges Ritz (1960) has traced the friendship with Robert Bridges, adding some new details. Pick summarizes the state of Hopkins studies in the Faverty *Guide to Research* (1956). (*CBEL*, III, 325 f.)

Robert Louis Stevenson (1850–1894). Collected works: edited by S. Colvin (28 vols., 1894–98; Edinburgh edition); edited by L. Osbourne and F. Van de G. Stevenson (26 vols., 1922–23; Vailima edition). Collected poems, edited by Janet A. Smith (1950; definitive edition). Selected novels and stories, edited by V. S. Pritchett (1945). Letters, edited by S. Colvin (4 vols., 1912), also letters to Henry James (ed. Janet A. Smith, 1948), to Charles Baxter (ed. J. De L. Ferguson and M. Waingrow,

1956), etc.; a definitive edition is being prepared by Bradford A. Booth. The official life by Graham Balfour (2 vols., 1901) has not been surpassed; there is a judicious critical study by David Daiches (1947). Bibliography by W. F. Prideaux (1903, rev. Flora L. Livingston 1917). (*CBEL*, III, 520 f.)

Oscar Wilde (1854–1900). Works, 14 vols., 1908; edited by G. F. Maine (1948; uncritical). *The Importance of Being Earnest*, edited by V. Holland (2 vols., 1957; from original manuscript); *De Profundis*, edited by V. Holland (1949; first complete edition). The meticulous edition of Wilde's letters by Rupert Hart-Davis (1962) supersedes all the earlier biographies. Some sensible criticism will be found in St. John Ervine's study (1951), though it does not replace Arthur Ransome's admirable assessment (1912). See also F. Winwar, *Oscar Wilde and the Yellow Nineties* (1941). (*CBEL*, III, 620 f.)

George Bernard Shaw (1856–1950). Works, 33 vols., 1930–38 (uncritical); complete plays (1931); collected prefaces (1934). Collected letters in progress (ed. Dan H. Laurence, Vol. I [1874–97], 1964). Selected prose, edited by Diarmuid Russell (1952). Archibald Henderson's immensely detailed life (1932, revised and rewritten 1956) can be supplemented by Hesketh Pearson's gossipy *G.B.S.* (1942) and St. John Ervine's opinionated *Bernard Shaw* (1956). There is a brilliant early critical study by G. K. Chesterton (1909); Edmund Wilson's essay in *The Triple Thinkers* (1938) is worth reading but is less substantial than Eric Bentley's study *George Bernard Shaw* (1947). (*CBEL*, III, 617 f.)

George Gissing (1857–1903). No collected edition, miscellaneous pieces edited by A. C. Gissing (1938). *The New Grub Street* has been edited by G. W. Stonier (1958). Letters between Gissing and H. G. Wells edited by R. A. Geltman (1961), and those to Eduard Bertz edited by A. C. Young (1961). Studies by Mabel C. Donnelly (1954; mainly biographical) and J. Korg (1963). (*CBEL,* III, 525 f.)

Joseph Conrad (1857–1924), né Józef Konrad Korzeniowski. Works, 22 vols., 1923–28 (an important "Author's Note" prefixed to each volume except XXII). Collected letters (ed. Edward Garnett, 1928) must be supplemented from the individual correspondences, especially the letters to Richard Curle (1928) and to Marguerite Poradowska (1940). Selection (2 novels, 3 tales) edited by M. D. Zabel (1947; good introduction). *Lord Jim:* edited by R. Heilman (1957; excellent critical apparatus); *Nostromo,* edited by R. P. Warren (1961). Also paperback editions by M. D. Zabel (1956–63), all with good introductions, of *Lord Jim, Under Western Eyes, The Nigger of the "Narcissus," Youth, Heart of Darkness,* and *The End of the Tether.* The two best biographies are by G. Jean-Aubry (1957; supersedes his earlier *Joseph Conrad: Life and Letters,* 2 vols., 1927) and Jocelyn Baines (1960; first-class); his widow's reminiscences of Conrad and his friends (1926 and 1935) and Richard Curle's *Last Twelve Years of Conrad* (1928) are also important. Of the numerous critical studies those of Muriel C. Bradbrook (1941; very short), Albert Guérard (1947), Douglas Hewitt (1952), and Thomas Moser (1957) are perhaps the most useful. The bibliography by K. A. Lohf and E. P. Sheehy (1957) lists other editions and studies 1895–1955.

Alfred Edward Housman (1859–1936). Collected poems, edited by John Sparrow (1956; some notes); manuscript poems, edited by T. B. Haber (1955; unreliable texts). *A Shropshire Lad,* edited by C. J. Weber (1946; some notes). Selected prose, edited by John Carter (1961). Biographical matter will be found in A. S. F. Gow (1936), Laurence Housman (1937), Grant Richards (1941), Percy Withers (1940), and George L. Watson (1957), though none of these memoirs constitutes a thorough biography. Criticism of Housman has been limited hitherto to essays and articles; details are provided by Lionel Stevenson in the Faverty *Guide to Research* (1956). There is a Housman concordance by C. K. Hyder (1940) and a bibliography by John Carter and John Sparrow (1952). (*CBEL*, III, 326.)

Francis Thompson (1859–1907). Works, edited by Wilfrid Meynell (3 vols., 1913; uncritical); collected poems, edited by L. Connolly (1941; with useful notes); literary criticism, edited by Connolly (1948; includes unidentified reviews). Engaging official life by Everard Meynell (1913) is supplemented by Viola Meynell's *Francis Thompson and Wilfrid Meynell* (1952). There is a good new life by Paul van K. Thomson (1961). Two useful general studies are those of J. C. Reid (1959) and Pierre Danchin (1959; in French). (*CBEL*, III, 326 f.)

James Matthew Barrie (1860–1937). Plays, edited by A. E. Wilson (1928, rev. 1942; twenty-six plays, no notes). Letters, edited by Viola Meynell (1942). See also Denis Mackail, *The Story of JMB* (1941), and Cynthia Asquith's *Portrait of Barrie* (1955). Bibliography by H. Garland (1928). (*CBEL*, III, 623 f.)

Rudyard Kipling (1865–1936). Complete works, 31 vols., 1913–38 (Bombay edition, includes pieces not published elsewhere). Complete poetry (1940); selected poems, edited by T. S. Eliot (1941; critical introduction reprinted in Eliot's *On Poetry and Poets*, 1957). The authorized biography is by C. E. Carrington (1955). There are full-length critical studies by Edward Shanks (1940), Hilton Brown (1945), J. M. S. Tompkins (1959; most perceptive but deals mainly with the later stories), and C. A. Bodelsen (1964). See also the acute essays by Edmund Wilson (in *The Wound and the Bow*, 1941) and George Orwell (in his *Critical Essays*, 1946), both of which have been reprinted (with nine less familiar appreciations) by A. Rutherford as *Kipling's Mind and Art*

(1964). Bibliography by J. McG. Stewart (ed. A. W. Yeats, 1959). (*CBEL*, III, 527 f.)

William Butler Yeats (1865–1939). Collected poems: 1950 (first complete edition); edited by P. Allt and R. K. Alspach (1957; gives variant readings from all printed editions). Collected plays, 1952 (first complete edition). Autobiographies, 1953 (complete). Collected essays and introductions, 1961 (adds two unpublished essays). Letters, edited by Allan Wade (1954). The official life is by J. M. Hone (1943, rev. 1962). Perhaps the best critical studies of Yeats are those of Richard Ellmann (1948 and 1954; based on Yeats's manuscripts); others of some distinction are those of Louis MacNeice (1941), Norman Jeffares (1949; useful for manuscripts quoted), T. R. Henn (1950), Peter Ure (1963; on the plays), and Jon Stallworthy (1963; Yeats's methods of composition in eighteen poems). Frank Kermode's influential *Romantic Image* (1957) is largely concerned with Yeats. Shorter critical discussions have been assembled by James Hall and Martin Steinmann (1950). A useful factual poem-by-poem commentary has been compiled by John Unterecker (1959). Somewhat similar are the two *Prolegomena* by G. B. Saul—to the poems (1957) and to the plays (1958). Of the specialist studies Mrs. H. H. Vindler's *Yeats's "Vision" and the Later Plays* (1962) is outstanding. Concordance by S. M. Parrish and J. A. Painter (1963). Bibliography by Allan Wade (1951, rev. 1958). (*CBEL*, III, 1059 f.)

Herbert George Wells (1866–1946). Collected works, 28 vols., 1924–27 (Atlantic edition, revised text with new prefaces). Collected short stories, 1927. Letters to and from Henry James, edited by L. Edel and G. N. Ray (1958), to and from George Gissing, edited by R. A. Gettmann (1961). A recent biography is by Vincent Brome (1951). Critical discussions by Antonina Vallatin (1950) and Bernard Bergonzi (1960; a perceptive study of the scientific romances). The bibliography by Geoffrey H.

Wells (1926) includes a Wells dictionary and a subject index.

Arnold Bennett (1867–1931). No collected edition of novels. Journals: edited by Newman Flower (3 vols., 1932–38); selection edited by Hugh Swinnerton (1954). *Anna of the Five Towns,* edited by Swinnerton (1954); *The Grand Babylon Hotel,* edited by Swinnerton (1954); *The Old Wives' Tale,* edited by Swinnerton (1954); *Clayhanger,* edited by Swinnerton (1954); *Riceyman Steps,* edited by Swinnerton (1954). There is a life of Bennett by Reginald Pound (1952). In addition to Virginia Woolf's gayly depreciatory *Mr. Bennett and Mrs. Brown* (1924) there are substantial critical studies by Georges Lafourcade (1939), Walter Allen (1948), and John Wain (in *Preliminary Essays,* 1957).

Ernest Dowson (1867–1900). Standard edition of poems by Mark Longaker (1963). (*CBEL*, III, 339 f.)

John Galsworthy (1867–1933). *The Man of Property* has been edited by Lionel Stevenson (1949). The official *Life and Letters of John Galsworthy* (1935) is by H. V. Marrot. There is also a critical study by Dudley Barker (1963).

Hilaire Belloc (1870–1953). Selected essays, edited by J. B. Morton (1948). Collected verse, edited by W. N. Roughead (1954). The official life of Belloc is by Robert Speaight (1957).

"Saki" (Hector Hugh Munro, 1870–1916). Short stories (1930, enlarged 1948; with memoir by Ethel M. Munro). Novels and plays (1933).

John Millington Synge (1871–1909). Collected works, edited by Robin Skelton (5 vols., Vol. I, 1962; definitive edition); edited by T. R. Henn (1963; good notes, etc., but includes only items published by Synge himself). Authorized life by David H. Greene and Edward M.

Stephens (1959). A short autobiography has been reconstructed by Alan F. Price from Synge's notebooks (1963); Price's *Synge and Anglo-Irish Drama* (1961) is the best critical study so far. (*CBEL*, III, 1062 f.)

Max Beerbohm (1872–1956). Selection, edited by S. C. Roberts (1962). Official life by David Cecil (1964). J. G. Riewald's elaborate study (The Hague, 1953) discusses the uncollected articles as well as the books; Riewald has also collected Beerbohm's scattered verse (1964).

William H. Davies (1871–1940). Collected poems (1963; introduction by Osbert Sitwell). An excellent critical biography by Richard J. Stonesifer (1963).

Ford Madox Ford, earlier Hueffer (1873–1939). Novels, edited by Graham Greene (4 vols., 1962–63). *The Good Soldier*, edited by Mark Schorer (1951). There are critical studies of the novels by R. A. Cassell (1962), John A. Meixner (1963), and Carol Ohmann (1964). D. D. Harvey's bibliography (1963) gives extracts from principal critiques of Ford. (BCB by Kenneth Young.)

Walter de la Mare (1873–1956). Collected poems (1942); collected rhymes and verses (1944); collected stories for children (1947). Selections from the verse by W. H. Auden (1963). There are critical studies by R. L. Mégroz (1924) and Forrest Reid (1929).

Gilbert Keith Chesterton (1874–1936). Selection from uncollected prose by A. L. Maycock (1963; good introduction). Lives by Maurice Evans (1939) and Maisie Ward (1944).

William Somerset Maugham (b. 1874). Collected plays, 6 vols., 1931–32. Complete short stories (3 vols., 1951). Selected novels (3 vols., 1953). *Of Human Bondage*, edited by R. A. Cordell (1956; good introduction). *The Maugham Enigma*, edited by Klaus W. Jonas (1954), is a collection of essays and reviews on Maugham, 1908–54.

There are competent critical studies by Richard A. Cordell (1961) and Laurence Brander (1963). (BCB by J. Brophy.)

Harley Granville-Barker (1877–1946). There are two recent studies of Granville-Barker—by C. B. Purdom (1955) and Margery M. Morgan (1961; thorough and level-headed).

John Masefield (b. 1878). Collected works, 5 vols., 1935–37. There is a clever study of Masefield by Muriel Spark (1953). (BCB by L. A. G. Strong.)

Edward Thomas (1878–1917). Collected poems, edited by W. de la Mare (1920, enlarged 1928). The life of Thomas has been written by John Moore (1939); there is a perceptive critical study by H. Coombes (1956). Biographical bibliography by R. P. Eckbert (1937).

Edward Morgan Forster (b. 1879). Collected short stories, 1947. Rose Macaulay's *The Writings of Forster* (1938) is readable but thin critically and not in the same class with Lionel Trilling's short study, *E. M. Forster* (1943). The best critical study of Forster so far is probably that by Frederick C. Crews (1962), but three recent surveys by James MacConkey (1957), K. W. Gransden (1962), and J. B. Beer (1961) are all of critical interest. See also J. K. Johnstone's *The Bloomsbury Group* (1954). Bibliography by B. J. Kirkpatrick (1964). (BCB by Rex Warner.)

Lytton Strachey (1880–1932). Collected works, 6 vols., 1948–52 (incomplete). The letters to and from Virginia Woolf have been edited by Leonard Woolf and James Strachey (1956). There is a useful study by C. P. Sanders, *Strachey: His Mind and Art* (1957); J. K. Johnstone's *The Bloomsbury Group* (1954) gives a lively account of Strachey and his circle. (BCB by R. A. Scott-James.)

Leopold Hamilton Myers (1881–1944). *The Near and the Far* (1943; collected edition of the four novels set in sixteenth-century India). There is a very good critical study of Myers's novels by G. H. Bantock (1956).

James Joyce (1882–1941). Collected poems, 1936. *Stephen Hero*, edited by Theodore Spencer (1944, enlarged 1955; first draft of *Portrait of the Artist*). Selections: edited by T. S. Eliot (1942); edited by Harry Levin (1947). Letters, edited by Stuart Gilbert (1957). Critical writings, edited by Ellsworth Mason and Richard Ellman (1959). There is a first-rate life of Joyce by Ellman (1959), and an extremely interesting account of his early years by his brother Stanislaus, *My Brother's Keeper* (1958). The best general book on Joyce is probably Harry Levin's short *Joyce: a Critical Introduction* (1941); Hugh Kenner's *James Joyce* (1956) and the Richard McKain and Marvin Magalaner *Joyce* (1956) are more ambitious —and pretentious—appreciations. There is also a judicious, level-headed study by S. L. Goldberg (1961). For *Ulysses* the standard aid is Stuart Gilbert's interpretation (1930, rev. 1952), as the Joseph Campbell and Henry M. Robinson *Skeleton Key* (1944) is to *Finnegan's Wake*—of which David Hayman has edited the first draft (1963) and Clive Hart has now compiled a special concordance (1963). T. E. Connolly has assembled twenty essays on *The Portrait of the Artist* (1964). Bibliography by J. J. Slocum and H. Cahoon (1953). (BCB by J. I. M. Stewart.)

Virginia Woolf (1882–1941). Uniform edition, 14 vols., 1929–52 (novels and essays). Diary, edited by Leonard Woolf (1953; extracts only). Letters to and from Lytton Strachey, edited by Leonard Woolf and James Strachey (1956). Of the numerous studies of the novels the best are probably those by D. Daiches (1942), Bernard Blackstone (1949), Joan M. Bennett (1954), and Dorothy Brewster (1963; woolly but factual). Leonard Woolf's own autobiography (especially Part II, 1964) is indispensable.

See also J. K. Johnstone's *The Bloomsbury Group* (1954).
Bibliography by B. J. Kirkpatrick (1957). (BCB by Virginia Woolf.)

Wyndham Lewis (1884–1957). Letters, edited by
W. K. Rose (1963). Hugh Kenner (1954) and Geoffrey
Wagner (1957) have both discussed Lewis's literary
achievement in some detail. (BCB by Clifford Dyment.)

David Herbert Lawrence (1885–1930). Works, 33
vols., 1936–39. Letters, edited by Aldous Huxley (1932;
good introduction); selection by Diana Trilling (1958;
adds to Huxley). *Phoenix: Posthumous Papers*, edited
by Ed. D. McDonald (1936; collected essays, reviews,
etc.). Complete poems, 3 vols., 1957. Selected literary
criticism, edited by Anthony Beal (1955). Selected writings, edited by Diana Trilling (1947). *Sons and Lovers*,
edited by Mark Schorer (1955; good introduction); *The
Plumed Serpent*, edited by W. Y. Tindall (1951; excellent introduction). J. Middleton Murry's account of Lawrence (1931, with new introduction 1954) is the most
informative of those written by his personal friends, but
the best life to date is Harry T. Moore's *The Intelligent
Heart* (1955, rev. 1960). Moore is also the author of a
useful *Reader's Guide to D. H. Lawrence* (1951, rev.
1964). The two best critical studies to date in their very
different ways are probably F. R. Leavis's *D. H. Lawrence, Novelist* (1955) and Graham Hough's *The Dark
Sun* (1956). There are recent studies by Kingsley Widmer
(1962), Julian Moynahan (1963), and E. W. Tedlock
(1963). (BCB by Kenneth Young.)

Ronald Firbank (1886–1926). Collected works: edited
by Arthur Waley (5 vols., 1929; with memoir by Osbert
Sitwell); edited by Anthony Powell (1961). Critical study
by Jocelyn Brooke (1951). Bibliography by Miriam J.
Benkowitz (1963).

Edith Sitwell (b. 1887). Collected poems, 1957. (BCB
by John Lehmann.)

Rupert Brooke (1887–1915). Collected poems, 1918 (with memoir by Edward Marsh); edited by Geoffrey Keynes (1946; no notes). Collected prose, edited by Christopher Hassall (1956). Hassall also wrote the best life of Brooke (1964).

Edwin Muir (1887–1959). Collected poems, edited by J. C. Hall (1952; no notes). There is a short critical study by P. H. Butter (1962). (BCB by J. C. Hall.)

Joyce Cary (1888–1957). Carfax edition of novels in progress (1951–   ; with prefaces). *The Horse's Mouth,* edited by Andrew Wright (1957; good introduction, includes discarded chapter). Miss M. M. Mahood's *Joyce Cary's Africa* (1964) is an account of the African novels and Cary's period in Nigeria. Critical study of the novels by Robert Bloom (1963). (BCB by Walter Allen.)

Thomas Stearns Eliot (b. 1888). Complete poems and plays, 1952 (omits *Confidential Clerk* and *Elder Statesman*). Collected poems (1963). Selected prose, edited by John Hayward (1953). The best introduction to Eliot is F. O. Matthiessen's lucid and level-headed book *The Achievement of T. S. Eliot* (1935, enlarged by C. L. Barber 1947); Hugh Kenner's *Invisible Poet* (1960) is almost too clever. Some interesting critical-biographical odds and ends are to be found in the homages edited by B. Rajan (1947), and that edited by R. March and Tambimuttu (1948). Helen Gardner's *The Art of Eliot* (1949) is mainly useful for *Four Quartets;* George Williamson's *A Reader's Guide to Eliot* (1953) and Grover Smith's *Eliot's Poetry and Plays* (1956) are both careful and helpful primers, identifying quotations, references, etc. Genesius Jones's *Approach to the Purpose* (1964) is a more sophisticated critical survey (confined to the poetry). Leonard Unger assembled some of the best of the earlier discussions of Eliot in 1948. Bibliography by Donald Gallup (1952). (BCB by M. C. Bradbrook.)

"Katherine Mansfield" (Kathleen Mansfield Beauchamp, 1888–1923). Collected stories, 1945. Selected stories: edited by J. Middleton Murry (1930); edited by D. M. Davin (1953). Journal, edited by J. Middleton Murry (1927, enlarged 1954). Letters, edited by J. Middleton Murry (2 vols., 1928). See Ruth E. Mantz and J. Middleton Murry, *The Life of Katherine Mansfield* (1933). There is a critical study by Antony Alpers (1954) and a bibliography by Ruth E. Mantz (1931). (BCB by Ian Gordon.)

Robin George Collingwood (1889–1943). (BCB by E. W. F. Tomlin.)

Ivy Compton-Burnett (b. 1892). Robert Liddell has written judiciously on *The Novels of I. Compton-Burnett* (1955). (BCB by Pamela Hansford-Johnson.)

"Hugh MacDiarmid" (Christopher Murray Grieve, b. 1892). Collected poems, 1962.

Wilfrid Owen (1893–1918). Poems: edited by Siegfried Sassoon (1920); edited by Edmund Blunden (1931; adds many poems and fragments to the Sassoon collection); edited by C. Day Lewis (1963; includes other unpublished poems). There is a careful critical study of Owen's work by D. S. R. Welland (1960), and his brother Harold's reminiscences (Vol. I, 1963) are of interest.

Ivor Armstrong Richards (b. 1893). See p. 203 below.

Aldous Huxley (1894–1963). Collected short stories, 1956. Collected essays, 1960. Collected criticism, 1960. Selections: 1937 (Everyman's Library); edited by C. J. Rolo (1947). *Point Counter Point,* edited by H. H. Watts (1947); *Brave New World,* edited by C. J. Rolo (1960; includes *Brave New World Revisited*). (BCB by Jocelyn Brooke.)

John Boynton Priestley (b. 1894). Plays, 3 vols., 1948–

50. (BCB by Ivor Brown.) There is an "informal" study by David Hughes (1958).

Leslie Poles Hartley (b. 1895). *Eustace and Hilda,* edited by David Cecil (1947). There is a critical study by Peter Bien (1963). (BCB by P. Bloomfield.)

Robert Graves (b. 1895). Collected poems, 1959 (in fact a selection by Graves himself, the latest of a series of such collections from 1926, each professing to be the definitive text of the corpus). The short critical study by J. M. Cohen (1960) has been superseded by Douglas Day's more ambitious *Swifter than Reason* (1964). (BCB by M. Seymour Smith.)

Edmund Blunden (b. 1896). Selected poems, edited by Rupert Hart-Davis (1957). (BCB by Alec M. Hardie.)

Elizabeth Bowen (b. 1899). (BCB by Jocelyn Brooke.)

Roy Campbell (1901–1957). Collected poems, 2 vols., 1949–57. (BCB by David Wright.)

Evelyn Waugh (b. 1903). See the study by Frederick T. Stopp (1958) and, for the Catholic novels only, A. A. DeVit (1958). (BCB by Christopher Hollis.)

"George Orwell" (Eric Arthur Blair, 1903–1950). Collected essays, 1961. There are books on Orwell by John Atkins (1954), Laurence Brander (1954), and Christopher Hollis (1956), all personal acquaintances, and a more academic study by Richard J. Voorhees (1961). (BCB by Tom Hopkinson.)

Graham Greene (b. 1904). There is a first-rate critical study by Kenneth and Miriam Allott (1951). (BCB by Francis Wyndham.)

"Henry Green" (Henry Vincent Yorke, b. 1905). See Edward Stokes, *The Novels of Henry Green* (1959).

Samuel Beckett (b. 1906). There is a critical study of

Beckett of great interest by Hugh Kenner (1962). J. Fletcher's study (1964) is confined to the novels.

William Empson (b. 1906). Collected poems (1955). See also p. 204 below.

Wystan Hugh Auden (b. 1907). Collected shorter poems, 1950. Richard Hoggart's *Introductory Essay* (1951) is level-headed and well-informed, *The Making of the Auden Canon* (1952) by Joseph W. Beach polemical but substantial, but both are superseded by the detailed study by Monroe K. Spears, *The Poetry of W. H. Auden* (1963). (BCB by Richard Hoggart.)

Roy Fuller (b. 1912). Collected poems (1962).

Dylan Thomas (1914–1953). Collected poems, 1934–52 (1952). Studies by Elder Olson (1954; ambitious, often unconvincing), and Ralph Maud (1963; the best critical study to date). See also the symposium edited by E. W. Tedlock (1960; biographical and critical). Bibliography by J. A. Rolph (1956). (BCB by G. S. Fraser.)

X.   Literary Criticism in English[1]

1. BIBLIOGRAPHIES AND HISTORIES OF CRITICISM

Contemporary Literary Scholarship, edited by Lewis Leary (1958), comments briefly in its chapters on criticism, poetry, the novel, and the drama on most of the post-1930 books—and a few articles—of critical interest in English, but the two indispensable works are *Theory of Literature* (1949, rev. 1956 and 1964) by René Wellek and Austin Warren, and *Literary Criticism: a Short History* (1957) by William K. Wimsatt and Cleanth Brooks. Although both are much more than guidebooks, they are of great value simply as works of reference because of the range and inclusiveness of their references; the bibliographies are especially thorough. *Theory of Literature* is arranged by topics (e.g. "Literature and Biography," "Evaluation") and is in effect more or less restricted to the last one hundred years, whereas the Wimsatt–Brooks *History* (which is "short" only in name) proceeds from Plato and Aristotle to the present day, though tending to concentrate in modern times mainly on English and American criticism. Of the older surveys George Saintsbury's *A History of Criticism and Literary Taste in Europe* (3 vols. 1900–4; English sections revised as *A History of English Criticism*, 1911) remains engagingly readable, but theoretically it is naïve; J. W. H. Atkins's *English Literary Criticism* (3 vols., 1943–51; only completed to *c.* 1800) is in the same tradition, if much duller. More sophisticated and more ambitious is René Wellek's *A History of Modern Criticism: 1750–1950* (4 vols., 1955–65), which de-

[1] Foreign critics have been omitted unless of exceptional importance in English criticism.

votes separate chapters full of meticulous detail to all the
principal European and American critics; the bias is toward critical *theory* throughout. A detailed if often superficial account of the most recent English and American criticism will be found in Stanley E. Hyman's *The
Armed Vision* (1948, rev. 1955), which also has useful
bibliographies. See also Murray Krieger, *The New Apol-
ogists for Poetry* (1956), a much abler book. For those
impatient of theory, George Watson's short and lively
Penguin paperback *The Literary Critics* (1962) can be
recommended. *Encyclopaedia of Literature* (2 vols., 1946,
rev. 1953 as *Dictionary of World Literature;* general editor Joseph T. Shipley) has some good critical articles as
well as many indifferent ones; William Elton's short *A
Glossary of the New Criticism* (1949, rev. 1951 as *A
Guide to the New Criticism*) is exactly what it proclaims
itself.

2. ANTHOLOGIES AND SYMPOSIA

GENERAL

The Great Critics, edited by James H. Smith and Edd
W. Parks (1932, enlarged 1939; gives the principal texts
in full—from the *Poetics,* translated by S. H. Butcher, to
Sainte-Beuve and Arnold—with extracts from Dionysius of
Halicarnassus, Castelvetro, Pater, etc.; pedestrian notes,
the non-English texts translated); *Criticism: the Major
Texts,* edited by Walter J. Bate (1948; contents similar to
Smith and Parks but fewer snippets; much better notes
and bibliographies). Alan H. Gilbert, *Literary Criticism,
Plato to Dryden* (1940), is notable for translations of
Continental Renaissance critics. The post-Renaissance
critics are covered by G. W. Allen and H. H. Clark (1963;
Pope to Croce).

ENGLISH CRITICISM

G. Gregory Smith's *Elizabethan Critical Essays* (2 vols.,
1904), J. E. Spingarn's *Critical Essays of the Seventeenth*

Century (3 vols., 1908), and Scott Elledge's *Eighteenth-Century Critical Essays* (2 vols., 1961) combine to provide a detailed and fully annotated panorama from Ascham to Alexander Knox (1796). A less scholarly and wide-ranging series are the World's Classics selections (without introductions or notes): sixteenth to eighteenth centuries edited by Edmund D. Jones (1922); nineteenth century edited by E. D. Jones (1916); twentieth century (to 1930) edited by Phyllis M. Jones (1933); 1933–57 edited by Derek Hudson (1958).

MODERN CRITICISM (mainly American)

Norman Foerster: *American Critical Essays* (1930); sequel edited by Harold Beaver (1959). These two World's Classics collections include essays by thirty-seven critics, from Poe to Irving Howe.

Morton D. Zabel: *Literary Opinion in America* (1937, enlarged 1951).

Donald A. Stauffer: *The Intent of the Critic* (1941).

Mark Schorer, Josephine Miles, and Gordon McKenzie: *Criticism* (1948). Includes *Poetics,* translated by S. H. Butcher, but mainly post-1900.

Robert W. Stallman: *Critiques and Essays in Criticism: 1920–1948* (1949).

Ray B. West: *Essays in Modern Literary Criticism* (1952).

E. Vivas and M. Krieger: *The Problems of Aesthetics* (1953). Several literary or semi-literary essays.

Irving Howe: *Modern Literary Criticism* (1958).

Gerald J. Goldberg: *The Modern Critical Spectrum* (1962).

Carroll Camden: *Literary Views: Critical and Historical Essays* (1964). Only Americans represented.

CRITICAL SYMPOSIA

Allen Tate (ed.): *The Language of Poetry* (1942).

Eric Bentley (ed.): *The Importance of Scrutiny* (1948). Excludes items in the earlier *Scrutiny* collection *Deter-*

minations (ed. F. R. Leavis, 1934), as well as those reprinted elsewhere by Leavis and L. C. Knights.

Ronald S. Crane (ed.): *Critics and Criticism* (1951). Chicago Aristotelianism. Abridged edition 1957.

Brewster Ghizelin (ed.): *The Creative Process* (1952).

John Wain (ed.): *Interpretations* (1955). Twelve well-known English poems "explicated" by Oxford-Cambridge critics of the post-Leavis generation.

A number of collections of modern essays, chapters or articles on single authors (or groups of authors, or periods) has been appearing recently, e.g. on Chaucer, Shakespeare, Jonson, Donne, Milton, Jane Austen, Dickens, Conrad, and Kipling. Details will be found above under the authors in question. The critical level is generally not very high.

3. CRITICAL JOURNALS (quarterly unless otherwise indicated)

The Times Literary Supplement. London, 1902– . Weekly.

Essays and Studies by Members of the English Association. Annually with change of editor each year from Vol. I (1910).

The Athenaeum. Edited by J. M. Middleton Murry for two brilliant years (1919–21). Weekly. Its earlier history (from 1828) is of intermittent critical interest. In 1921 it was taken over by *The Nation* (London), a general weekly, which was later itself absorbed by *The New Statesman.*

The Criterion, 1922–39. Quarterly (except briefly in 1927 when it became a monthly). Founded and edited by T. S. Eliot.

Scrutiny, 1932–53. Founded and edited by F. R. Leavis. Reissued with "Retrospect" and index 1963. Selection edited by Eric Bentley 1948 as *The Importance of Scrutiny.*

The Sewanee Review. 1892– . Critical metamorphosis only dates from 1944.

English Institute Essays. Annually, under a variety of titles, from 1939. Selection edited by W. K. Wimsatt 1963.

The Kenyon Review. 1939– . Founded and edited by John Crowe Ransom.

The Hudson Review. 1948– .

Essays in Criticism. 1951– . Founded and edited by F. W. Bateson.

The Critical Quarterly. 1959– . Founded and edited by C. B. Cox and A. E. Dyson.

4. GENERAL CRITICAL THEORY

i. Aristotle's *Poetics.* Standard translation by Ingram Bywater (1898; with Greek text and philological commentary); also separately with illuminating introduction by Gilbert Murray (1920). Latest translation by W. H. Fyfe (1927) and L. J. Potts (1953; has useful critical appendixes). See also the inferior translation by S. H. Butcher (1894, ed. John Gassner, 1951) which has an elaborate critical commentary. Humphry House's *Aristotle's Poetics* (1956) is a lucid exposition of the argument and is more reliable than F. L. Lucas's *Tragedy* (1928), which is not confined to the *Poetics.* Gerald F. Else's enormous and drastic reinterpretation (1957) is for addicts only.

ii. *Renaissance and Neo-Classical Criticism.* See J. E. Spingarn's *History of Literary Criticism in the Renaissance* (1899, rev. 1908), a competent introduction which is still respected, though it has been superseded by the more elaborate treatment by Bernard Weinberg (2 vols., 1962). The standard account of French neo-classicism is René Bray's *La Formation de la doctrine classique en France* (Dijon, 1927); A. F. B. Clark's *Boileau and the French Classical Critics in England* (Paris, 1925) is a useful guide down to *c.* 1830. *The Continental Model* (ed. Scott Elledge and Donald Schier, 1960) gives translations of eighteen French critical treatises of the seventeenth century with useful notes.

iii. *The Germans.* The non-German reader will find most of what he needs in René Wellek's *History of Modern Criticism* (Vols. I, II, 1955). The standard translation of Lessing's *Laokoön* is by Robert Phillimore (1874, often reprinted); a more recent one is by E. A. McCormick (1962). For Coleridge, the English heir par excellence, see p. 160 above.

iv. *Nineteenth Century.* See M. H. Abrams, *The Mirror and the Lamp* (1953), a model account of Romantic critical theory. Alba H. Warren, *English Poetic Theory, 1825–1865* (1950) is useful within its narrower limits.

v. *Twentieth Century.*

Lascelles Abercrombie: *The Theory of Poetry* (1924).

I. A. Richards: *Principles of Literary Criticism* (1924); *Science and Poetry* (1926); *Practical Criticism* (1929); *Coleridge and Imagination* (1935).

Kenneth Burke: *Attitudes towards History* (2 vols., 1937); *The Philosophy of Literary Form* (1941); *A Grammar of Motives* (1945); *A Rhetoric of Motives* (1950).

Susanne K. Langer: *Philosophy in a New Key* (1942); *Feeling and Form* (1953).

George Whalley: *Poetic Process* (1953).

Philip Wheelwright: *The Burning Fountain: a Study in the Language of Symbolism* (1954).

Hans Meyerhoff: *Time in Literature* (1955).

Eliseo Vivas: *Creation and Discovery* (1955).

Northrop Frye: *Anatomy of Criticism* (1957). Persuasive proposals for a new critical system.

Laurence Lerner: *The Truest Poetry* (1960). Unoriginal but a lucid introduction.

William K. Wimsatt: *The Verbal Icon* (1954). Seventeen important theoretical essays, two in collaboration with Monroe Beardsley.

Monroe C. Beardsley: *Aesthetics: Problems in the Philosophy of Criticism* (1958).

R. C. Elliott: *The Power of Satire: Magic, Ritual, Art* (1960).

René Wellek: *Concepts of Criticism* (1963). Detailed surveys of terms like the Baroque and Romanticism.

Angus Fletcher: *Allegory: the Theory of a Symbolic Mode* (1964).

5. Criticism of Poetry

The older English critics (Sidney, Dryden, Johnson, Coleridge, Hazlitt, Arnold, Pater), appear in the preceding sections. For T. S. Eliot see p. 194. Many of the following works are not limited to poetry. See also 8 and 9 below.

T. E. Hulme: *Speculations* (1924); *More Speculations*, edited by S. Hynes (1955).

Owen Barfield: *Poetic Diction* (1925).

Herbert Read: *Phases of English Poetry* (1928).

George W. H. Rylands: *Words and Poetry* (1928).

William Empson: *Seven Types of Ambiguity* (1930); *Some Versions of Pastoral* (1935); *The Structure of Complex Words* (1951).

G. Wilson Knight: *The Wheel of Fire* (1930, rev. 1949; introduction by T. S. Eliot); *The Burning Oracle* (1939); *The Sacred Dome* (1941).

Edmund Wilson: *Axel's Castle: a Study in the Imaginative Literature of 1870–1930* (1931).

F. R. Leavis: *New Bearings in English Poetry* (1932); *Revaluation* (1936); *The Common Pursuit* (1952).

E. M. W. Tillyard: *Poetry Direct and Oblique* (1934, rev. 1945).

R. P. Blackmur: *The Double Agent* (1935); *Form and Value in Modern Poetry* (1952).

Allen Tate: *Reactionary Essays on Poetry and Ideas* (1936); *Reason in Madness* (1941); *On the Limits of Poetry* (1948).

John Crowe Ransom: *The World's Body* (1938); *The New Criticism* (1941).

Cleanth Brooks: *Modern Poetry and the Tradition* (1939); *The Well-Wrought Urn* (1947).

C. S. Lewis: *Rehabilitations* (1939).

L. C. Knights: *Explorations* (1946).

F. A. Pottle: *The Idiom of Poetry* (1946).

Donald Stauffer: *The Nature of Poetry* (1946).

Yvor Winters: *In Defence of Reason* (1947); *The Function of Criticism* (1957).

A. R. Thompson: *The Dry Mock* (1948). Irony.

Philip Rahv: *Image and Idea* (1949).

W. H. Auden: *The Enchafèd Flood* (1950). Analysis of sea-imagery. *The Dyer's Hand* (1963). Miscellaneous critical aphorisms.

Donald Davie: *Purity of Diction in English Verse* (1952).

John Wain: *Preliminary Essays* (1957). *Essays on Literature and Ideas* (1963).

A. Alvarez: *The Shaping Spirit: Studies in Modern English and American Poets* (1958).

Isabel C. Hungerland: *Poetic Discourse* (1958). Analysis by a professional philosopher.

J. V. Cunningham: *Tradition and Poetic Structure* (1960). A collection of essays.

Robert Penn Warren has also collected his scattered critical pieces (1963).

CRITICAL ANTHOLOGIES

A Survey of Modernist Poetry (ed. Robert Graves and Laura Riding, 1938) and the more pedagogic *Understanding Poetry* (ed. Cleanth Brooks and Robert Penn Warren, 1938) set a fashion for anthologies of English and/or American short poems which are more or less fully "explicated." Such critical analyses appear regularly in *The Explicator* (from 1944), which also includes an annual check-list of the genre. *Poetry Explication* (by George Arms and Joseph M. Kautz, 1950) lists over seventeen hundred items for the period 1925–49. Competent recent anthologies of the explicatory type are:

Earl Daniels: *The Art of Reading Poetry* (1941).

Louis G. Locke, William M. Gibson, and George Arms: *Introduction to Literature* (1948, rev. 1952). Poems and short stories with explanatory critiques from *The Explicator* and other sources.

Fred B. Millet: *Reading Poetry* (1950).

Kimon Friar and John M. Brinnin: *Modern Poetry, American and British* (1951). Copious notes.

Frederick L. Gwynn, Ralph W. Condee, and Arthur O. Lewis: *The Case for Poetry* (1954).

6. CRITICISM OF DRAMA

The older critics have been listed separately in the preceding sections. See especially Dryden (p. 111), Lamb (p. 162), and Hazlitt (p. 163). There is a bibliography Aristotle's *Poetics* see p. 202 above. Nietzsche's *Birth of Tragedy* was not translated until 1909 (*Complete Works,* ed. Oscar Levy, Vol. I). See also *Playwrights on Playwriting* (ed. T. Cole, 1960).

George Meredith: *On the Idea of Comedy* (1877).

Henri Bergson: *Le Rire* (Paris, 1900, tr. 1928).

A. B. Walkley: *Dramatic Criticism* (1903); *Drama and Life* (1907).

A. C. Bradley: *Shakespearean Tragedy* (1904).

William Archer: *Play-Making: a Manual of Craftsmanship* (1912); *The Old Drama and the New* (1923).

W. Macneile Dixon: *Tragedy* (1924).

Harley Granville-Barker: *Prefaces to Shakespeare* (5 series, 1927–48).

J. W. Krutch: *The Fool* (1935). From ancient Greece to Chaplin.

A. R. Thompson: *The Anatomy of Drama* (1942).

Eric Bentley: *The Playwright as Thinker* (1946); *In Search of Theatre* (1953).

Una Ellis-Fermor: *The Frontiers of Drama* (1946).

Moody E. Prior: *The Language of Tragedy* (1947).

Stark Young: *Immortal Shadows* (1948).

Francis Fergusson: *The Idea of a Theatre* (1949).

Alan S. Downer: *The British Drama* (1950). Critical analyses: *King Lear* to *Getting Married*.

A. P. Rossiter: *English Drama from Early Times to the Elizabethans* (1950).

J. V. Cunningham: *Woe or Wonder* (1951).

Herbert Weisinger: *Tragedy and the Paradox of the Fortunate Fall* (1953).

Raymond Williams: *Drama from Ibsen to Eliot* (1953); *Modern Tragedy* (1964).

T. R. Henn: *The Harvest of Tragedy* (1956).

H. D. F. Kitto: *Form and Meaning in Drama* (1956).

Mary McCarthy: *Sights and Spectacles, 1937–1956* (1956).

H. J. Muller: *The Spirit of Tragedy* (1956).

Ronald Peacock: *The Art of Drama* (1957). Theoretical analysis.

Richard B. Sewall: *The Vision of Tragedy* (1959). Definition and examples.

Of the recent collections of plays, three at least have critical interest:

Understanding Drama, edited by Cleanth Brooks and Robert Heilman (1945, rev. 1948).

The Play, edited by Eric Bentley (1951).

The Art of the Play, edited by Alan S. Downer (1955).

The Brooks–Heilman discussions of each play are particularly searching.

7. CRITICISM OF PROSE FICTION

I. F. Bell and D. Baird's *The English Novel, 1578– 1956: a Checklist of Twentieth Century Criticisms* (1959) is useful. See also Warren S. Walker, *Twentieth-Century Short Story Explication* (1961), which lists discussions of particular short stories (all post-1800) since 1900. *Short Fiction Criticism* (ed. Jarvis Thurston, 1960), is a similar check-list from 1925. Useful collections of critical essays on the novel are *Forms of Modern Fiction* (ed. W. V. O'Connor, 1948), *Critiques and Essays on Modern Fic-*

tion, *1920–1951* (ed. J. W. Aldridge, 1952), and *Modern British Fiction* (ed. Mark Schorer, 1961). Miriam K. Allott has collected pronouncements by novelists on their art in *Novelists on the Novel* (1959). Somewhat similar is Roger Sale's *Discussion of the Novel* (1960). The following are the principal recent (i.e. post-Henry James) critical studies:

Percy Lubbock: *The Craft of Fiction* (1921).

Virginia Woolf: *Mr. Bennett and Mrs. Brown* (1924).

Edith Wharton: *The Writing of Fiction* (1925).

Ramon Fernandez: *Messages* (Paris, 1926; tr. English 1927).

Albert Thibandet: *Le liseur de romans* (Paris, 1925); *Réflexions sur le roman* (1938).

E. M. Forster: *Aspects of the Novel* (1927).

Ortega y Gasset: *Ideas sobra la novela* (Madrid, 1925; tr. as *Notes on the Novel,* 1948).

Edwin Muir: *The Structure of the Novel* (1929).

Edmund Wilson: *Axel's Castle* (1931; includes Proust and Joyce); *The Wound and the Bow* (1941; includes Dickens and Kipling).

Joseph W. Beach: *The Twentieth Century Novel: Studies in Technique* (1932).

Q. D. Leavis: *Fiction and the Reading Public* (1932). The nineteenth-century background.

Granville Hicks: *The Great Tradition* (1933). Marxist interpretation of American literature since the Civil War with main emphasis on the novel.

The English Novelists (ed. Derek Verschoyle, 1936).

Cleanth Brooks and R. P. Warren: *Understanding Fiction* (1943). Texts analyzed mainly modern American short stories.

Phyllis Bentley: *Some Observations on the Art of Narrative* (1947).

Robert Liddell: *A Treatise on the Novel* (1947); *Some Principles of Fiction* (1953).

V. S. Pritchett: *The Living Novel* (1947); *Books in*

General (1953). Collected essays and reviews, mainly on novels or novelists.

Yvor Winters: *In Defence of Reason* (1947; for Hawthorne, Melville, etc.).

F. R. Leavis: *The Great Tradition: George Eliot, Henry James, Joseph Conrad* (1948); *D. H. Lawrence, Novelist* (1955).

Richard Chase: *Quest for Myth* (1949); *The American Novel and Its Tradition* (1957).

E. K. Brown: *Rhythm in the Novel* (1950).

Lionel Trilling: *The Liberal Imagination* (1950).

Arnold Kettle: *Introduction to the English Novel* (2 vols., 1951–52). Marxist interpretations of key novels from Defoe to Graham Greene.

Marius Bewley: *Eccentric Design: Form in the Classical American Novel* (1952).

A. A. Mendilow: *Time and the Novel* (1952).

Robert Humphrey: *Stream of Consciousness in the Modern Novel* (1954). For a history of the mode, see Melvin J. Friedman (1955).

Leon Edel: *The Psychological Novel, 1900–1950* (1955).

Frank O'Conner: *Mirror in the Roadway: a Study of the Modern Novel* (1957).

Sean O'Faolain: *The Vanishing Hero: Studies in Novelists of the Twenties* (1956).

Morton D. Zabel: *Craft and Character in Modern Fiction* (1957).

John Bayley: *Characters of Love: a Study in the Literature of Personality* (1960).

Wayne Booth: *Rhetoric of Fiction* (1961). Masterly analysis of the theory of the novel.

W. J. Harvey: *The Art of George Eliot* (1961). Important for general theory of the novel.

Bertil Romberg: *Studies in the Narrative Technique of the First-Person Novel* (Stockholm, 1962).

Paul West: *The Modern Novel* (1963; critical survey of European and American fiction since 1900).

8. Style and Stylistics

Robert Louis Stevenson: "On Some Technical Elements of Style in Literature," *Contemporary Review,* April (1885). Reprinted in *Essays in the Art of Writing* (1905).

Walter Pater: *Appreciations. With an Essay on Style* (1889).

Walter Raleigh: *Style* (1897).

Remy de Gourmont: *Le problème du style* (Paris, 1902). An important influence on T. S. Eliot and Middleton Murry.

Lane Cooper: *Theories of Style* (1907).

Morris W. Croll: Introduction to Lyly's *Euphues* (ed. Harry Clemons, 1916); "The Baroque Style in Prose" (in Klaeber Miscellany, 1929).

T. S. Eliot: *The Sacred Wood* (1920).

J. Middleton Murry: *The Problem of Style* (1922).

"Vernon Lee" (Violet Paget): *The Handling of Words* (1923).

Herbert Read: *English Prose Style* (1928). Wide range of examples.

H. C. Wyld: *Some Aspects of the Diction of English Poetry* (1933). The philological aspects.

W. K. Wimsatt: *The Prose Style of Samuel Johnson* (1941).

Robert Graves and Alan Hodge: *The Reader over Your Shoulder* (1943).

Erich Auerbach: *Mimesis* (Berne, 1946; tr. 1953). Progress of realism from Homer to Virginia Woolf.

Leo Spitzer: *Linguistics and Literary History: Essays in Stylistics* (1948).

George Williamson: *The Senecan Amble* (1951). Seventeenth-century prose style.

Donald Davie: *Purity of Diction in English Verse* (1953); *Articulate Energy: an Enquiry into the Syntax of English Poetry* (1955).

Ernest Gowers: *Plain Words: Their ABC* (1954).

Bernard Groom: *The Diction of Poetry from Spenser to Bridges* (1955). Unpretentious but reliable.

Geoffrey Tillotson: *Augustan Studies* (1961). Useful for eighteenth-century poetic diction.

Winifred Nowottny: *The Language Poets Use* (1962). A scrupulous and sensitive analysis.

Stephen Ullmann: *Language and Style* (1964). The semantic approach.

9. PROSODY

J. M. Schipper: *English Metrik* (3 vols., Bonn, 1881–88; abridged translation 1910).

Robert Bridges: *Milton's Prosody* (1901, with W. J. Stone, "On the Use of Classical Metres in English"). Written 1887, final revision 1921.

George Saintsbury: *A History of English Prosody* (3 vols., 1906–10); *A History of English Prose Rhythm* (1912).

Paul Verrier: *Essai sur les Principes de la Métrique anglaise* (3 vols., Paris, 1909–10).

A. C. Clark: *Prose-Rhythm in English* (1910).

W. M. Patterson: *The Rhythm of Prose* (1916).

T. S. Omond: *English Metrists* (1921).

P. F. Baum: *The Principles of English Versification* (1922); *The Other Harmony of Prose* (1952).

George R. Stewart: *Modern Metrical Techniques as Illustrated by Ballad Meter, 1700–1920* (1922); *The Techniques of English Verse* (1930).

E. A. Sonnenschein: *What Is Rhythm?* (1925).

John H. Scott: *Rhythmic Prose* (1925).

Henry Lanz: *The Physical Basis of Rime* (1931).

Wilbur L. Schramm: *Approaches to a Science of Verse* (1925).

André Classe: *The Rhythm of English Prose* (1939).

John C. Pope: *The Rhythm of Beowulf* (1942).

Walter J. Bate: *The Stylistic Development of John Keats* (1945).

Karl Shapiro: *English Prosody and Modern Poetry* (1947).

Paul Fussell: *The Theory of Prosody in Eighteenth-Century England* (1954).

F. T. Prince: *The Italian Element in Milton's Verse* (1954).

J. Thompson: *The Founding of English Metre* (1961).

XI. Literary Scholarship:[1] an Introduction to Research in English Literature

The subject matter of this section is covered in greater detail in the four American bibliographical handbooks already referred to in the Preface:

T. P. Cross: *A List of Books and Articles Designed to Serve as an Introduction to the Bibliography and Methods of English Literary History* (1919). Latest revision by D. F. Bond as *A Reference Guide to English Studies* (1962).

J. W. Spargo: *A Bibliographical Manual for Students of the Language and Literature of England and the U. S.* (1939, rev. 1941 and 1956).

A. G. Kennedy: *A Concise Bibliography for Students of English* (1940). Latest revision by D. B. Sands (1960) is greatly enlarged (mainly extra-literary titles).

R. D. Altick and Andrew Wright: *Selective Bibliography for the Study of English and American Literature* (1960, rev. 1963).

These handbooks were all designed for the "beginning" graduate student and all suffer from the twin defects of overinclusiveness and illogical arrangement. The Bond revision of Cross is the least expensive of the four, but the Altick–Wright is decidedly the most useful in every other way: it excludes most of the inessentials, has a sensible preliminary section "On the Use of Scholarly Tools," and attaches "A Glossary of Useful Terms" (from "A.L.S." = "autograph letter, signed," to "watermark," "wire-lines," and "xerox"). What is lacking in it and the other hand-

[1] This section has been compiled in collaboration with Harrison T. Meserole.

books is a proper attention both to the techniques of literary research—such as textual criticism, source-hunting, influences—and the semi-critical areas (process of composition, key terms and concepts, the literary audience). An attempt is made in this section to fill some of these gaps, however perfunctorily. The annual *English Institute Essays* (from 1939) can be recommended to those interested in a more sophisticated approach to literary technique.

1. Literary Research: Primers and Style Sheets

The most acute discussion of the special problems created by literary research is still André Morize's *Problems and Methods of Literary History: a Guide for Graduate Students* (1922), but unfortunately almost all his examples are drawn from modern French literature. In the English field R. D. Altick's *The Art of Literary Research* (1963) is the most comprehensive, accurate, and up-to-date introduction, though his habit of talking down to the reader is irritating. The same defect is even more prominent in Jacques Barzun and Henry F. Graff's *The Modern Researcher* (1957), which is intended in any case for historians and draws most of its examples from American history, though young literary scholars will also find it well worth dipping into. *An Introduction to Research in English Literary History* (1952) by Chauncey Sanders has useful simplified sections on "The Materials of Research" (handwriting, paper, printing, engraving) and "The Tools of Research" (good on bibliographical description and collation), but the later chapters are naïve critically and the hundreds of examples of modern research cited are not properly discussed. The more mature scholar will find matter to interest him in *The Aims and Methods of Scholarship in Modern Languages and Literatures* (ed. James Thorpe, 1963). Prepared at the request of the (American) Modern Language Association, this pamphlet consists of four essays: William G. Moulton on linguistics; Fredson

Bowers on textual criticism; Robert E. Spiller on literary history; Northrop Frye on literary criticism. An earlier set of similar essays, still well worth reading, by A. H. Marckwardt, L. P. G. Peckham, René Wellek, and James Thorpe, appeared in *PMLA*, LXVII (1952), No. 6, 3–37. The essays are too short, however, to carry their very abstract arguments at all far and cannot be compared with René Wellek and Austin Warren's masterly *Theory of Literature* (1949, rev. 1956). These are all American works; their only English equivalent is R. B. McKerrow's shrewd and down-to-earth article "Form and Matter in the Publication of Research" (*RES*, XVI [1940], 116–21; also *PMLA*, LXV [1950], No. 3, 3–8).

For modern presentation conventions see:

W. R. Parker: *The MLA Style Sheet* (1951, rev. 1954). Now standard for more than eighty journals and forty university presses.

[Helen Gardner and Humphry House]: *Notes on the Presentation of Theses on Literary Subjects* (1952). Standard in England; much less detailed than the preceding item.

James Thorpe: *Literary Scholarship: a Handbook for Advanced Students of English and American Literature* (1964). Not confined to conventions of style; also briefly covers research methods.

2. IDENTIFYING AND LOCATING THE TEXTS

GENERAL BIBLIOGRAPHIES

The most ambitious of these is *CBEL* (*The Cambridge Bibliography of English Literature,* ed. F. W. Bateson, 4 vols., 1940) which aimed at a complete coverage of the books by the writers included (apart from those in the "background" and supplementary sections) and, up to 1800, of all editions up to fifty years from the first. Manuscripts were only included in the medieval sections and virtually no attempt was made to locate actual copies of any edition. A complete revision is in progress under the general editorship of George Watson. Watson's Supplement (1957) is restricted to recent books and articles on English literature, but his epitome *The Concise Cambridge Bibliography of English Literature* (1958) has the advantage of including the principal twentieth-century authors; the main work stopped with those who were "established" by 1900. A discussion of the virtues and limitations of *CBEL* will be found in the Altick–Wright *Selective Bibliography* (1960, rev. 1963), pp. 7–9, where the principal reviews are listed.

Earlier compilations still of some value are:

Robert Watt: *Bibliotheca Britannica; or a General Index to British and Foreign Literature* (4 vols., 1824). Arranged by authors and subjects—latter especially useful for tracking down authors of minor eighteenth-century works published anonymously.

W. T. Lowndes: *The Bibliographer's Manual of English Literature* (rev. H. G. Bohn, 6 vols., 1857–64). More selective than Watt but includes far more sixteenth- and seventeenth-century items of literary interest with occasional notes.

BIBLIOGRAPHIES OF BIBLIOGRAPHIES

C. S. Northup: *A Register of Bibliographies of the English Language and Literature* (1925, reissued 1962). Supplement to 1932 by N. Van Patten (1934).

Theodore Besterman: *A World Bibliography of Bibliographies* (3d ed., 4 vols., 1955–56). Eighty thousand titles (separately published items only: no articles) arranged by subject, with an author index, and occasionally annotated.

Useful in bringing bibliographic material up to date is *The Bibliographic Index: a Cumulative Bibliography of Bibliographies*, edited by Dorothy Charles and Beatrice Joseph (1938–). Begun as a quarterly series, in 1945 all materials (1937–45) were gathered into a single volume of 50,000 entries arranged and indexed by subjects. It is annotated, and now appears semi-annually.

PERIOD BIBLIOGRAPHIES

N. R. Ker: *Catalogue of Manuscripts containing Anglo-Saxon* (1957). Not confined to works of literary interest, for which see A. H. Heusinkveld and E. J. Bashe, *A Bibliographical Guide to the Language, Literature, and History of the Anglo-Saxons* (1931) and *CBEL*, I, 53–98. The period's Latin writings are listed in *CBEL*, I, 98–110.

J. E. Wells: *A Manual of the Writings in Middle English, 1050–1400* (1916). Nine Supplements (1919–52); a revised edition now in progress will consolidate all Wells's material in one volume and extend the terminal date to 1500. Confined to Middle English literature (which Wells repeated in *CBEL*, I, 113–272); the period's Latin writings are in *CBEL*, I, 280–314. At present the fullest list of fifteenth-century writings in English is that appended to H. S. Bennett's volume in *The Oxford History of English Literature* (II [Part 1], 1947).

A. W. Pollard and G. R. Redgrave: *A Short-Title Catalogue of Books Printed in England, Scotland, and Ireland, and of English Books Printed Abroad, 1475–1640* (1926; reissued 1946, 1948, 1950, 1956). Elaborate revised edition in progress by W. A. Jackson and others. Complete and includes books in Latin. Copies located. See Paul G. Morrison, *Index of Printers, Publishers, and Booksellers [in the Short-Title Catalogue]* (1950).

Copies of *STC* books in the United States are listed in William Warner Bishop, *A Checklist of American Copies of "Short-Title Catalogue" Books* (2nd ed., 1950), and David Ramage provides *A Finding List of English Books to 1640 in Libraries in the British Isles* (1958). In progress at University Microfilms, Ann Arbor, Michigan, is a project to microfilm all works listed in the *STC*.

Donald Wing: *Short-Title Catalogue of Books Printed in England, Scotland, Ireland, Wales, and British America and of English Books Printed in Other Countries, 1641–*

1700 (3 vols., 1945–51). Complete except for periodicals. Extends the *STC* to the year 1700, and there is in preparation by the (London) Bibliographical Society an eighteenth-century supplement to Wing. Paul Morrison has also compiled an index of the Wing printers and publishers (1955). For the occasional errors and omissions see the references in the Cross–Bond *Reference Guide to English Studies* (1962), No. 676. Microfilming of a selection of Wing titles is in progress at University Microfilms.

For the bibliographies of nineteenth- and twentieth-century literature see Chapter IX, and under "Trade Lists and National Bibliographies" and "Genre Bibliographies" below.

TRADE LISTS AND NATIONAL BIBLIOGRAPHIES

Forerunners of the modern national bibliography and trade list are the Stationers' Company's Register and the Restoration Term Catalogues, both of which have been edited by Edward Arber: *A Transcript of the Registers of the Company of Stationers of London, 1554–1640* (5 vols., 1875–77, 1894; reissued 1950). This is continued by G. E. B. Eyre's *Transcript, 1640–1708* (3 vols., 1913–14; reissued 1950) and *The Term Catalogues, 1668–1709: a Contemporary Bibliography of English Literature in the Reigns of Charles II, James II, William and Mary, and Anne* (3 vols., 1903–6). For other early trade lists see *CBEL*, II, 93–95.

The most important of the later lists is *The London Catalogue of Books in All Languages, Arts, and Sciences, Printed in Great Britain and Published in London 1700–1855* (8 vols., 1773–1855; various editions with varying titles, 1786–1855), which is arranged by authors. The *British Catalogue* was merged with the *London Catalogue* in the *English Catalogue of Books* [*1801–*] which is still published annually, cumulated in larger volumes at various intervals, and arranged by authors and titles. There are useful indexes by Sampson Low up to 1889.

The standard modern index is the *British National*

Bibliography (1950–), issued weekly and cumulated quarterly, annually, and quinquennially, and arranged by author, title, and subject. Also occasionally useful are *Whitaker's Cumulative Booklist* (1924–), based on weekly lists appearing in *The Bookseller,* and (Whitaker's) *Reference Catalogue of Current Literature: a National Inclusive Book-Reference Index of Books in Print and on Sale in the United Kingdom* (1874–), arranged by subjects and now issued at approximately five-year intervals.

GENRE BIBLIOGRAPHIES (BOOKS)

Poetry

W. Carew Hazlitt: *Hand-Book to the Popular, Poetical, and Dramatic Literature of Great Britain* (1867; supplements, 1876, 1882, 1889–92, 1903). Indexed by G. J. Gray, *A General Index to Hazlitt's Handbook and His Bibliographical Collections, 1867–89* (1893).

Carleton Brown: *A Register of Middle English Religious and Didactic Verse* (2 vols., 1916–20). Volume II now superseded by Carleton Brown and Rossell Hope Robbins, *The Index of Middle English Verse* (1943), which in turn is supplemented by William Ringler's bibliographical essay in *PBSA,* XLIX (1955).

Arthur E. Case: *A Bibliography of English Poetical Miscellanies, 1521–1750* (1935). See also Richard C. Boys, "A Finding-List of English Poetical Miscellanies, 1700–1748, in Selected American Libraries," *ELH,* VII (1940); Norman Ault's list in *CBEL,* II, 173–256, is fuller than Case for 1660–1750 and continues to 1800. Both the British Museum and Bodley have card indexes of the first lines of the poems in their manuscripts.

Drama

A. B. Harbage: *Annals of English Drama, 975–1700: an Analytical Record of All Plays, Extant or Lost,* chronologically arranged (1940; rev. S. Schoenbaum 1964); Carl J. Stratman: *Bibliography of Medieval Drama* (1954: ch. V, "Medieval English Drama"); W. W. Greg: *A Bibliography of the English Printed Drama to the Restoration* (4 vols., 1939–59); Gertrude L. Woodward and James G. Mc-Manaway: *A Check List of English Plays, 1641–1700* (1945), with a Supplement by Fredson Bowers (1949); *The London Stage, 1660–1880: a Calendar of Plays, Entertainments, and Afterpieces* (1960– ; in progress); Allardyce Nicoll, *A History of English Drama, 1660–1900* (6 vols., 1952–59; Vol. VI is *A Short-Title Alphabetical Catalogue of Plays Produced or Printed in England from 1660 to 1900*); and Blanch M. Baker, *Theatre and Allied Arts: a Guide to Books Dealing with the History, Criticism, and Technic of the Drama and Theatre and Related Arts and Crafts* (1952).

Prose

Sterg O'Dell, *A Chronological List of Prose Fiction in English Printed in England and Other Countries, 1475–1600* (1954); Charles C. Mish, *English Prose Fiction, 1600–1700* (3 vols., 1952); William H. McBurney, *A Check List of English Prose Fiction, 1700–39* (1960); R. M. Wiles, *Serial Publication in England before 1750* (1957, mainly non-fiction); Andrew Block, *The English Novel, 1740–1850: a Catalogue Including Prose Romances, Short Stories, and Translations of Foreign Fiction* (1939; new edition 1961; to be used with caution, see *TLS*, March 25, 1939, and April 21, 1961); Michael Sadleir, *Nineteenth Century Fiction: a Bibliographical Record Based on His Own Collection* (2 vols., 1951); C. N. Greenough, *A Bibliography of the Theophrastan Character in English* (1947).

NEWSPAPERS AND OTHER PERIODICALS (LISTS AND INDEXES)

Ulrich's Periodicals Directory: a Classified Guide to a Selected List of Current Periodicals, Foreign and Domestic (10th ed., 1963) is an excellent source for finding titles because it is international in scope, it contains a detailed index and cross-reference system, it lists titles by subject group, and it is revised often enough (every three to four years) to be conveniently up-to-date. For English periodicals the standard finding list and location guide is the *British Union-Catalogue of Periodicals* (4 vols. plus supplement, 1955–58; 1962). This may be supplemented by the *Guide to Current British Periodicals,* edited by Mary Toase (1962), which classifies (but does not locate) some 3800 current journals.

Supplementary special tools for English periodicals are: the British Museum's *Periodical Publications* (3 vols., 1963); William S. Ward, *Index and Finding List of Serials Published in the British Isles, 1789–1832* (1953); Katherine K. Weed and Richmond P. Bond, *Studies of British Newspapers and Periodicals from Their Beginning to 1800: a Bibliography,* in SP, extra series No. 2 (1946). Particularly useful in locating runs of seventeenth- and eighteenth-century English periodicals and newspapers in American libraries is Ronald S. Crane and F. B. Kaye, *A Census of British Newspapers and Periodicals, 1620–1800* (1927; also in SP, XXIV [1927]); four later monographs locate special collections of English periodicals: R. T. Milford and D. M. Sutherland, *A Catalogue of English Newspapers and Periodicals in the Bodleian Library, 1622–1800,* in the Oxford Bibliographical Society *Proceedings and Papers,* IV (1934–35); G. A. Cranfield, *A Hand-List of English Provincial Newspapers and Periodicals, 1700–1760,* Cambridge Bibliographical Society Monograph No. 2 (1952; addenda in *Transactions* of the CBS, II, iii [1956] and V [1959]); A. J. Gabler, "Check-List of English Newspapers and Periodicals before 1801 in the Huntington Library," *HLB,* No. 2 (1931); and Powell Stewart, *British Newspapers and Periodicals, 1632–1800* [*in the University of Texas Library*] (1950).

The standard guide to English newspapers is *Willing's Press Guide* (89th issue, 1963), which is published annually and kept up to date by quarterly supplements. R. L. Munter, *A Hand-List of Irish Newspapers, 1685–1750,* Cambridge Bibliographical Society Monograph No. 4 (1962), Crane and Kaye, and the four monographs listed as supplementary to Crane and Kaye, provide additional finding lists and location guides, as does [J. G. Muddiman], *The Times Tercentenary Handlist of English and Welsh Newspapers, Magazines, and Reviews* [*1620–1920*] (1920; see *Notes and Queries* [1921–22] for corrections and additions). In all other respects Muddiman is superseded by *CBEL*, I, 736 ff., II, 688 ff., III, 779 ff.

Copies of books and periodicals can also be located by the use of the two Union catalogues (actually card catalogues, not to be confused with the printed catalogues of the same names). The British Union Catalogue in the National Central Library in London contains roughly a million entries, each directing the user to one of the British regional catalogues in which actual locations of copies may be found. The National Union Catalog in the Library of Congress contains well over fifteen million cards which locate copies of books in American libraries (any book acquired by these libraries after 1952 is listed in the printed *NUC*).

AUTHOR BIBLIOGRAPHIES

Bibliographies that include lists of reviews and other secondary matter (biographies, critical studies, etc.) have been listed above under the principal writers, but those limited to detailed descriptions of the title page and format of each printed book by a particular author were normally excluded. They will be found in *CBEL* at the head of each list of an author's works. Some of the more important are listed in A. J. Walford's *Guide to Reference Material* (1959), pp. 366–78.

LIBRARY CATALOGUES

The British Museum: *Catalogue of Printed Books* (95 vols., 1881–1900) and its Supplement (15 vols., 1900–5), the whole reprinted in 58 volumes (1948–50) with a Supplement of 10 volumes (1950). See also *Rules for Compiling the Catalogues in the Department of Printed Books in the British Museum* (2nd ed., 1936). The Museum's *General Catalogue of Printed Books* (51 vols., 1931–54) adds materials published after 1905, and is in turn being continued by the *General Catalogue of Printed Books: Photolithographic Edition to 1955* (1960–   ), which when completed in approximately 300 volumes will supersede earlier catalogues. Lists of special collections and classes of books (such as incunabula, seventeenth-century pamphlets, and books printed before 1641) may be consulted in separate printed catalogues published by the Museum.

The Library of Congress: *Catalog of Books Represented by Printed Cards Issued to July 31, 1942* (167 vols., 1942–46), its Supplement, 1942–47 (42 vols., 1948), and the Library of Congress *Author Catalog* [*1948–52*] (24 vols., 1953). *The National Union Catalog: a Cumulative Author List* (1953–   ), issued monthly and cumulated quarterly and annually, continues the listings.

Other libraries: The best general guide to other British libraries is the *ASLIB* (Association of Special Libraries and Information Bureaux) *Directory: a Guide to Sources of Specialized Information in Great Britain,* edited by Miriam Alman (2 vols., 1957; supplement 1962). Reginald Rye, the *Student's Guide to the Libraries of London* (3rd ed., 1927), and Raymond Irwin and Ronald Stavely (eds.), *The Libraries of London* (2nd ed., 1961), are useful special sources. For American libraries see Robert B. Downs, *American Library Resources: a Bibliographical Guide* (1951).

William Andrews Clark (now the University of California): 19 volumes, 1920–31 (by R. E. Cowan and Clark himself).

S. Christie-Miller: *The Britwill Handlist* (2 vols., 1933).

Edinburgh Faculty of Advocates (now the University of Edinburgh): 7 volumes, 1867–78.

Carl H. Pforzheimer: *English Literature, 1475–1700* (3 vols., 1940).

Lord Rothschild: 2 volumes, 1954. Additions and corrections in *The Library*, 5th series, X (1955).

John Rylands (now a public library, Manchester): 3 volumes, 1899 (by E. Gordon Duff). A semiannual *Bulletin* gives details of new acquisitions in early printed books.

Chauncey Brewster Tinker (now in Yale University Library): 1959 (by R. F. Metzdorf).

Thomas J. Wise (now in the British Museum): *The Ashley Library* (11 vols., 1922–36; compiled by Wise himself).

John Henry Wrenn (now the University of Texas): 5 volumes, 1920 (by H. B. Wrenn and T. J. Wise).

Except in some cases for special collections there are no published catalogues of the Bodleian Library (Oxford), the Pierpont Morgan Library, New York City, the Folger Library, Washington, D.C., the Widener and Houghton Library at Harvard, the Yale University Library, the Huntington at San Marino, California, the Newberry at Chicago, and the John Carter Brown Library at Brown University, Providence, Rhode Island, the New York Public Library, the American Antiquarian Society in Worcester, Massachusetts, the Boston Public Library, the Victorian fiction collection at the University of Illinois, or the Browning Library at Baylor University, Waco, Texas, though there are guides to some of them (e.g., W. S. Lewis, *The Yale Collections,* 1946) and catalogues of several of the special collections in others (e.g., A. S. W. Rosenbach's catalogue of the Widener collection now at Harvard, 2 vols., 1918).

CATALOGUES OF BOOK SALES

American Book Prices Current (1895–   ), *Book Prices Current* (1886–   ), George L. McKay, *American Book Auction Catalogues, 1713–1934: a Union List* (1937; addenda in *Bulletin of New York Public Library,* L [1946], LII [1949]), *Book Auction Records, 1902–* (1903), and the British Museum special *List of Catalogues of English Book Sales, 1676–1900* (1915) provide records of sales, auctions, and owners of books in the United States and Great Britain.

Bibliographie générale de littérature comparée [1949–] (Paris, 1950–).

Rudolf Hirsch and Howell J. Heaney compile a "Selective Check List of Bibliographical Scholarship" which is published in the annual *Studies in Bibliography* (Vol. X, 1957, collected and indexed the issues for 1949–55). *Bibliography in Britain*, edited by John Simmons (Oxford Bibliographical Society, 1963–), includes the whole field of book production in an annual survey.

There are other special serial lists in *Modern Drama, Journal of Aesthetics and Art Criticism, Journal of American Folklore, Southern Folklore Quarterly, Journal of English and Germanic Philology* (Anglo–German scholarship), *Studies in the Renaissance, Speech Monographs* (rhetoric, public addresses, dissertations completed and in progress), *Onoma* (onomastics), *Babel* (translation), *Bulletin bibliographique de la Société Internationale Arthurienne, New England Quarterly, Revue d'histoire ecclésiastique* (medieval studies), *Romanic Review* (Anglo–French and Franco–American studies, 1938–48), and *Zeitschrift für Anglistik und Amerikanistik* (dissertations in English and American literature).

Shakespeare Quarterly provides an annotated list annually (1950–), as does the *Keats–Shelley Journal* (on Keats, Shelley, Byron, Hunt, et al.). *The Shaw Review* includes in each issue "A Continuing Check-List of Shaviana."

Some of these serial bibliographies have been collected and published separately. The *PQ* bibliographies of Restoration to eighteenth-century studies (1925–60) have been collected in four volumes, edited by Louis A. Landa, et al. (1950–52, 1962), the *MP* and *Victorian Studies* lists for 1837–1901 (1932–54) in two volumes, edited by William D. Templeman and Austin Wright (1945, 1956).

Work in progress is not nearly so easily located. James M. Osborn's *Work in Progress in the Modern Humanities, 1938–42* (1939–43) was continued in part by "Research in

Progress in the Modern Languages and Literatures" in *PMLA* from 1950 to 1960 but is no longer being compiled. Some scholars had used Osborn's public-spirited experiment to corner projects that they never followed up. *Contemporary Literary Scholarship: a Critical Review*, edited by Lewis Leary (1958), may be consulted in this connection. Though rapidly becoming outdated, it describes in separate chapters recent trends in scholarship in each area of English and American literature, suggests topics that need study within each area, and notices important contributions recently published and in progress. A somewhat similar function is now being performed by *Studies in English Literature* (founded 1960) with its recurrent critical surveys of "Recent Studies" (each issue either non-dramatic Renaissance literature or Elizabethan–Jacobean drama, or Restoration and eighteenth century, or nineteenth century).

The standard index to theses completed in Great Britain is *Index to Theses Accepted for Higher Degrees in the Universities of Great Britain and Ireland* [*1950/51–*] (1950–), which is arranged by author and subject. Not an index but useful for the period before 1950 is P. D. Record, *A Survey of Thesis Literature in British Libraries* (1950). Standard for the United States is *Dissertation Abstracts: a Guide to Dissertations and Monographs Available on Microfilm* (1938–). Published monthly, arranged and indexed by author and subject, it is nonetheless incomplete and must be supplemented by consulting lists published at various intervals by universities which do not contribute abstracts of their theses to it (Harvard, Yale, Chicago, *inter alia*). For the period before 1938 in America the Library of Congress published *A List of American Doctoral Dissertations Printed* [*1912–1938*] (1913–40), and the index of *Doctoral Dissertations Accepted by American Universities* [*1933/34–1954/55*] was combined from 1955–56 with the list in *Dissertation Abstracts*. The American counterpart to Record's *Survey* is T. R. Palfrey and H. E. Coleman, *Guide to Bib-*

liographies of Theses—U.S. and Canada (2d ed., 1940), which must be supplemented by R. P. Rosenberg, "Bibliographies of Theses in America" in *Bulletin of Bibliography*, XVIII– (1945/46–).

There are, in addition, a few special-area compilations. Richard D. Altick and W. R. Matthews's *Guide to Doctoral Dissertations in Victorian Literature, 1886–1958* (1960) is international in scope, indexed by author, and provides a fully cross-referenced list of those theses that deal wholly or principally with the literature of England, 1837–1900. Richard Mummendey's *Language and Literature of the Anglo-Saxon Nations as Presented in German Doctoral Dissertations, 1885–1950* (1954) is incomplete and must be supplemented by consulting the standard source for German dissertations, *Jahresverzeichnis der deutschen Hochschulschriften, 1885–* (Berlin and Leipzig, 1887–), and the lists of German dissertations on English and American literature published periodically in *Zeitschrift für Anglistik und Amerikanistik* (1953–).

The biennial *Progress of Medieval Studies in the United States and Canada* (1923–) contains lists of masters' and doctors' theses in progress or completed; since 1940 Renaissance studies are also included.

An Index to Book Reviews in the Humanities (1960–), though not limited to literary matters, is the most useful of the general sources. It indexes reviews from some three hundred English and American periodicals. The *Essay and General Literature Index* (see p. 226 above) lists some reviews that have appeared in scholarly journals but it is not comprehensive in coverage. The *Book Review Digest* (1905–), which appears monthly (omitting February and July) and is cumulated annually, indexes and provides excerpts from reviews of current books appearing in some seventy-five English and American general magazines. The *International Index to Periodicals* (see p. 227 above) also lists some reviews from scholarly journals. For earlier periods *Poole's Index* and the indexes to the London *Times* and the New York *Times* are helpful.

CRITICAL SURVEYS OF MODERN SCHOLARSHIP

For some areas of English studies there are books which review the scholarship in a particular period more intensively. In Middle English John E. Wells's *Manual of Writings in Middle English, 1050–1400* (1916) and its nine supplements (1916–51) account for material published up to 1945; a revision is now in preparation. Two composite MLA volumes evaluate the work in the Romantic Period: Thomas M. Raysor (ed.), *The English Romantic Poets: a Review of Research* (rev. ed., 1956), deals with Wordsworth, Coleridge, Keats, Shelley, and Byron; C. W. and L. H. Houtchens (eds.), *The English Romantic Poets and Essayists: a Review of Research and Criticism* (1957), adds chapters on Blake, Lamb, Hazlitt, Scott, Southey, Campbell, Moore, Landor, Hunt, and De Quincey. In the same MLA series Frederic E. Faverty has edited *The Victorian Poets: a Guide to Research* (1956), which reviews scholarship since 1920 on Tennyson, the Brownings, FitzGerald, Clough, Arnold, Swinburne, the Pre-Raphaelites, Hopkins, and others. Lionel Stevenson is editing a companion volume on the Victorian novelists.

THE LEARNED JOURNALS

The following selective list includes the principal journals now being published in the various fields of literary study together with their standard abbreviations (when no abbreviation is given, the short title of the journal, omitting "A," "An," "The," is used in citation). Titles marked with an asterisk (*) indicate journals that review books. The subdivisions are intended to indicate the main areas of interest and are not mutually exclusive.

Bibliography
   Cambridge   Bibliographical   Society: Transactions
       (1949–   ).

Edinburgh Bibliographical Society: Transactions
  (1938–).
*The Library (1889–). Incorporated from 1920 the
  transactions of the London Bibliographical Society
  (1893–).
Oxford Bibliographical Society: Proceedings and Papers
  (1923–).
*Papers of the Bibliographical Society of America [PBSA]
  (1904/5–).
Studies in Bibliography (University of Virginia) [SB]
  (1948/49–).

Comparative Literature, General Literature, and Miscellaneous

Bulletin of the New York Public Library [BNYPL]
  (1897–).
*Comparative Literature [CL] (1949–).
Comparative Literature Studies [CLS] (1963–).
Harvard Studies and Notes in Philology and Literature
  (1892–).
*Journal of Aesthetics and Art Critisicm [JAAC]
  (1941–).
*Journal of the History of Ideas [JHI] (1940–).
Notes and Queries [N&Q] (1849/50–).
*Revue de littérature comparée [RLC] (1921–).
Speculum (1926–).
*Yearbook of Comparative and General Literature
  [YCGL] (1951–).

English Literature

Abstracts of English Studies (1958–).
*Anglia: Zeitschrift für englische Philologie (1877–).
*Criticism (1959–).
ELH [Journal of English Literary History] (1934–).
Englische Studien: Organ für englische Philologie (1877–
  1939).

English Institute Essays [EIE] (1939–   ).
English Studies: a Journal of English Letters and Philology [ES] (1919–   ).
Essays and Studies by Members of the English Association (1910–   ).
*Essays in Criticism [EIC] (1951–   ).
*Etudes anglaises [EA] (1937–   ).
Huntington Library Quarterly [HLQ] (1937/8–   ).
*Medieval Studies (Toronto) *[MS]* (1939–   ).
*Medium Aevum [MÆ] (1932–   ).
*Nineteenth Century Fiction [NCF] (1945–   ).
Philological Quarterly [PQ] (1922–   ).
Review of English Literature [REL] (1960–   ).
*Review of English Studies [RES] (1925–   ).
Studies in English Literature, 1500–1900 [SEL] (1961–   ).
Studies in Philology [SP] (1906–   ).
Studies in Romanticism [SIR] (1961–   ).
*University of Toronto Quarterly [UTQ] (1930–   ).
*Victorian Studies [VS] (1957/8–   ).
Year's Work in English Studies [YWES] (1919/20–   ).
*Zeitschrift für Anglistik und Amerikanistik [ZAA] (1953–   ).

Modern Languages and Literatures (including English)

*Critique: Studies in Modern Fiction (1956–   ).
*Journal of English and Germanic Philology [JEGP] (1897–   ).
*Modern Language Notes [MLN] (1886–   ).
*Modern Language Quarterly [MLQ] (1940–   ).
*Modern Philology [MP] (1903/4–   ).
*Modern Language Review [MLR] (1905/6–   ).
Modern Fiction Studies [MFS] (1955–   ).
PMLA: Publications of the Modern Language Association of America (1884/5–   ).
*Wisconsin Studies in Contemporary Literature [WSCL] (1960–   ).

Year's Work in Modern Language Studies [*YWMLS*]
(1931–   ).

Journals for Individual Literary Figures; Newsletters

Brontë Society Transactions [*BST*] (1898–   ).
The Dickensian (1905–   ).
James Joyce Miscellany [*JJM*] (1957–   ).
James Joyce Quarterly [*JJQ*] (1963–   ).
James Joyce Review [*JJR*] (1957–   ).
Johnsonian News Letter (1940–   ).
Keats–Shelley Journal [*KSJ*] (1951–   ).
Literature and Psychology [*L&P*] (1950–   ).
Renaissance News [*RN*] (1947–   ).
Seventeenth-Century News and *Neo-Latin News* [*SCN; NLN*] (1942–   ).
Shakespeare Newsletter [*ShN*] (1951–   ).
Shakespeare Quarterly [*SQ*] (1950–   ).
Shakespeare Survey [*ShS*] (1948–   ).
Shavian (1953–   ).
Shaw Review [*ShawR*] (1951–   ).
Victorian Newsletter [*VN*] (1953/4–   ).

Literary Periodicals (semi-scholarly)

Critical Quarterly (1959–   ).
Hudson Review [*HudR*] (1948–   ).
Kenyon Review [*KR*] (1938–   ).
Partisan Review [*PR*] (1934–   ).
Sewanee Review [*SR*] (1892–   ).
Thought (1926–   ).
* (London) *Times Literary Supplement* [*TLS*] (1902–   ).
Virginia Quarterly Review [*VQR*] (1925–   ).
Yale Review [*YR*] (1892–   ).
  Contributions of scholarly interest on English literature
are also to be found in the proceedings of such bodies as
the British Academy, the Connecticut Academy of Arts

and Sciences, the Leeds Philosophical Society, and the Michigan Academy of Science, Arts, and Letters.

COMPOSITE MISCELLANIES (FESTSCHRIFTEN)

Much literary scholarship, sometimes of the highest quality, is tucked away in the volumes of academic piety that celebrate perhaps the seventieth birthday of some distinguished professor. Among the best of the species are those dedicated to Furnivall (1901), Kittredge (1913), Klaeber (1929), Grierson (1938), Nichol Smith (1945), Sherburn (1949), Tinker (1949), F. P. Wilson (1959), Marjorie Nicolson (1962), and McKillop (1963).

THE BOOK TRADE

F. A. Mumby, *Publishing and Bookselling: a History from the Earliest Times to the Present Day* (3d ed., 1954), is the standard history and contains the fullest bibliography of materials relating to the literature on English publishing and book-selling. Specialist studies are Cyprian Blagden, *The Stationers' Company: a History, 1403–1959* (1960); Marjorie Plant, *The English Book Trade: an Economic History of the Making and Sale of Books* (1939); E. Gordon Duff, *A Century of the English Book Trade* [1457–1577] (1905); and H. S. Bennett, *English Books and Readers, 1475 to 1557* (1952).

E. Gordon Duff, *The Printers, Stationers, and Booksellers of London from 1476 to 1535* (1906), and his *Hand-lists of English Printers, 1501–1556* compiled, with other scholars' help, in four parts (1895, 1896, 1905, 1913), begin a chronological series of special dictionaries and check-lists in the field. Ronald B. McKerrow, *A Dictionary of Printers and Booksellers in England, Scotland, and Ireland, and of Foreign Printers of English Books, 1557–1640* (1910), comes next, and is in turn continued by Henry R. Plomer's three volumes: *A Dictionary of the Booksellers and Printers Who Were at Work in England, Scotland, and Ireland from 1641 to 1667* (1907); *A Dic-*

tionary [as above] *from 1668 to 1725* (1922); *A Dictionary* [as above] *from 1726 to 1775* (1932). Joseph Moxon's
Mechanical Exercises on the Whole Art of Printing (1683–
84), the earliest treatise on printing in English, has been
edited by Herbert Davis and Harry Carter (1958). Graham Pollard's sections on "Book Production and Distribu-
tion" (*CBEL*, I, 345 f., II, 81 f., and III, 70 f.) provide
a complete bibliography of the subject.

BIOGRAPHICAL DICTIONARIES

For biographical information on English figures no
longer living the standard source is the *Dictionary of National Biography* [*DNB*], edited by Leslie Stephen and
Sidney Lee (63 vols.; reprinted in 22 vols., 1922–50)
and its supplements (1901–1950). Summaries of each life
are collected into the *Concise DNB* (Part I [1953] includes figures to 1900; II [1961], 1901–50). *Who's
Who*, published annually since 1849, includes data on
English and Commonwealth figures in all fields and is
standard for living persons. Its companion source, *Who
Was Who* (4 vols., 1929–52), contains final entries in
Who's Who of persons who have died in preceding
quinquennia, with death date.

Biographical data on university figures may be found in
*Alumni Cantabrigienses: a Biographical List of All Known
Students, Graduates, and Holders of Office at the University of Cambridge from the Earliest Times to 1900*, edited
by John and J. A. Venn (10 vols., 1922–54) and in
*Alumni Oxonienses: the Members of the University of Ox-
ford* [*1500–1886*], edited by Joseph Foster (8 vols.,
1887–92). For Oxonians before 1500 consult A. B.
Emden, *A Biographical Register of the University of Oxford to A.D. 1500* (3 vols., 1957–59).

For information on titled persons there are G. E.
C[okayne]'s two sources, *The Complete Peerage of Eng-
land, Scotland, Ireland, Great Britain, and the United
Kingdom, Extant, Extinct, or Dormant* (new ed., 14 vols.,

1910–59) and *Complete Baronetage, 1611–1800* (5 vols. plus index, 1900–9); and *Burke's Landed Gentry*, edited by L. G. Pine (17th ed., 1952).

Two special sources particularly good for minor figures not found elsewhere are William Musgrave, *Obituary Prior to 1800 as Far as Relates to England, Scotland, Ireland*, edited by Sir G. T. Armytage (6 vols., 1899–1901), and Frederick Boase, *Modern English Biography, Containing Many Thousand Concise Memoirs of Persons Who Have Died Since the Year 1850* (3 vols. plus 3-vol. supplement; Truro, 1892–1901; 1908–21), which continues Musgrave.

Although not precisely biographical dictionaries, William Matthews's two volumes will often reward by providing leads to sources not immediately locatable elsewhere: *British Autobiographies: an Annotated Bibliography of British Autobiographies Published or Written before 1951* (1955) and *British Diaries: an Annotated Bibliography of British Diaries Written between 1442 and 1942* (1950).

For biographical information on persons not included in the special sources, one may consult a group of general tools, the most useful of which are Phyllis M. Riches, *An Analytical Bibliography of Universal Collected Biography, comprising Books Published in the English Tongue in Great Britain and Ireland, America, and the British Dominions* (1934); J. O. Thorne, *Chambers' Biographical Dictionary* (rev. ed., 1961); and Helen Hefling and Jessie Dyde, *Hefling and Richards' Index to Contemporary Biography and Criticism* (2d ed., 1934), which includes persons born in 1850 and later. *The Biography Index: a Cumulative Index to Biographical Material in Books and Magazines* [1946–   ] (1947–   ) is issued quarterly and cumulated annually and triennially; it locates biographical data in current books and periodicals in the English language and thus provides up-to-date material to supplement Riches, Thorne, and the older general and special sources.

4. The Techniques of Literary Research

PALEOGRAPHY

A good introduction to paleography, the study of earlier handwriting and its particular habits of abbreviation, contraction, capitalization, etc., is H. G. T. Christopher's *Palaeography and Archives: a Manual for the Librarian, Archivist, and Student* (1938), and there is an excellent essay by Stanley Morison on the development of handwriting in Ambrose Heal, *The English Writing-Masters and Their Copybooks, 1570–1800: a Biographical Dictionary and a Bibliography* (1931). W. W. Greg's *English Literary Autographs, 1550–1650* (3 vols., 1932) expands the discussion of Renaissance hands begun in R. B. McKerrow's *An Introduction to Bibliography for Literary Students* (1927) and provides facsimile models of the various hands, as does C. E. Wright's *English Vernacular Hands from the Twelfth to the Fifteenth Centuries* (1960). See also R. B. Haselden, *Scientific Aids for the Study of Manuscripts* (1935). The standard treatises on the "English" hand are Charles Johnson and Hilary Jenkinson, *English Court Hand* (1915) and Jenkinson's *The Later Court Hand in England from the Fifteenth to the Seventeenth Century* (2 vols., 1927). The literary relevance of paleography is simply exemplified in C. J. Sisson's *New Readings in Shakespeare* (2 vols., 1956); E. Maunde Thompson's *Shakespeare's Handwriting* (1916) and his chapter in *Shakespeare's Hand in the Play of Sir Thomas More* (ed. A. W. Pollard, 1923) are more technical.

ANALYTICAL BIBLIOGRAPHY

The standard full-length introduction is Ronald B. McKerrow's *An Introduction to Bibliography for Literary Students* (1927), the material in which each student of literature must master. Arundell Esdaile and Roy Stokes's *A Student's Manual of Bibliography* (3d ed., 1954) occasionally elucidates passages in McKerrow and has had the advantage of studies made in the field since the earlier work appeared. The more important articles have been printed in *The Library* (1889–   ), which was merged in 1920 with the *Transactions* of the (London) Bibliographical Society and is indexed in George W. Cole, *An Index to Bibliographical Papers Published by the Bibliographical Society and the Library Association, London, 1877–1932* (1933); the *Papers of the Bibliographical Society of America [PBSA]* (1904/5–   ), for which there are cumulative indexes to Volumes I–XXV, XXVI–XLV; and the annual *Studies in Bibliography. Papers of the Bibliographical Society of the University of Virginia* (1948/9–   ), which contains an annual bibliography of scholarship in bibliography, as does the Oxford Bibliographical Society's *Bibliography in Britain* (1963–   ). The most elaborate recent study is Fredson Bowers's *Principles of Bibliographical Description* (1949), but more relevant for the ordinary literary researcher are R. W. Chapman's *Cancels* (1930) and Percy Simpson's *Proof-Reading in the Sixteenth, Seventeenth, and Eighteenth Century* (1935). More recent problems are discussed in entertaining detail by Michael Sadleir in his *XIX Century Fiction: a Bibliographical Record* (2 vols., 1951). The most acute discussion of the practical problems involved in bibliographical description is the introduction to the last volume of W. W. Greg's *A Bibliography of the English Printed Drama to the Restoration* (4 vols., 1929–59). At a lower level John Carter's *ABC for Book-Collectors* (1952, rev. 1961) is indispensable (technical terms expounded alphabetically with lucidity and wit).

TEXTUAL CRITICISM

The methodology of Greek and Latin scholarship is brilliantly epitomized by Paul Maas, *Textual Criticism* (tr. from German 1958). W. W. Greg's short *The Calculus of Variants* (1927) was intended to make the classical methods available for editors of English texts, though more is in fact to be learned from A. E. Housman's introductions to his Manilius (1903), Juvenal (1905), and Lucan (1926), and his entertaining "The Application of Thought to Textual Criticism" (reprinted with various reviews, etc., by John Carter in *A. E. Housman: Selected Prose,* 1961).

Modern English textual criticism begins with R. B. Mc-Kerrow's enormously elaborate edition of Thomas Nashe (5 vols., 1904–10), which first introduced the term (and concept) "copy-text." When it was reissued by F. P. Wilson with supplementary notes (5 vols., 1958), McKerrow's old colleague W. W. Greg controverted his recommendations in an important appendix. Earlier, McKerrow's *Prolegomena for the Oxford Shakespeare* (1939) stimulated Greg to his own "Prolegomena," which was prefixed to his *The Editorial Problem in Shakespeare* (1942, rev. 1950). Other important contributions have been made by J. Dover Wilson (*The Manuscript of Shakespeare's Hamlet,* 1934), Alice Walker (*Textual Problems of the First Folio,* 1953), Fredson Bowers (*On Editing Shakespeare and the Elizabethan Dramatists,* 1955, *Textual and Literary Criticism,* 1959, and *Bibliography and Textual Criticism,* 1964), and Charlton Hinman (*The Printing and Proof-reading of the First Folio of Shakespeare,* 1963). Articles on every aspect of the textual study of Elizabethan drama will be found in *Studies in Bibliography,* which is edited by Bowers, the inventor of the term "biblio-textual" and the prophet of the method.

Outside Shakespeare, textual criticism has been especially active with Langland (important edition of *A* text of *Piers Plowman* by G. A. Kane, 1960), Chaucer (edition of *Canterbury Tales* by J. M. Manly and Edith Rickert, 8 vols., 1940), Rochester and his associates (D. M. Vieth, *Attribution in Restoration Poetry,* 1963), Pope ("General Note on the Text" in *Epistle to Several Persons,* ed. F. W. Bateson, rev. 1961), and Addison (*The Spectator,* ed. D. F. Bond, 4 vols., 1964).

A mathematical approach to textual criticism has been worked out and illustrated by V. A. Dearing in *A Manual of Textual Criticism* (1960); he has recently harnessed the computer to the text of Dryden now being issued by the University of California Press as described in his pamphlet *Methods of Textual Editing* (Clark Memorial Library, Los Angeles, 1962).

SOURCES AND INFLUENCES

The best general introduction is in André Morize, *Problems and Methods of Literary History*, Chapters V and X, and R. D. Altick provides a readable survey of both aspects in *The Art of Literary Research*, pp. 79–102. The chapters in Chauncey Sanders, *An Introduction to Research in Literary History*, are useful for their detailed notes which list several hundred books and articles, mainly from the 1920s and 1930s, devoted either to "Source-Study" or to "Sources and Influence." One of the few discussions of the principles involved is Hardin Craig's "Shakespeare and Wilson's *Arte of Rhetorique*, an Inquiry into the Criteria for Determining Sources" (*SP*, XXVIII [1931], 618–30). The topic is also examined by Kenneth Muir and F. W. Bateson, *Essays in Criticism*, IV (1954), 432–40.

Some classic examples of source-influence scholarship are: R. D. Havens, *Milton's Influence on English Poetry* (1922); J. L. Lowes, *The Road to Xanadu* (1927, rev. 1930; Coleridge's knowledge of travel books, etc.); Janet Scott, *Les sonnets élisabéthains: les sources et l'apport personnel* (Paris, 1929); Huntington Brown, *Rabelais in English Literature* (1930); W. F. Bryan and Germaine Dempster, *Sources and Analogues of Chaucer's Canterbury Tales* (1940); Grover Smith, *T. S. Eliot's Poetry and Plays: a Study in Sources and Meaning* (1956); and R. W. Dent, *John Webster's Borrowing* (1960).

Of the many refutations of proposed sources two of the most effective are D. L. Clark's "What Was Shelley's Indebtedness to Keats?" (*PMLA*, LVI [1941], 479–97) and W. B. C. Watkins, "The Plagiarist: Spenser or Marlowe?" (*ELH*, XI [1944], 249–65). Until recently a degree of plagiarism was ethically respectable because of the neo-classic doctrine of *imitatio* (see H. O. White, *Plagiarism and Imitation during the English Renaissance,* 1935). Useful summaries of the classical influences will be found in J. A. K. Thomson's *Classical Influences on English Poetry* (1948) and *Classical Influences on English Prose* (1956). A more critical account is Gilbert Highet's *The Classical Tradition: Greek and Roman Influences on Western Literature* (1949).

Accounts of an author's after-fame have been of two types. In Caroline Spurgeon's *Five Hundred Years of Chaucer Criticism and Allusion* (3 vols., 1925) and John Munro's *The Shakspere Allusion-Book* (rev. E. K. Chambers, 2 vols., 1932) every discoverable reference—for Chaucer to 1900, for Shakespeare to 1700—is transcribed in chronological order. The more usual selective treatment in a continuous narrative is ably represented by A. B. Howes, *Yorick and the Critics: Sterne's Reputation in England, 1760–1868* (1958), and G. H. Ford, *Keats and the Victorians: a Study of His Influence and Rise to Fame, 1821–95* (1944).

ATTRIBUTION AND AUTHENTICITY

Morize, *Problems and Methods of Literary History,* Chapter VII, is a good introduction to the topic, which is also surveyed by Altick, *Art of Literary Research,* pp. 63–79. Sanders, *Introduction to Research,* deals briefly with nearly a hundred examples of the genre, pp. 142–61, 343–47.

The standard work of reference is Samuel Halkett and John Laing, *Dictionary of Anonymous and Pseudonymous English Literature* (new edition, 9 vols. plus supplement, 1926–62), revised and enlarged by J. Kennedy, W. A. Smith, and F. A. Johnson. The Library of Congress *Catalog of Printed Books: Supplement* (42 vols.; see p. 223) also identifies the authors of approximately 26,000 anonyma and pseudonyma. J. M. Quérard, *Les supercheries littéraires dévoilées* (7 vols., Paris, 1869–79), and William Cushing's two books, *Anonyms* (1889) and *Initials and*

Pseudonyms (2 vols., 1886–88), are occasionally useful. For the most part reliable, none of these is infallible because each derives its identifications from a variety of sources, some dependable, some not. A more scholarly venture, still in progress, is W. E. Houghton's gradual identification of the anonymous reviews in the great nineteenth-century journals (from office copies, correspondence, etc.). Indexes of the contributors to the *Monthly Review* (1749–1815) have already been brought out by B. C. Nangle (2 vols., 1934–55).

A greater objectivity in the use of internal evidence is the most important recent advance. The happy-go-lucky methods in Elizabethan drama, including Shakespeare, of F. G. Fleay and J. M. Robertson (and the more responsible Charles Crawford and Dugdale Sykes) were pilloried by E. K. Chambers in "The Disintegration of Shakespeare" (*Proceedings of British Academy,* XI [1925], 89–108, and in *Shakespeareian Gleanings,* 1944). The next stage—represented by the more cautious E. H. C. Oliphant, *The Plays of Beaumont and Fletcher: an Attempt to Determine Their Respective Shares and the Shares of Others* (1927) —has given place to the meticulous linguistic re-examination typified by Cyrus Hoy, "The Shares of Fletcher and His Collaborators in the Beaumont and Fletcher Canon" (*Studies in Bibliography,* VIII–XV [1956–63]). The turning point was perhaps the collaborative *Shakespeare's Hand in the Play of Sir Thomas More* by A. W. Pollard, W. W. Greg, E. M. Thompson, J. D. Wilson, and R. W. Chambers (1923), which remains a model of method, as in another field does R. S. Crane's recovery of unsigned essays in *New Essays by Oliver Goldsmith* (1927). G. Udny Yule's *The Statistical Study of Literary Vocabulary* (1944), an attempt to determine the authorship of *De Imitatione Christi,* opened a door for the use of computers; Alvar Ellegård has applied similar methods to the "Junius" problem in *A Statistical Method for Determining Authorship* (Stockholm, 1962). *The Bulletin of the New York Public Library* (LXI–LXIV [1957–60]) included an interesting symposium on internal evidence with illustrations from different periods and genres.

The most spectacular modern exposure of literary forgery is John Carter and Graham Pollard's *An Enquiry into the Nature of Certain Nineteenth Century Pamphlets* (1934), which has recently been supplemented by D. F. Foxon's *Thomas J. Wise and the Pre-Restoration Drama: a Study in Theft and Sophistication* (1959).

THE PROCESSES OF COMPOSITION

Robert Graves: *On English Poetry* (1922). Includes expositions of the origination and development of a few of his own poems.

E. de Selincourt: *The Prelude, by William Wordsworth, Edited from the Manuscripts* (1926, rev. Helen Darbishire, 1960).

J. L. Lowes: *The Road to Xanadu: a Study in the Ways of the Imagination* (1927, rev. 1930). "The Ancient Mariner" and "Kubla Khan."

R. L. Purdy: *The Rivals, by Richard Brinsley Sheridan. Edited from the Larpent MS* (1935).

Josephine W. Bennett: *The Evolution of "The Faerie Queene"* (1942).

C. D. Abbott: *Poets at Work* (1948). Based on manuscripts of modern poets at the Lockwood Memorial Library, Buffalo.

A. H. Gilbert: *On the Composition of "Paradise Lost"* (1948).

Grace J. Calder: *The Writing of "Past and Present"* (1949).

Neville Rogers: *Shelley at Work* (1956). Study of manuscripts in Bodleian.

John Butt and Kathleen Tillotson: *Dickens at Work* (1957).

Jerome Beaty: *"Middlemarch" from Notebook to Novel: a Study of George Eliot's Creative Method* (1960).

J. H. Buckley: *Tennyson: the Growth of a Poet* (1960).

E. R. Wasserman: Pope's *Epistle to Bathurst* (1960).

Jon Stallworthy: *Between the Lines: Yeats's Poetry in the Making* (1963).

R. W. Rader: *Tennyson's "Maud"* (1963).

THE LITERARY PROFESSION AND AUDIENCE

Alexandre Beljame: *Le public et les hommes de lettres en Angleterre au dix-huitième siècle, 1660–1744* (Paris, 1881: English tr. with new notes, etc., by Bonamy Dobrée, 1948).

A. C. Bradley: *Oxford Lectures on Poetry* (1904). Includes "Shakespeare's Theatre and Audience."

Leslie Stephen: *English Literature and Society in the Eighteenth Century* (1904).

Phoebe Sheavyn: *The Literary Profession in the Elizabethan Age* (1909). Revision by J. W. Saunders in preparation.

John Palmer: *The Comedy of Manners* (1913). Restoration comedy.

C. B. Tinker: *The Salon and English Letters* (1915). Later eighteenth century.

K. J. Holzknecht: *Literary Patronage in the Middle Ages* (1923).

L. L. Schücking: *Die Soziologie der literarischen Geshmacksbildung* (Munich, 1923: English translation 1941).

A. S. Collins: *Authorship in the Days of Johnson, 1726–1780* (1927) and *The Profession of Letters, 1780–1832* (1928).

Amy Cruse: *The Englishman and His Books in the Early Nineteenth Century* (1930), *The Victorians and Their Books* (1935), and *After the Victorians* (1938).

Q. D. Leavis: *Fiction and the Reading Public* (1932).

R. J. Allen: *The Clubs of Augustan London* (1933).

L. B. Wright: *Middle-Class Culture in Elizabethan England* (1935).

"Christopher Caudwell" (Christopher St. J. Sprigg): *Illusion and Reality* (1937). An ambitious Marxist theory of literature.

L. C. Knights: *Drama and Society in the Age of Jonson* (1937).

Alfred Harbage: *Shakespeare's Audience* (1941).

George Thomson: *Marxism and Poetry* (1945).

Dorothy Whitelock: *The Audience of Beowulf* (1951).

H. S. Bennett: *English Books and Readers, 1475 to 1557* (1952).

Arnold Kettle: *Introduction to the English Novel* (2 vols., 1952–53). Intelligent Marxist approach.

G. H. Ford: *Dickens and His Readers* (1955).

R. K. Webb: *The British Working Class Reader, 1790–1848* (1955).

R. D. Altick: *The English Common Reader* (1957). Mainly the nineteenth-century reading public.

Alvar Ellegård: *The Readership of the Periodical Press in Mid-Victorian Britain* (Gothenburg, 1957).

Lennox Grey: "Literary Audience." A good introductory survey in *Contemporary Literary Scholarship,* edited by Lewis Leary (1958).

John Loftis: *Comedy and Society from Congreve to Fielding* (1960) and *The Politics of Drama in Augustan England* (1963).

Louis James: *Fiction for the Working Man, 1830–1850* (1963).

KEY LITERARY TERMS AND CONCEPTS

The best general surveys are: for the Middle Ages, E. R. Curtius, *Europäische Literatur und lateinsches Mittelalter* (Berne, 1948; English translation 1953); for the Renaissance and neo-classicism, W. K. Wimsatt and Cleanth Brooks, *Literary Criticism: a Short History* (1957; especially Part II); for the later eighteenth and nineteenth centuries, M. H. Abrams, *The Mirror and the Lamp: Romantic Theory and the Critical Tradition* (1953); for the twentieth century, Frank Kermode, *Romantic Image* (1957).

Some important shorter and more specialized accounts will be found in the *Journal of the History of Ideas*

(1940–   ) and in the following collections of essays, etc.:

Logan P. Smith: *Four Words: Romantic, Originality, Creative, Genius* (1924). Reprinted in *Words and Idioms* (1925).

A. O. Lovejoy: *Essays in the History of Ideas* (1948). Nature, classicism, Romanticism, Gothic, etc.

C. S. Lewis: *Studies in Words* (1960). Nature, wit, sense, simple, conscious, etc.

George Williamson: *Seventeenth Century Contexts* (1960). Mutability, "strong lines," enthusiasm, wit.

J. B. Leishman: *Themes and Variations in Shakespeare's Sonnets* (1961). Poetry as immortalization (from Pindar to Shakespeare), devouring time and fading beauty (from Greek anthology to Shakespeare).

René Wellek: *Concepts of Criticism* (1963). Literary criticism, baroque, Romanticism, realism, etc.

The terms most elaborately discussed recently have been:

CLASSICISM: Henri Peyre, "Le mot Classicisme" (in *Le classicisme français*, 1942). Also Lovejoy (above).

COURTESY: Ruth Kelso, *The Institution of the Gentleman in English Literature of the Sixteenth Century* (1929) and *Doctrine for the Lady of the Renaissance* (1956).

CULTURE: Raymond Williams, *Culture and Society, 1780–1950* (1958).

DISSOCIATION OF SENSIBILITY: F. W. Bateson, *Essays in Criticism*, I (1951), 302–12. Also Kermode (above).

GOTHIC: Samuel Kliger: *The Goths in England* (1952). Also Lovejoy (above).

IMAGINATION: M. W. Bundy, "'Invention' and 'Imagination' in the Renaissance," *JEGP*, XXIX (1930), 535–45; A. S. P. Woodhouse, "Collins and the Creative Imagination" (in *Studies in English by Members of University College, Toronto*, ed. M. W. Wallace, 1931).

IRONY: Norman Knox, *The Word* Irony *and Its Context, 1500–1755* (1961).

NATURE: J. W. Beach, *The Concept of Nature in Nine-*

teenth-Century English Poetry (1936). Also Lovejoy and Lewis (above).

NOVELTY: C. de W. Thorpe, "Addison and Some of His Predecessors on 'Novelty,'" *PMLA*, LII (1937), 1114–29.

PICTURESQUE: Elizabeth W. Manwaring, *Italian Landscape in Eighteenth Century England* (1925); J. H. Hagstrum, *The Sister Arts* (1958).

PLENITUDE: A. O. Lovejoy, *The Great Chain of Being* (1936); Maynard Mack, introduction to edition of Pope's *Essay on Man* (1950). Lovejoy's book demonstrates brilliantly his approach to the history of thought via single "unit-ideas."

PRIMITIVISM: H. N. Fairchild, *The Noble Savage* (1928); Lois Whitney, *Primitivism and the Idea of Progress in English Popular Literature of the Eighteenth Century* (1934); Margaret M. Fitzgerald, *First Follow Nature: Primitivism in English Poetry, 1725–50* (1947).

REALISM: Harry Levin, "What Is Realism?" (in *Contexts of Criticism*, 1957, pp. 67–75). Also Wellek (above).

ROMANTICISM: Fernand Baldensperger, "'Romantique,' ses analogues et ses équivalents: tableau synoptique de 1650 à 1810," *Harvard Studies and Notes in Philology and Literature*, XIX (1937), 13–105 (examples from French, English, and German in parallel columns); Northrop Frye, M. H. Abrams, Lionel Trilling, and René Wellek, *Romanticism Reconsidered* (1963). Also Lovejoy and Kermode (above).

SENTIMENTAL: E. Erämetsä, *A Study of the Word "Sentimental"* (Helsinki, 1951).

SIMPLICITY: R. D. Havens, "Simplicity, a Changing Concept," *Journal of the History of Ideas*, XIV (1953), 3–32. From 1700 to *c.* 1815.

SUBLIME: S. H. Monk, *The Sublime: a Study of Critical Theories in 18th Century England* (1935); J. T. Boulton, introduction to edition of Burke's *Sublime and Beautiful* (1958).

WIT: George Williamson, *The Proper Wit of Poetry* (1961).

Index